THE COMMON CORE STATE STANDARDS IN LITERACY SERIES

A series designed to help educators successfully
implement CCSS literacy standards in K–12 classrooms

SUSAN B. NEUMAN AND D. RAY REUTZEL, EDITORS

SERIES BOARD: Diane August, Linda Gambrell, Steve Graham, Laura Justice,
Margaret McKeown, and Timothy Shanahan

Reading, Thinking, and Writing About History

Teaching Argument Writing to Diverse Learners in the Common Core Classroom, Grades 6–12

CHAUNCEY MONTE-SANO, SUSAN DE LA PAZ, AND MARK FELTON

Engaging Students in Disciplinary Literacy, K–6

Reading, Writing, and Teaching Tools for the Classroom

CYNTHIA H. BROCK, VIRGINIA J. GOATLEY, TAFFY E. RAPHAEL,
ELISABETH TROST-SHAHATA, AND CATHERINE M. WEBER

All About Words

Increasing Vocabulary in the Common Core Classroom, PreK–2

SUSAN B. NEUMAN AND TANYA WRIGHT

READING, THINKING, *and* WRITING ABOUT HISTORY

Teaching Argument Writing to Diverse Learners in the Common Core Classroom, Grades 6–12

Chauncey Monte-Sano
Susan De La Paz
Mark Felton

Foreword by Sam Wineburg

TEACHERS COLLEGE PRESS

TEACHERS COLLEGE | COLUMBIA UNIVERSITY

NEW YORK AND LONDON

NATIONAL WRITING PROJECT

National Writing Project
Berkeley, CA

Published simultaneously by Teachers College Press, 1234 Amsterdam Avenue, New York, NY 10027 and the National Writing Project, 2105 Bancroft Way, Berkeley, CA 94720-1042

The National Writing Project (NWP) is a nationwide network of educators working together to improve the teaching of writing in the nation's schools and in other settings. NWP provides high-quality professional development programs to teachers in a variety of disciplines and at all levels, from early childhood through university. Through its network of nearly 200 university-based sites, NWP develops the leadership, programs, and research needed for teachers to help students become successful writers and learners.

Library of Congress Cataloging-in-Publication Data

Monte-Sano, Chauncey.
   Reading, writing, and thinking about history : teaching diverse learners in the common core classroom, grades 6–12 / Chauncey Monte-Sano, Susan De La Paz, and Mark Felton.
      pages cm
   Includes bibliographical references and index.
   ISBN 978-0-8077-5530-3 (pbk.)—ISBN 978-0-8077-7287-4 (ebook)
   1. History—Study and teaching (Elementary)—United States. 2. History—Study and teaching (Secondary)—United States. 3. History—Study and teaching—Standards—United States. 4. Language arts—Correlation with content subjects. I. Title.
   LB1582.U6M66 2014
   372.89′044—dc23
                                                                    2013047386

ISBN 978-0-8077-5530-3 (paperback)
ISBN 978-0-8077-7287-4 (ebook)

Printed on acid-free paper
Manufactured in the United States of America

21 20 19 18 17 16   8 7 6 5 4 3

*We dedicate this book
to the students, teachers, and administrators
who worked in partnership with us
as we developed this curriculum.*

Contents

Foreword

WHO OWNS BRAGGING rights for the American form of constitutional government? If the names Jefferson, Adams, or Madison come to mind, think again. The Founding Fathers, according to some historians, were rank imitators. It is not the Founding Fathers who invented this system, these scholars claim, but our "Forgotten Fathers." Long before the Articles of Confederation and the drafting of the Constitution in Philadelphia, the sachems of the Iroquois League had invented a system of "sovereign units united into one government." We now refer to this as the "federal" system. The anthropologist Jack Weatherford wastes no time: "the Indians invented it."[1]

Did they? The historian, Samuel B. Payne, Jr., says no. In an article that challenges the "Iroquois Influence" thesis, Payne first examines "the most detailed and authoritative statements" of scholars like Weatherford and others.[2] He then tells us he will prove the "Forgotten Fathers" thesis false. Next, he lays out the evidence for and against the Iroquois' influence on the colonists. He concludes that the entire thesis is "unfounded."

The path this argument takes seems straightforward, even linear. But if you have ever watched middle school students trying to traverse it, you know it is anything but. How do young writers select evidence most relevant to their argument? How do they provide warrant for the facts presented, explaining how each fact supports their overall argument? In what order should points be arrayed? Each compositional decision demands subtle judgment. Historical writing is harder than it looks.

How does Payne do it? He begins by telling us of the establishment of the New England Confederation in 1643, which wedded Massachusetts Bay, Plymouth, Connecticut, and New Haven into common bond, with each colony sending representatives to yearly meetings to forge agreements and public laws. The group authored a document with the prescient title "Articles of Confederation," formalizing its governing structure.

The New England Confederation of 1643 is a historical fact. But why does Payne bother? Because it wasn't until 1672, 29 years after the establishment of the New England Confederation, that colonists first made contact with the Iroquois. How could the Iroquois have bequeathed notions of confederation to the colonists if the colonists themselves were already practicing it? Indeed, multiple models of confederation, from the Swiss system of canons to the United Provinces of the Netherlands, had long been a fixture in the European conceptual universe. Political writings of the 17th and 18th centuries abound with references to confederated systems, some tracing back to the Achaean League (266 B.C.E.) in ancient Greece. Just as the Iroquois did not need the Europeans to come up with their idea of confederation, so the Europeans did not need the Iroquois to come up with theirs.

How can we teach students to make arguments like this? Sadly, our assignments often have the opposite effect. We throw young writers to the wolves, expecting them to absorb complex skills by osmosis. We hope that by providing many examples, the inner structure of argumentation will seep into young people's brains. For a lucky few, this may happen. Most others will struggle. But if anything is "struggling" here, it is a pedagogy that perpetuates inequality and widens the disparity between have and have-nots.

Learning to write, as Chauncey Monte-Sano, Susan De La Paz, and Mark Felton argue in this important book, is a complex act of cognition with many moving parts. At the heart of their approach is the idea of *cognitive apprenticeship*. Writing differs a great deal from dance. In dance, for example, we can see and feel the moves we are supposed to make. In writing, however, the most important moves are invisible to the naked eye.

How, then, are students supposed to master something no one has ever explicitly modeled for them? Ask yourself: As a teacher do you *explicitly* explain to students how you approach a historical document, how you make choices about which facts to include and which are expendable? Do you let students in on the reasoning behind your written choices? Our students can only become apprentices of our thinking if we, as teachers, make what is normally tacit explicit. Our own inner thoughts, hidden from view, must become part of our curriculum.

Making our thinking visible is only the first step. That's where this invaluable book comes in. The tools it provides—from graphic organizers, to lesson plans, to the accompanying documents—demystify the writing process and offer a sequenced path toward attaining proficiency. To cite one of this book's many examples: Sentence starters are crucial aids when students first try on the unfamiliar voice of argumentative writing. As they become proficient in using this genre, such tools can be put to the side. But until then, it is precisely such scaffolds that allow students to get to places they could never have reached unaided. No carpenter goes to a worksite without a toolbox. Similarly, teachers who want to help students become effective writers will ignore this book at their peril.

Historical writing is more than mastering a set of rhetorical skills. It is a way of thinking about what ideas are most worthy of our belief. In our networked society, where conflicting information bombards us from all sides, learning the skills of historical argumentation will not only make your students better writers. These skills will make them more thoughtful and discerning citizens.

NOTES

1.   Jack Weatherford. 1988. *Indian Givers: How the Indians of the Americas Transformed the World.* New York: Crown.

2.   Samuel B. Payne, Jr. 1996. "The Iroquois League, the Articles of Confederation, and the Constitution." *The William and Mary Quarterly 53,* 605–620.

Acknowledgments

MANY PEOPLE HAVE made this book possible. We are grateful to the Institute of Education Sciences, U.S. Department of Education, for their generous grant to the University of Maryland (Grant No. R305A090153) that funded this project. We thank those who helped us develop the university-school partnership that made this work possible, including Ken Estes, Phyllis Evans, Sandy Jimenez, Bruce Katz, Steve Koziol, Blesilda Lim, Margaret McLaughlin, Kara Miley-Libby, Sandra Rose, Kola Sunmonu, and Gladys Whitehead. Finally, we thank the teachers and students in each classroom who experimented with this curriculum, learned with us, and gave us valuable feedback. We are especially grateful to the students whose work we share throughout this book, Tamia Wren and Aaron Boston.

We thank the team of people we worked with while developing and testing this curriculum. Many research assistants scanned and scored student essays over the years. Roderick Carey, David Draa, Jeehye Deogracias, Liliana Maggioni, Dan Wissinger, Kelly Worland, and Laura Yee helped collect, organize, and analyze data. In addition to this work, Jared Aumen attended to last-minute details and editing in the final production of this manuscript. Teacher-in-Residence Denise Miles and Project Directors Christopher Budano and Ben Hoffman organized our collective efforts, worked closely with our partner schools, and managed day-to-day operations. Finally, Bob Croninger and Cara Jackson conducted statistical analyses and helped us analyze results from the project, enabling us to make claims about the curriculum's effectiveness.

In transforming the project into a book, Flannery Burke advised us on matters of historical accuracy and representation of historiography, and Mary Ryan strengthened our prose, helping us keep the reader in mind.

Last, we thank our families for their support throughout the entirety of this project.

CHAPTER 1

On Integrating History and Literacy

MOST PEOPLE THINK of literacy as the domain of language arts classes. The truth is, we ask students to read and write many times and in many ways during the course of a school day. In looking closely at the reading and writing that occur in classrooms, it's clear that studying history presents students with literacy demands.

Consider the following:

In an 8th-grade U.S. history class we recently observed, the teacher posed the essay question, "Did Andrew Jackson exceed the constitutional powers of the president when he forcefully relocated Native Americans out west?" Students were given a selection of primary and secondary sources to read as they constructed their responses. The assignment directed students to explain their responses in an essay, citing at least three pieces of evidence to support their views. Evidence included interviews with survivors of the forced Native American emigration known as the Trail of Tears, diary entries from military officers, legal documents, and speeches by President Andrew Jackson. To ensure basic understanding, students answered comprehension questions about each source. As they read and discussed, the students were expected to develop content knowledge, consider the different perspectives presented, and critique sources at the teacher's prompting (who is the author, what do we know about him that might help us anticipate his perspective, etc.). After analyzing the readings as a class, each student completed the essay independently. As they constructed their interpretations, students were asked to convince their audience of their argument, using selected evidence to support their ideas.

This scenario features disciplinary literacy, an instructional approach that highlights subject-specific ways of reading, writing, and thinking that are the hallmarks of advanced literacy practice in a discipline. By adolescence, students begin to confront texts and tasks that require specialized forms of knowledge. Developers of the Common Core State Standards ("Common Core") recognize the disciplinary nature of literacy practices;[1] many of these goals align with aspects of this first vignette—comprehending and critiquing while reading informational texts, working with historical sources, writing informative texts in response to reading, and composing arguments in an essay. By embracing subject matter, inquiry, and disciplinary ways of thinking, this approach also reflects the new College, Career, and Civic Life Framework for Social Studies State Standards ("C3 Framework").[2]

A few weeks later, the same teacher presented a different kind of literacy task using an essay question: "What problems did our new nation face?" Students read a corresponding textbook passage, took notes on the reading, and wrote a summary of what the textbook said about this topic. In doing so, they had to comprehend the text on a literal level and report this information. Such reading and writing experiences helped the students build background knowledge about the challenges faced by the United States in its first 50 years, and grasp an overall sense of the topic. Preparing the summary also facilitated basic comprehension of the text. Having completed this kind of task many times, students were able to work independently. Even so, the approach did not encourage the students to critique what they read, deliberate about evidence, incorporate it into their writing, or consider multiple perspectives and the demands of an audience.

This second set of literacy practices is common in history class and supported by the mainstream resources found in most classrooms.[3] Students are generally used to working with a textbook and viewing history as a collection of right answers. Yet the authoritative tone found in most textbooks (along with a lack of footnotes or links to primary sources) can obstruct historical thinking and argument.[4] While textbook readings and summary writing may help students develop background knowledge and literal comprehension, skills that are useful in studying any content area, this approach reinforces the notion that the history classroom is no place for questioning, analysis, or students' ideas, all of which are foundational to disciplinary literacy. Certainly the literacy practices featured in this scenario are necessary, but they are not sufficient when it comes to meeting the demands of either disciplinary literacy or the Common Core. Further, the second vignette thwarts the inquiry process and social studies concepts outlined in the four dimensions of the C3 Framework.[5]

WHERE WE FIT IN

This book emphasizes the types of disciplinary literacy practices found in the first scenario, where students analyze a range of historical sources and construct a written argument in response.[6] We believe that such experiences foster a greater appreciation of history and the literacy practices central to history, and do more to prepare students for the demands they will face as adults. Analyzing sources and constructing a written argument are skills that go beyond basic literacy practice or simple memorization; they rely on historical thinking. When students analyze historical sources, they ask critical questions. When students build arguments, they weigh the reliability of the evidence. Social studies teachers are well suited to teaching literacy practices, because such approaches are embedded in the study of historical topics and concepts.

The curriculum in this book contributes to history educators' efforts in four ways. It:

1. Prepares academically diverse and younger students to engage in historical investigations (i.e., to inquire, analyze, and interpret), introducing them to historical thinking and literacy practices gradually, and helping them become independent over time.

2. Teaches argument writing not simply through the inclusion of writing assignments, but through structured opportunities to learn, and supporting tools that facilitate student growth.
3. Shares a research-tested program to improve students' historical thinking and evidence-based argument writing.[7]
4. Integrates background knowledge of specific U.S. history topics with historical analysis and literacy practices.

We have spent years devising ways to help students develop the reading, thinking, and writing practices that are central to history—in a nutshell, a disciplinary literacy approach to history. Collectively, we have taught in elementary and high schools, worked alongside middle and high school teachers to differentiate instruction, and integrated reading and writing into our K–12 efforts. We have worked closely with teachers in preservice teacher education and professional development programs, and developed expertise as researchers and curriculum developers. As a culmination of those efforts, this book will explain *how* students can develop disciplinary literacy, using resources that have proven effective in our research. As we have found, teaching reading and writing does not mean history gets swept aside to make room for literacy instruction. Engaging students in historical inquiry doesn't exclude literacy practices. Instead, teaching students the critical reading and argument writing skills laid out in the Common Core, and the inquiry practices and disciplinary concepts in the C3, can give them a better understanding of history. This book not only shows you how to incorporate these approaches, it provides classroom-ready resources to use with your students.

THE CHALLENGE OF THE CCSS AND C3

The advent of the Common Core and the C3 Framework presents opportunities to use curriculum that targets and builds literacy practices and historical concepts. In the context of social studies classrooms, the Common Core offers a chance to integrate reading informational text and crafting argument into historical study. And the C3 Framework supports this initiative, as historical inquiry relies on reading, analyzing, and constructing texts, as well as disciplinary concepts such as context, perspectives, evidence, and argumentation.[8] The foundational concepts that motivate this curriculum provide the rationale behind these intersections; the teaching principles offer a road map to bring these ideas into the classroom.

To be sure, the Common Core and the C3 set the bar high for students and teachers. How can social studies teachers prepare students for college, career, and civic life when they are already asked to cover huge swaths of information? Although the Common Core and C3 Framework outline clear goals, they do not explain how to achieve them. Today's schools have few available curriculum resources to help teachers offer enriched experiences to students, and teachers have little time to develop their own. When they do salvage the time to plan experiences, they are faced with sifting through online archives, or trying to make arcane historical sources accessible to students with a range of literacy skills. Such tasks can overwhelm even the best-intentioned educator.

Even when students are given the chance to develop literacy practices and content knowledge, the essays they produce are often lacking. In the classroom where we observed the first two vignettes, students either didn't use enough detail or explain how the evidence supported a claim; in some cases they didn't write anything at all unless the teacher was at their sides—difficult to do in a class of 32 students who have a broad range of skills.

Such experiences are common in education: While it's the teacher's job to adapt instruction, results don't always match a teacher's instructional vision; and getting there can be frustrating for both teachers and students. One way to address this problem involves setting students up for success by selecting historical thinking and literacy practices with an eye on what we want them to learn, starting early, and practicing often. Students won't pick up historical thinking or literacy practices through occasional assignments; the effort must be strategic and sustained.

This is where we come in. This book presents classroom-ready materials that target historical reading and writing for teachers who have little time to create materials beyond the textbook. Primary sources have been modified to allow struggling readers access to the material. If teachers wish to challenge students, Web links to the original, unmodified sources are provided, along with other sources that may be used to extend investigations.[9] We share examples of student writing for each curriculum module and identify ways to support students, depending on their incoming literacy skills. All of these practices are designed to support real teachers working in today's busy, challenging classrooms.

OVERVIEW OF THE CURRICULUM AND ITS DEVELOPMENT

The curriculum materials in this book were based on our work with 8th-grade U.S. history classes in a large school district in the Mid-Atlantic region that includes urban, suburban, and rural communities. Middle schools that were identified by the district had significant numbers of struggling readers (a third of all students below grade level in reading). At the same time, these schools clearly supported learning for more successful students (45% of students were proficient, and just over 20% were advanced readers). Data from state reading tests indicated that over half the 8th-graders were proficient in reading. Demographic and economic data showed that 45% of the district's students received free and reduced-price meals, 8.5% received ESL services, and 10% received services for identified disabilities. African American students made up the majority of the district (67%), followed by 23% Hispanic students, 5% non-Hispanic Whites, 3% Asian, and 2% other races.

As we collaborated with social studies teachers, it became clear that students brought a wide range of literacy practices and diverse background knowledge. A curriculum was needed that would meet their varying needs. With this background information in mind, we set out to improve students' historical thinking and evidence-based, argumentative essays. The targeted skills included learning to take a position in response to a question, supporting an argument with evidence, and explaining how a piece of evidence supports a position. We also wanted to address history-specific aspects of writing arguments: in particular, judging the quality of evidence by the reliability of the author, the time period in which the evidence was created, and the legitimacy and strength of an author's supporting evidence. Students were asked to consider counterevidence and multiple perspectives. Last, we focused on major topics found in a typical U.S. history class.

The curriculum we propose for U.S. history classes involves six 3-day investigations (see Table 1.1). Each investigation features reading, discussing, and evaluating evidence from sources, as well as planning and writing. All of the investigations follow a similar path: Students are asked to work with two primary source excerpts that reflect different perspectives on a controversial historical topic. Day 1 contains background information and involves reading and annotating, while Day 3 culminates in a written essay and reflection. The activities presented during Day 2 shift over the course of the six investigations, as students gain facility in reading and evaluating evidence and move toward using sources to plan their culminating essay. Along the way, disciplinary literacy tools offer strategies for historical reading, analysis, and argument writing. For example, *IREAD* supports historical thinking and reading, while *H2W* (How to Write Your Essay) and Planning Your Essay involve historical thinking and argumentative writing. (All of these disciplinary literacy tools can be found in Appendix A and are discussed in Chapter 2.) Throughout the investigations, these tools scaffold student work and help them grasp disciplinary approaches to reading and writing. At various points in the earlier investigations, teachers model specific skills and let students practice using the disciplinary literacy tools. In the final investigations, student independence is promoted by gradually removing the supports built into the curriculum.

During the time this curriculum was tested, an essay task that involved primary sources was used to determine students' incoming skills. The students proved to be academically diverse. Some students wrote a single sentence, others wrote a few words and then crossed them out. Some students wrote several paragraphs, sharing great insights that lacked a coherent argument. At the end of the year, another test was given to measure writing improvement.

When teachers used the curriculum and participated in this professional development program, students consistently had significantly better writing outcomes than other 8th-graders in the same district.[10] As we discovered, the extent to which teacher and student engaged with the curriculum made a big difference. In other words, when teachers followed the lessons and students completed activities such as reading and annotating primary sources, generating a plan before composing an essay, and writing essays that incorporated explanation and evaluation of evidence, students were able to write stronger disciplinary arguments.

TABLE 1.1. Six Historical Investigations and Disciplinary Literacy Practices

Chapter	Historical Investigation	Disciplinary Literacy Practices Introduced (After each strategy is introduced they are practiced in subsequent investigations)
3	**#1, Lexington Green**[11] Who fired the first shot at Lexington Green?	**Historical reading:** Sourcing and annotating sources **Historical writing:** Taking a position in response to a controversial question; Composing an introduction and conclusion
4	**#2, Shays' Rebellion** Were Daniel Shays and his followers rebels or freedom fighters?	**Historical reading:** Contextualizing and annotating sources **Historical writing:** Identifying the components and structure of a historical argument; Planning and composing supporting and rebuttal paragraphs
5	**#3, Alien and Sedition Acts** Did the Alien and Sedition Acts violate the U.S. Constitution?	**Historical reading:** Considering authors' claims and the evidence provided for them **Historical writing:** Planning an entire essay and composing most (or all) of it
6	**#4, Indian Removal** What path offered the best chance of survival for the Cherokee in the early 1800s: staying in their original territory or removal to the West?	**Historical reading:** Deliberating about and evaluating evidence **Historical writing:** Composing a full essay
7	**#5, Abolitionism** What was the most effective way to free slaves in the United States before the Civil War: nonviolence or more aggressive action?	**Students set goals to read, analyze, plan, and compose with greater independence**
8	**#6, Mexican American War** Was the United States justified in going to war with Mexico in 1846?	**Students integrate reading, analysis, planning, and composing independently**

FOUNDATIONAL CONCEPTS FOR INTEGRATING LITERACY AND HISTORY

Three concepts form the foundation for integrating literacy and history into the curriculum: Historical interpretation or argument is a central aim in studying history; analyzing and questioning historical sources and artifacts are crucial to historical learning; and in studying history, reading, thinking, and writing are interconnected. Each concept reinforces key aspects of the Common Core and C3.

History as Evidence-Based Interpretation

If students are to develop the literacy practices they need, social studies educators must embrace inquiry and interpretation. Students will not learn to consider multiple perspectives, critique what they read, or develop an argument if history lessons focus solely on memorizing names and dates or filling in bubbles on a Scantron sheet. A better idea is to frame history around the discipline's central goal: evidence-based interpretation. The hope is that when students are asked "How do you know?" they will respond, "By questioning historical evidence" rather than "The textbook says so." Our approach highlights making claims based on analyzing evidence, and the notion that historical knowledge is a product of historical study, not a foregone conclusion.[12] By focusing on historical interpretation, students have the chance to read critically and form their own ideas, as they investigate historical sources and craft arguments. In this way, literacy becomes an integral part of learning history.

The relationship works both ways: Knowledge of history is also essential to reading and crafting historical arguments. Students need strong background knowledge to consider the content, sources, and context of the documents as they interpret history. In its emphasis on writing arguments, the Common Core aligns with this notion of history as interpretation;[13] in emphasizing inquiry practices, the C3 aligns with our approach as well. Among other goals, the Common Core suggests that students need to know how to make claims, recognize alternative claims, support claims with reasoning and credible evidence, and make concluding statements. The C3 Framework highlights perspectives, argumentation, evaluating sources, using evidence, and communicating conclusions. But, when history presents only one storyline, there is no place for competing claims, evidence, or inquiry; students see the story as a given. Using an interpretive approach that opens up the subject, students have the chance to develop arguments.

Learning History Through Analysis and Questioning

Our curriculum holds that people learn history not by memorizing copious amounts of information, but by looking critically at historical artifacts and asking questions about them—not just by rote regurgitation, but by thinking historically.[14] While historical artifacts encompass a wide range of documentary evidence from paintings and objects to diary entries and speeches, this curriculum relies for the most part on written texts, so that students can improve their textual reading practices at the same time they are sharpening their critical skills.

Wineburg's seminal research deals with three historical reading practices used by experts: sourcing, contextualization, and corroboration.[15] Historians interrogate historical texts by recognizing authors and their biases ("sourcing"), situating texts in the time and place of their creation ("contextualization"), and comparing texts ("corroboration") in order to find points of agreement and contradiction. Confronted with a historical text, a historian first asks who wrote it and when, as well as its author's perspective or motives ("sourcing"). Historians also ask what was happening when and where the text was created ("contextualization"), and compare the details of one text to another ("corroboration"). Through this process of questioning texts, historians analyze and make sense of historical documents as they develop an interpretation of the past.

Although not all of the historical reading practices are cited in the Common Core (particularly contextualization), our curriculum emphasizes them because they are crucial to helping students understand historical texts and concepts, as well as construct historical arguments. Along with historical reading practices, the curriculum supports many of the goals in the Common Core's *Reading Standards for Literacy in History/Social Studies 6–12*. Students using this curriculum will learn to "cite specific textual evidence to support analysis of primary and secondary sources," "determine the central ideas or information of a primary or secondary source," "define the meaning of words and phrases as they are used in a text," and "identify aspects of a text that reveal an author's point of view or purpose," among other standards.[16] The Common Core's reading standards for informational text[17] are similar to their reading standards for literacy in history/social studies, as our curriculum covers many of the goals laid out for ELA classes as well. Using combined historical reading and general reading practices, students will hit the Common Core and then some. The curriculum supports major aspects of Dimensions 2, 3, and 4 of the C3 Framework by "applying disciplinary concepts and tools," "evaluating sources and using evidence," and "communicating conclusions."[18] Using this curriculum, students will learn to comprehend *and* critique what they read, recognize multiple perspectives, situate sources and people in their historical context, determine the credibility of the evidence before them, and convey their ideas to others.

Reading, Thinking, and Writing Are Interconnected

Reading, thinking, and writing are aspects of the same activity, aimed at fostering content learning. Learning historical ways of reading and thinking can help students become better writers, while constructing cogent arguments helps them to read more critically. Intense scrutiny of a historical topic offers students the chance to understand a historical event or person as well as remember relevant details. Our curriculum asks students to annotate while reading, helping make sense of what they read. Planning an essay prompts students to reread texts as they map out a claim while learning about the topic under investigation.

The Common Core's design considerations state that literacy practices should be integrated; we couldn't agree more. We also agree that literacy practices are key to subject-area learning, especially where inquiry is paramount. Reading, writing, and thinking are all interconnected in the study of history. Because learning a new discipline involves mastering its oral and written language, it is often difficult to distinguish between content learning and content *literacy* learning.[19] For the students using this curriculum, learning history is as much about learning to read, write, and think historically as it is about mastering the content in each module. Rather than being discrete skills, these practices overlap and mutually reinforce one another.

TEACHING PRINCIPLES FOR INTEGRATING LITERACY AND HISTORY

Beyond the foundational concepts of disciplinary literacy in history, we have identified teaching principles that guided our integration of literacy and history in the classroom. Because integrating literacy with the interpretive aspects of history can pose a challenge for students, with the help of teachers who piloted the project, we've designed a curriculum based on the following principles:

- Pose central historical questions that have multiple possible answers, and present historical sources for students to investigate.
- Develop students' background knowledge to support their historical thinking and literacy practices.
- Present content in developmentally appropriate ways.
- Employ a cognitive apprenticeship approach to support students in learning new literacy practices.
- Adapt the curriculum to students' needs while continuing to highlight disciplinary thinking and writing.

Pose Central Historical Questions and Present Sources

Each investigation centers on a historical question with several different answers. Rather than explore obscure events or people, we selected questions and sources that address common topics in the middle school U.S. history curriculum, with others from elementary and high school classes. Each investigation includes two historical sources that feature alternate perspectives about the central question. All texts are primary sources by witnesses or contemporaries of the events in question.

The purpose is to have students develop interpretations or arguments, consulting source texts for evidence. By offering debatable questions and conflicting sources, the study of history is framed as a process of inquiry and analysis rather than recording and reporting fixed knowledge. And, because questions drive the literacy practices and disciplinary concepts embedded in each investigation, students must read, think, and write in order to figure out a response.

Develop Students' Background Knowledge

While we don't encourage teaching history with a sole focus on memorization of facts, students cannot investigate or consider historical topics without some knowledge. Students may be able to source texts using helpful headnotes and attributions, but would have trouble contextualizing texts, understanding their situated meaning, or identifying a historical perspective without knowledge of the time period. Our emphasis on inquiry is intended to shift the conventional focus of history classrooms, not dismiss it entirely.

An inquiry approach gives students the opportunity to make sense of past events so that their historical significance and meaning become apparent. Connecting background knowledge to each investigation supports students' historical understanding and thinking; integrating background knowledge using an inquiry approach and literacy practices allows teachers to cover necessary content while fostering disciplinary concepts and literacy. To this end, we provide introductory readings, video clips, timeline activities, and tasks to augment content knowledge. Each investigation begins with an activity that gives background knowledge so that students are able to read and reason about the controversy at hand.

> *Teachers Reflect:* "I was basically able to use that investigation [#6] almost as half of a chapter. . . . All of the concepts I needed to cover were taken care of in the investigation, so it supplemented and took the place of things to help me with my pacing. It was another way to look at material and analyze it."

Use Developmentally Appropriate Tasks

Although many of the aspects that students encounter are authentic, we have deviated from a historian's process to accommodate their range of literacy practices and knowledge. While it is important to challenge students to improve their skills, for those who struggle with literacy, the gap between what they know and what they are asked to do can be frustrating and overwhelm learning.

To address this challenge, we simplified historical questions so that two of the responses would be obvious. When asked, "Were Daniel Shays and his followers rebels or freedom fighters?" two responses are clear: "Daniel Shays and his followers were rebels" and "Daniel Shays and his followers were freedom fighters." Professional historians ask open-ended questions with a plethora of possible answers. By using a more limited structure, students can formulate an argument in a more concrete way.

To address other challenges faced by struggling readers, we preselected two compelling texts. In contrast, historians search a wide array of sources as they explore questions. While multiple texts may be crucial to students' argument writing and history learning, two texts may be sufficient for studying a controversy.[20] For this curriculum, sources came not from a textbook but authors who represent the opinions and ideas involved in the events under scrutiny. Richard Paxton found that students who read and wrote about sources with a "visible author," as opposed to the third-person anonymity of a textbook, are more likely to interact with the text, and write longer essays.[21]

We moderated complex reading by excerpting and modifying primary sources in each investigation, making them accessible to students reading 2 years below grade level. We don't aim to make reading easy—students should after all be challenged—instead, we aim to inspire students accustomed to failure to try and make sense of a text. These changes are designed to give students a foothold in the world of historical analysis; we fully expect such scaffolds should be removed over time. In modifying historical texts,[22] we include a headnote at the top of the page and an attribution at the bottom, information designed to encourage historical reading practices (locating the author, author's position, date and place of the text's creation, audience, type of text, etc.). An excerpt of the original text relevant to the central question is intended to both focus and shorten reading time.

Finally, we altered and clarified complex sentence structure or vocabulary, removing ellipses or brackets that may distract struggling readers. While a historical purist would find such practices anathema, we believe they are necessary steps to make historical materials accessible to struggling or younger students, giving them the same opportunity to improve their disciplinary literacy practice as more skilled or older readers. Able readers can always use the original texts by following links in the first footnote in the "Reading History" sections of Chapters 3–8.

Take a Cognitive Apprenticeship Approach to Thinking and Literacy Practices

These kinds of literacy and historical thinking practices aren't always obvious, and it's unfair to expect students to acquire them without providing some clear expectations. One helpful model for instruction is cognitive apprenticeship,[23] which makes expert thinking and literacy practices visible to novices through teacher modeling. As students gain practice in new ways of reading, thinking, and writing, less modeling is required, but regular feedback is given to support learning, so that students can use these practices independently (see Chapter 2 for a complete discussion). When it comes to modeling and guiding historical reading and writing practices, it's sometimes hard to know where to start, especially if students already struggle with reading and writing; for many social studies teachers, addressing literacy is a new frontier. This curriculum simplifies the process by introducing tools that structure historical reading and writing practices for students and teachers. Both *IREAD* and *H2W* (How to Write Your Essay) scaffold work for students just learning to use complex literacy practices in history (see Appendix A).

Adapt to Students' Needs While Emphasizing Disciplinary Thinking and Writing

This curriculum lays out an instructional plan for six 3-day investigations. These have proven successful for improving students' historical thinking and writing, especially when teachers use the materials faithfully and provide time to practice key literacy activities. But student success can also come from how teachers adapt the curriculum to meet their own needs and those of their students. This could mean spending more time modeling skills for struggling readers, providing extensive background knowledge to help students connect topics to their own lives, or letting students discuss and deliberate out loud.

Although the goals should remain consistent, how teachers and students reach them will vary. One size does not fit all. We count on the fact that teachers will use knowledge of their own students to make instructional decisions. Along the way, we include samples of student writing, typical challenges, and ways to help teachers think about their students and adapt the curriculum to their needs.

HOW TO USE THIS BOOK

This book is meant to serve as both a guide and model for teachers interested in integrating historical thinking and literacy in their curriculum. The six historical investigations we present come with the materials and tools teachers need to implement the curriculum in their classrooms. To make the most of the curriculum, we recommend that teachers implement all six investigations. For one thing, students need time to get used to the complex history and literacy practices in this curriculum; they need feedback to refine their skills and a coordinated plan to become more independent over time.

We recommend that these investigations be used along with—rather than instead of—a more traditional textbook or curriculum. Historical background materials support each investigation, but students will benefit from a broader perspective on U.S. history. Teachers can use this book as a model and resource to develop curriculum for other grade levels and different social studies content.

This chapter is designed to give a rationale for integrating history and literacy in social studies along with an overview of our proposed curriculum. The next chapter will describe the cognitive apprenticeship model for instruction, and the disciplinary literacy tools used throughout the curriculum to support the development of students as readers, thinkers, and writers. Chapters 3–8 present the materials behind the six historical investigations and the rationales for each. Along the way, we highlight the links between the curriculum modules, the Common Core, and the C3. Finally, Chapter 9 examines the goals of the curriculum by assessing student learning and progress. A set of rubrics that we share can be used to trace student progress on pre- and posttests in different areas, including advancing and substantiating claims, addressing counterarguments, recognizing perspectives and contextualizing.

Investigation Materials

To use each investigation teachers will need a copy of the lesson plan (Chapters 3–8); a reproducible student packet containing the historical question, background materials, and primary source documents (Chapters 3–8); the disciplinary literacy tools that students will need across multiple investigations, including *IREAD*, *H2W*, Planning Your Essay, Essay Response Template, and the Reflection Guide (Appendix A); and optional materials to support students (Appendix B). If they wish, teachers can make posters of the *IREAD* and *H2W* tools to display in the classroom. Students with whom we worked kept folders to store copies of all of their investigation materials in a portfolio, which facilitated reflection as they had easy access to their completed essays.

Student Work Samples

At the end of Chapters 3–8, we provide student writing samples from each investigation with formative feedback to illustrate the progress of two different learners and help teachers support student development. To prepare for teaching each investigation, we suggest that teachers analyze student work— the samples from Tamia and Aaron as well as their own—to anticipate students' needs and adapt instruction when needed. In Chapter 9, we analyze our two focal students' pre- and posttests to discuss their overall progress over the course of the year (see Appendix C for these students' pre- and posttests).

Tamia is an African American girl identified as a basic reader on her state standardized reading assessment. She always has a smile on her face and is the kind of person that other people like to be around. On grammar and story-writing subtests of a standardized test of written language she earned "below average" and "significantly below average" scores, respectively (Test Of Written Language, 4th edition, or TOWL4). We looked at Tamia's work across investigations and saw she had completed about 80% of the reading and 50% of the planning activities, and wrote essays averaging 1.5 paragraphs across all investigations. It is possible that Tamia struggled to complete her work on our lessons in part due to the effort she needed for extended reading and writing activities. Tamia's teacher was very supportive—she modeled, promoted students' independence, delivered accurate historical content, and created a positive learning environment for students in her classes.

Aaron is an African American boy identified as an advanced reader on state-administered standardized reading assessment. He is an avid football player and a hard worker who holds himself to high standards. He earned average and above average scores, respectively, on the grammar and story-writing subtests of a standardized test of written language (TOWL4). As we looked at Aaron's work across investigations, we noticed that he completed about 90% of the reading and planning activities and wrote an average of three paragraphs across all investigations. It is possible that Aaron's advanced literacy skills enabled him to complete his work easily within the time expected for our lessons. Like Tamia's teacher, Aaron's teacher was supportive in modeling and promoting student independence, presenting historical content, and offering a positive learning environment.

Given the goals of the curriculum, we focused formative student feedback on historical thinking and evidence-based, argument writing. These comments are not meant to be exhaustive, and teachers may choose to comment on other aspects of writing, such as grammar, mechanics or organization. We also recognize that some teachers may not wish to comment on all aspects of historical reasoning and disciplinary literacy for each essay. We are more thorough in order to provide a detailed analysis of two distinct types of learners.

A FINAL WORD

These materials have been examined by teachers from academically diverse classrooms who share concerns about student learning. The lessons in them have significantly improved students' argument writing and historical thinking across reading levels when teachers have fully implemented them. This curriculum moves teachers and students beyond treating historical sources as purely informational texts and toward authentic historical study that provides engaging opportunities for students to learn content and think historically. The curriculum in this book will open up opportunities to develop the disciplinary literacy practices targeted in the Common Core State Standards and C3 Framework, deepening student understanding of historical events, people, and controversies as well as concepts. Because content area literacy is no longer content-free, but instead, deeply embedded in subject-matter learning, we believe, history teachers may be best situated to lead this work.

CHAPTER 2

Teaching Disciplinary Literacy Through a Cognitive Apprenticeship

E ACH YEAR, the teachers on our project are asked to reflect on the curriculum, sharing what they liked and what might improve. For one teacher, the cognitive apprenticeship model was helpful because:

> [It helped students] reach that point where they're engaged in the process of critically thinking. Sometimes I would ask them why, and then we would walk through it together, we would talk through it together, but now I can ask them why and just walk away and let them think about things on their own, and then come back and say, "What do you think?" And it's great because it's not so much them relying on me. I feel they have gotten a really valuable skill early . . . when they go to high school, they can cultivate it and get better and better. By the time they go to college I think a lot of these kids are going to be amazing writers, because they're amazing now.

WHAT IS COGNITIVE APPRENTICESHIP?

Chapter 1 explained why we took a cognitive apprenticeship approach to teaching literacy and historical thinking, and gave an overview of the *IREAD* and *H2W* tools central to our curriculum. This chapter goes into depth on what cognitive apprenticeship means, and how teachers can use this model of instruction to help students learn to write historical arguments.

A cognitive apprenticeship is both an instructional model that teachers use to organize the learning environment and an approach to learning that helps students see the processes involved in complex learning activities.[1] Tracing the origins of cognitive apprenticeship takes one deeper into the literature, and the story that unfolds is rich and multifaceted. Early pioneers were Ann Brown and her colleagues[2] and Michael Pressley, whose seminal 1979 review established metacognitive approaches. Collectively, the work of Karen Harris and Steve Graham (1992), Carol Sue Englert and her colleagues (1991), Carol Lee (1995), and Bernice Wong (1997) show that an important zeitgeist of the 1980s and 1990s in the United States and Canada was to develop effective approaches for teachers and students to navigate authentic reading comprehension, literary interpretation, and writing activities as well as ways to improve students' academic performance.

Collins and his colleagues envisioned that cognitive apprenticeships could focus on complex, higher-order thinking; make visible heuristic strategies used by experts; model, coach, and scaffold for novices as they learn how to use those heuristics; and finally, through an evolving community of practitioners, achieve the habits of critical thinking.[3]

The value of cognitive apprenticeship has long been recognized among special educators, who found it beneficial for the students who struggle most with literacy. Harris and Graham's form of cognitive apprenticeship (called self-regulated strategy development, or SRSD)[4] provides a coordinated way for teachers to unpack important learning outcomes for students; their approach to teaching has been tested in more than 50 studies of youngsters with high-incidence[5] disabilities, English language learners, and "average" learners, as well as gifted and talented students from 2nd grade to high school, and adults in North America and Europe.

The SRSD approach provides a systematic teaching model that guides teachers to provide more help when starting and for students to gradually take on more responsibility for their learning. Though described sequentially in text, the stages of instruction are often used more flexibly in the classroom, with different goals for advanced and struggling learners. These stages call for teachers to move from modeling, to collaborative modeling, to supported and independent practice (e.g., from whole class to small groups and pairs, to students working independently). Transitioning through these stages enables students to learn how to use specific strategies on their own. As students gain mastery, teachers systematically remove scaffolds like the planning graphic organizer (called Planning Your Essay in this book) or the *IREAD* and *H2W* tools.

This book uses the more general term *cognitive apprenticeship*. Though we were positively influenced by the SRSD model in some of our early work, our approach here does not emphasize self-regulation in the learning process. While our curriculum emphasizes reflection throughout, by the time most students reach middle or high school, they can handle material independently without explicit instruction on self-regulating their learning, and it is cumbersome to customize these procedures.[6] Observing advanced as well as struggling readers over the past 3 years led us to make real changes to the SRSD instructional model, because content-area teachers work with a range of learners, and because our curriculum asks students to integrate reading and writing as they think about historical content. Thus, our apprenticeship is distinct because it privileges learning about history in secondary, inclusive classrooms.

Prior Disciplinary Cognitive Apprenticeships

While this curriculum employs a cognitive apprenticeship model of instruction for social studies, others like Engle and Conant provided earlier examples in disciplines such as science.[7] Some of our own work in history[8] has used a cognitive apprenticeship model with middle and high school students. This curriculum extends our early work by more fully developing the historical controversies students grapple with, including historical investigations that use primary sources, and showing teachers how to monitor students' improvement as they plan and compose their argumentative essays.

Using a cognitive apprenticeship model allows all learners—from struggling readers to the most capable learners—to benefit from high expectations and a supported learning environment. While we have seen that students capable of reading and writing at a high level will likely benefit most from our curriculum, even struggling readers and writers make demonstrable gains in general as well as disciplinary ways. Our curriculum was designed for a heterogeneous group of students, including those with academic challenges. Students often lack strong reading and writing skills for a host of reasons, including poor motivation, language and cultural differences, or because they have a disability such as ADHD, a learning disability, or another type of learning problem. Even capable readers and writers may be only beginning to develop knowledge about history.

A cognitive apprenticeship model of instruction is an excellent way to teach students who don't generally think historically or view history interpretively. In reading historical texts, students often focus on the literal meaning of documents but miss the intertextual reading strategies of interpretive work. Nor do they write the same way historians do. Armed with tools and a systematic approach to instruction, our curriculum helps students construct an original written argument after analyzing historical information. Teachers need support in guiding students to write arguments, especially if they have less experience in how to teach writing or in teaching outside the textbook. Cognitive apprenticeship can help teachers as well as students meet these challenges, and adapts well to today's larger, more diverse classrooms.

We recognize that some teachers will find this approach different from the way they typically organize teaching and learning. It will require them to rethink their roles and those of their students. They must learn how to systematically introduce and then reduce support, while thoughtfully considering the role of written analysis and feedback.

What Rethinking Roles for Teachers and Students Means

Throughout this book, we share ideas from watching the many teachers who have worked with us as they modeled, facilitated, and coached their students. We have watched their students learn to make sense of content, develop disciplinary understanding, and demonstrate competence in writing historical arguments. For some classes, it is helpful for teachers to first set common expectations or norms for learning by focusing on positive student actions before letting students work in small groups in the classroom. Thus, we suggest students try being "Good Detectives"[9] (see Appendix B, Figure B.1, for poster)—if doing so is difficult, teachers might try these skills during an introductory lesson (see the Food Fight Mystery in Appendix B, Figure B.5) to give students the experience of working together before beginning the investigations.

FIGURE 2.1. Instructional Stages or Phases of Instruction, with Accompanying Rationale

Stage 1. Prepare students to learn—The goal of this stage is to make a commitment to learn, and to build background knowledge for reading and writing historically. This is both a phase of instruction and something we do to prepare students for learning at the start of each lesson by setting goals that place activities within the process of historical investigation. [e.g., Investigation 1 and when beginning each subsequent investigation]

Stage 2. Model how to read and write like a historian—Teachers make disciplinary thinking visible using *IREAD* and *H2W* as a way to explore history. Teachers identify strategies and share their thinking out loud so that students can both hear and see what it means to use each strategy as it is modeled. [e.g., Investigations 1–2]

Stage 3. Support students' practice—Teachers guide the class while students attempt each step of *IREAD* and *H2W*, giving them a chance to identify information with guidance (prompting students or redirecting them to the tools), reminding them of the purpose and steps involved in planning, and highlighting supports for students as they compose their essays. Most students appreciate this level of support, as it helps them become more confident reading and writing about a historical question. [e.g., Investigation 3]

Stage 4. Provide additional, more challenging forms of practice—Students read, plan, and write with more autonomy, working in small groups or pairs. More nuanced thinking requires that teachers monitor student progress and explain how students can improve their reasoning along with reading and writing historically. [e.g., Investigations 4 and 5]

Stage 5. Promote independence—The last stage is the hardest but most rewarding for teachers and students. Teachers ask students to complete later investigations at their own pace. Give them plenty of time to read and write with documents, while systematically reducing supports. Students who engage with the curriculum meaningfully and independently make greater strides in disciplinary literacy. [e.g., Investigations 5 and 6]

ORGANIZING THE LEARNING ENVIRONMENT

Engaging in a cognitive apprenticeship is a powerful way to organize instruction. The distinct instructional stages shown in Figure 2.1 add structure to the cognitive apprenticeship. After learning the purpose of each stage and exploring how to use it with students, teachers can reorder, combine, modify, or reteach stages, based on their knowledge of learner characteristics, as needed.

Stages 1–3 allow teachers to systematically introduce supports that will help students understand what it means to think about historical problems, learn how to read historically, and plan and compose disciplinary arguments in history.

Stage 1: Prepare Students to Learn

When beginning this program, we suggest offering an overview of *IREAD* and *H2W* so that students can see the overarching goal of the curriculum. Because each tool is complex, students may not gain a complete understanding until they complete the first three investigations. To deepen their understanding, teachers can describe why each element is included and how to use the tools in more detail with successive investigations. The result is shared background information that corresponds to both learning and content in an integrated approach to the discipline.

Stage 2: Model How to Read and Write Like a Historian

In this stage of cognitive apprenticeship, teachers may feel like performers as they work to explain how they approach and engage in disciplinary reading and writing, and use the tools designed to scaffold student performance. When modeling, teachers should try to come up with plans and compositions that may be somewhat above students' current levels of performance but are within their reach. It is important for teachers to demonstrate how to define the problem at hand (explaining how to think through the reading and writing processes with phrases

> *Classroom Notes.* Try completing the investigation on your own and rehearsing before you model in class. A statement like "The first thing I do is write *IREAD* on the top of the paper, and cross out each step as I work" will be easier to remember when you've planned ahead what to model.

like "I'm thinking about how each step in *IREAD* helps me answer the historical question") and how to grapple with the purpose of each step of the strategy (saying, "Before reading this document, I make sure I understand the historical question"). Remember to make (and correct) intentional mistakes by refining judgments or discarding reasons that are not central to the argument, to show students that you expect them to do the same, as well as to demonstrate rhetorical decision making.

The fact is, teachers' naturally high metacognitive skills must be raised even higher to demonstrate all the thinking we want students to learn.

Stage 3: Support Students' Practice

This stage invites students to work as a class applying *IREAD* and *H2W* to the investigation. Chapters 3–8 provide lesson plans that will explain our general approach. Teachers model using the first document and then ask students to practice with the second.

As students complete Investigations 3–5, they become more skilled, confident, and ultimately independent in reading and writing. Dialogue plays an important role in fostering independence. It sharpens and refines their thinking about the content and skills in the curriculum, and uncovers gaps in their un-

> *Classroom Notes.* Some students may be overwhelmed. Let them know that you are there for support, and reassure them that not every student will complete every activity in each investigation. At the same time, encourage students to try composing at least part of an essay for each investigation.

derstanding. Dialogue also makes thinking "visible" to others by providing the chance to ask questions and get feedback. Students will learn to argue more effectively in writing as they prompt one another to produce the claims, evidence, and counterargument often missing in history essays. Over time, students will internalize such dialogue and begin to address a critical audience as they write.

By now, the astute teacher has noticed that by using cognitive apprenticeship, students engage in learning activities longer than in most programs. This is due to learning simultaneously how to read historically and write argumentatively, as well as the inherent challenges of historical controversies. Remember, instructional stages aren't distinct; they're connected. Teachers must decide when to have students work collaboratively rather than model a cognitive process for them.

We suggest that teachers set up their classrooms so they can move easily from modeling to supporting collaborative practice and back again for mini-modeling sessions. Calling on students and recording their ideas on a visualizer or interactive whiteboard requires space to move around the room, especially during the last two stages of instruction, when teachers circulate among students, who are working independently, to examine their papers and hold miniconferences.

The goal is to *begin* to transfer responsibility for learning from the teacher to the students in a way that ensures success. Before completing Investigation 3 or 4, most students are not able to work independently after simply watching the teacher perform a practice; however, most are ready to work in pairs or small groups equipped with tools and teacher guidance on their use.

Stage 4. Provide Additional, More Challenging Forms of Practice

> *Classroom Notes.* During Investigations 3–5, leverage the power of dialogue. As you walk around the room, encourage students to ask one another questions, restate ideas, and respond to opposing views.

During Stage 4, teachers ask students to work more independently and start to systematically fade out the use of tools such as *IREAD* and *H2W*. This stage invites students to work in pairs or small groups, whichever is most helpful in an individual learning community. Most students have a sense of disciplinary reading and writing by the time they complete Investigation 3, but may need teacher guidance in applying *IREAD* and *H2W*.

Teachers still guide students through annotating important points (perhaps 3–5 per letter), and forming judgments about both documents, using *EAD* as a guide rather than assigning one judgment to each letter of the acronym. As students work, they can share judgments with the class and learn from each other. Some teachers make this visible by recording ideas publicly on a teacher's version of the Investigation packet or on oversized chart paper, while others guide students by pacing instruction for 5 or 10 minutes at a time, depending on the needs of the class. Try to anticipate student needs by reviewing the documents and asking guiding questions as students begin to make judgments on their own.

Stage 5: Promote Independence

By this stage, most student writing will have improved, but their progress as a group will vary (this is clear in the examples provided throughout this book) because students begin and make progress at different rates. Although we expect that you already do so, be sure to take time to reflect on students' writing accomplishments at the end of each investigation. Most students should be well on their way to becoming competent historical detectives, so this is a good time to pause and remember where they began the year. Congratulate them and explain that they will soon be able to apply the *IREAD* and *H2W* tools to any document, either from these investigations or in future history classes.

At this stage of the cognitive apprentice-ship, students should be able to read, anno-tate, and judge documents independently; plan how to use evidence that supports their argument; and compose a five-paragraph es-say. We have specifically included two inves-tigations at this stage, because students are rarely able to meet this goal the first time they attempt to do so on their own. For their part, teachers will benefit from a close read-ing of the investigation in order to under-stand the historical controversies students will face.

> ***Classroom Notes.*** Work-ing with a colleague, take op-posing sides so you can share two perspectives with stu-dents. Seeing how two dif-ferent teachers annotate and plan can give students the confidence to develop their own ways of thinking about documents.

Because you are about to enter the hardest part of the curriculum, we ask you to pause and reconsider two questions at this time:

What are the strengths and weaknesses in students' use of evidence and his-torical writing? Here you can reflect on students' progress in demonstrat-ing a disciplinary use of evidence in writing historical arguments. Explore the Analysis of Student Writing Worksheet (see Appendix A, Figure A.12) to consider students' competencies and areas for improvement. Research shows that combining your feedback with having students complete at least three paragraphs per essay in Investigations 1–6 will improve their ability to write historical arguments. Not all students will benefit, but as an expert vested in their learning, your input is critical.

How can you help students improve? Look back to see how prior investiga-tions have gone, and set one goal for independent practice as you teach the remaining investigations. Perhaps you notice that your students re-spond to the historical question with an argument, or provide background in their introductions that explains the controversy. Some students fol-low the *H2W* text structure fairly well, and many use evidence to support their arguments. You will likely notice that students vary in their ability to explain how evidence supports an argument, and to judge the credibility of evidence according to disciplinary standards (author reliability, the influence of context, facts and examples), as well as their ability to rebut or reconcile the opposing side of an argument. Each scenario is important in deciding on ways to further their learning.

As we watched the teachers who worked with us to develop this curriculum, we observed how successful teachers:

- Began with students' misconceptions and guided them to make accurate judgments.
- Managed classroom interruptions in ways that kept students focused on learning.
- Asked students to justify ideas ("Why did you judge an author in that way?").
- Made reflection meaningful by pairing students with different perspectives and then asking them to exchange papers and note areas for improvement.

Successful teachers also considered whether their students had difficulty finishing a written essay within 3 days, whether they seemed to be "going through the steps" of *IREAD* without connecting it to the historical question, whether they chose quotes while planning without remembering how they related to one another, and whether students used the *H2W* tool without thinking of the entire argument. Finally, we noticed that successful teachers foster student independence by helping students see the big picture of overall literacy activities: That is, they reminded students how the steps of *IREAD*, planning, and *H2W* all fit together, and that understanding the historical question is part of writing an evidence-based argument.

Although it may seem that students are doing all the work in Stage 5, you will remain actively involved by teaching from "behind the scenes" by preparing for each class, actively reading the historical controversy, planning and composing a historical argument of your own, and responding to students' needs when they are working. This form of teaching can be difficult because it involves differentiation of instruction according to multiple students' needs; however, it is needed to promote their independence.

OVERVIEW OF THE DISCIPLINARY LITERACY TOOLS

In this reading and writing program, students engage in several important practices that support their literacy development: Students access and evaluate historical content through *IREAD*, build background knowledge about the writing process and historical argumentation through sample essays and *H2W*, learn to plan and compose as distinct phases, set goals and reflect on their progress from Investigations 1–6, and transition from guided practice to self-directed learning. To achieve this, we created two disciplinary tools for students (see Appendix A, Figures A.1–A.5), additional writing supports for

A student uses the IREAD foldable as he reads and analyzes a primary source. (Photograph by C.J. Breil.)

students (see Appendix A, Figures A.6–A.11) and one tool for teachers to use for analyzing written work (see Appendix A, Figure A.12).

IREAD

The mnemonic *IREAD* tool was developed to support historical thinking while reading. The tool teaches students to analyze and annotate primary sources, and was designed to address a problem many students face—grappling with basic reading comprehension when working with primary sources. Copy Figure A.1 and A.2 in Appendix A back to back on cardstock, fold in half, and cut along the lines separating each letter to create a "foldable" that students can use regularly as they read.

> **Classroom Notes.** Ask students to write and cross out the letters of each mnemonic on the top of their papers so you can spot where they are during the lesson. Encourage the students working more slowly to seek help from you or their group.

The letters *IR* support students' reading comprehension by prompting them to keep the historical question in mind when reading, and to look for authors' main ideas. *I* stands for "Identify the author's argument in response to the historical question." Students must determine how an author thinks about an issue and might respond to the historical question. Even though the author did not necessarily write in response to this question, giving students a purpose for reading supports comprehension. Students show their thinking by noting thoughts in response to this question directly on each primary source document. *R* cues students to "Read each paragraph and ask, what is the author's main idea?" We ask students to "shrink" each paragraph into a phrase or sentence that is written in the margins of each document, to help them grasp the essential ideas from each source.[10]

EAD prompts students to engage in historical thinking and analysis through specific annotation. The letters represent three ways of judging evidence: Examining authorship; Assessing the influence of context; and Determining the quality of facts and examples. *E* prompts students to "Examine the author's reliability," shorthand for considering the influence an author has on what is written and the usefulness of sources in considering a particular historical question. We ask: Who wrote this document, and what judgments can we make about him or her? Why did he or she write this document? Have students give a reason to trust each document and a reason to doubt it, given the type of document, its audience, and the occasion of its writing. *A* prompts students to "Assess the influence of context" so they can judge whether the author's argument makes sense, given what else was going on at that time and place. Students put arrows next to contextual information (dates and locations of documents, historical events). As they read, students construct a timeline using information from documents, headnotes, and source lines. These timelines will help students see how a place and events happening at the time can influence the writing of a given document. *D* cues students to "Determine the quality of the author's facts and examples." We suggest that students box or underline facts and examples cited by the author, and then judge whether or not they are convincing. Because this requires intertextual thinking, it is helpful for students to consider questions like: What facts or examples does the author give to support his or her argument? How do facts or examples support the author's argument? Where do the facts or examples come from? Which facts or examples are most persuasive?

How to Write (or, *H2W*)

This tool provides students with background knowledge about what good historical writing looks like so that they can learn about the ideas that good writers use when they work with historical sources. The *H2W* tool is presented on colored cardstock so that it can be used more than once and located easily. One side features a sample text structure and the other offers helpful transition phrases for introducing and explaining ideas (see Appendix A, Figures A.4 and A.5).

The term *text structure* refers to a visual representation of an organizational pattern that an author uses to structure ideas in a text (cause/effect, compare/contrast, problem/solution). *H2W* offers a five-paragraph format that teachers tell us is reasonable for 8th-graders to use. While teachers may find this structure restrictive or formulaic, it is appropriate for most middle school students to use when first developing disciplinary thinking skills. Throughout this book, we stress that capable students can and should write additional sup-

FIGURE 2.2. An Explanation of the *H2W* Tool

Introduction. The first paragraph in *H2W* is designed to establish the context and historical controversy so that students can formulate their arguments. Students are prompted to cite the source they select, so that their response to the historical question is clear and supported.

Supporting paragraphs. The next two paragraphs prompt students to think through two reasons that support their arguments, along with their accompanying evidence. As students often struggle in selecting and evaluating relevant evidence, they are prompted to compose a sentence that *explains* how their quote or evidence supports their argument as a scaffold to the culminating sentence of each supporting paragraph. They are also reminded to integrate historical thinking with primary sources by including "judgments" about the evidence they cite. Such analytical comments distinguish historical arguments and push students to go past inserting quotations to considering the credibility and relevance of their evidence to the central question.

Rebuttal paragraph. This paragraph is logically the most difficult to craft. One way to present its purpose to students is by presenting a scenario familiar to students that requires persuasion rather than historical thinking. For example, to convince a parent to give you spending money or a principal to allow longer recess, you must counter the anticipated point of contention with a benefit (more money can buy a healthier meal, a longer recess will refresh students working on state standards). Thus, mentioning an appropriate analogy can be helpful before explaining the text structure in this paragraph. Once students grasp how the reason, quote, or evidence they select for their rebuttal relates to their supporting evidence, they can plan this in subsequent essays.

Conclusion. The text structure in the last paragraph fosters interpretive thinking. Students are asked to corroborate evidence from both documents before developing their ideas. Because students may expend a great deal of energy on developing their supporting and rebuttal paragraphs, a short but nuanced ending is often best.

porting or rebuttal paragraphs, while students for whom this is too difficult may write less (i.e., an introduction and conclusion, perhaps one supporting paragraph). In our work, text structure seems to be an acceptable way to show students how to organize ideas for a historical argument. As students gain experience in this genre, they should be expected to experiment with different forms of historical argumentation, such as weaving narration and description into their arguments. For a description, see Figure 2.2.

ADDITIONAL WRITING SUPPORTS FOR STUDENTS

Sample Essays

Although many students find *H2W* useful by itself, we offer two sets of sample essays (see Appendix A, Figures A.8 and A.9) to give students a sense of the text structure so that they can craft historical arguments with confidence.

These sample essays on the topics of Lexington Green and Shays' Rebellion make text structure visible for students. Teachers can introduce them in different ways. For those new to writing historically, explain that *H2W* provides a road map for what to include when writing. Sample essays show students what an argument looks like. For younger or more hesitant writers, teachers can go over one of the essays and compare the content with the corresponding text structure. As students catch on, teachers need less time for formal review. Perhaps create a jigsaw with half the room continuing to inspect the sample essay and *H2W*, while the remaining students apply *H2W* to the second essay. Allow time for exploration, but not so much that students get bored or restless.

Students should see that the introductory paragraphs in each essay share the same contextual information but they differ in presenting opposing arguments. The supporting paragraphs give reasons that align, or "go along with," the writer's argument. Each sentence matches *H2W*. Thus, the rebuttal paragraph in Essay 1 opposes one of the supporting ideas in Essay 2, and so forth. Be sure to point out the helpful phrases from *H2W* used in the sample essays. If time and attention are short, return to this in later investigations as students begin to write in pairs or on their own. Teachers familiar with the curriculum can substitute their own or their students' essays as samples. This is a good way to relate sample essays to the text structure found in *H2W*.

Planning

Chapters 3–5 detail our approach to teaching students how to plan their essays, and Appendix A includes a graphic organizer called "Planning Your Essay" (Figure A.6) for each investigation. Suffice it to say here that our approach emphasizes having students plan before they compose in order to create a visible representation of their thinking. In creating a plan, students must decide what to include from their primary sources and how to organize their thoughts. We suggest teachers encourage students to create written plans as long as they are needed, and to allow students to shorten their planning processes as they gain competence. Many students will internalize how to plan a historical argument by the time they finish Investigation 6. Although the curriculum provides useful steps and notations, there is no right way to plan. It is more important that teachers and students create a shared understanding of how to organize reasons, quotes, and evidence. Remember that planning is only a means to an end! Expect that students may initially spend more time planning instead of writing. As your students work on later investigations, problem-solve ways to help students pace themselves to finish composing, perhaps by framing less complex arguments.

> *Classroom Notes.* One idea for modeling is to use colored pens to highlight how different parts of a document can be used when planning different paragraphs of an essay.

Student Reflection Guide

Student writing improves when they get feedback on how effective it is.[11] We developed the student Reflection Guide (see Appendix A, Figures A.10 and A.11) to promote systematic reflection on student writing on the six historical

A teacher works with and guides a small group of students as they analyze primary sources. (Photograph by C.J. Breil.)

investigations. The student Reflection Guide, aligned with our curriculum, prompts students to evaluate their writing after each investigation and set goals for the next investigation. It is designed to help students identify what works in their essays and what needs improvement.

Clearly, there are other ways that experienced teachers can have their students share and discuss compositions. We suggest caution, however, when it comes to some rubrics, as they may not specify the key attributes of the skills being assessed.[12] A low rating won't help a student figure out what's wrong.[13] Though it takes time for students to reflect on their learning, it will help their writing improve. Our reflection guide asks students if their essays include specific criteria (an introduction that sets up the controversy, a rebuttal that rejects the opposing side), and helps them decide on a substantive writing goal.

SUPPORT FOR TEACHERS: ANALYSIS OF STUDENT WRITING WORKSHEET

This tool for teachers (see Appendix A, Figure A.12) focuses on two questions that you can revisit after students finish each investigation: What are students' incoming strengths and weaknesses in their use of evidence and historical writing? How can you use this information to help students improve? The teachers in our project met once a month as a professional learning community to share students' progress in historical reading and writing. Meetings were spent discussing the historical background for each investigation, practicing how to use and model tools for reading and writing, anticipating challenges that a particular group of students might be facing, and planning when and how to integrate the investigations into the district curriculum. We also included time for teachers to analyze students' investigations and how to make instructional decisions based on what they noticed.

Each session began by celebrating what was going well with regard to literacy as well as contemplating what teachers or students were struggling with. Participants created a journal, attaching the analysis worksheet for students they followed, either in a notebook or digitally. Here are a few guiding principles to consider (preferably along with a colleague):

Select three students whose work you'd like to follow over the course of the year. Students should be chosen carefully. Do they attend school regularly? Do they represent a specific type of learner (a capable reader who struggles with writing, a proficient learner, a student who demonstrates advanced literacy or thinking skills, a student who struggles with literacy, etc.)? Evaluate the students' essays after each investigation, making brief notes next to each essay component. In meeting with your community, share the following points:

Praise: Include an excerpt from each student's essay that shows strength in his/her writing. Explain why you selected this example—what does this show?

Polish: Select an excerpt from each student's essay that shows a weakness in his/her writing. What does this show?

Goals: Given these students' strengths and weaknesses, set a goal for each student and identify feedback to help him/her achieve the goal. Ask: What are the similarities and differences between these students' work and the rest of the students you teach? What questions do you have about students' writing at this point? The teachers in our project found that the Analysis of Student Writing Worksheet helped them learn "in and from practice,"[14] especially as a way to monitor student progress. Teachers shared work examples and supported one another's attempts at interpreting meaning in their students' work. They used their knowledge of students' historical reading and writing abilities to set goals for learners with different learning profiles and to make instructional decisions to help students meet those goals.

We hope you are rewarded by your students' results, and by knowing that teaching this curriculum will get easier every year. In fact, we encourage you to share your successes (and challenges) with us!

CHAPTER 3

Who Fired the First Shot at Lexington Green?

Overview of Chapter 3

Investigation	Foundational Concepts	Disciplinary Literacy Practices	CCSS Links	C3 Links	Principles of Teaching
Investigation 1: *Who fired the first shot at Lexington Green?*	Historical argument, or interpretation, as foundational frame We learn history by analyzing and questioning historical sources or texts	Source and annotate historical texts Take a position in response to a controversial question Compose introduction and conclusion paragraphs	RI.5.6 (p. 14) RH.6–12.1 (p. 61) RH.6–12.2 (p. 61) RH.6–12.6 (p. 61) W.5.1a (p. 20) WHST.6–12.1a (p. 64)	D2.His.1.6–8 D2.His.4.6–12 D2.His.6.6–8 D2.His.10.6–8 D2.His.13.6–8 D2.His.16.6–12 D3.2.6–8 D4.1.6–12 D4.4.6–12	Pose central historical questions that have multiple possible answers and present historical sources to investigate Develop students' background knowledge Present developmentally appropriate representations of content using the *IREAD* and *H2W* tools and sample essays cognitive apprenticeship Stages 1 and 2: Prepare students to learn and model how to read and write like a historian

INVESTIGATION I INTRODUCES history as inquiry and interpretation, and exposes students to the strategies of sourcing historical texts, taking a position in response to a controversial question, and composing introductory and concluding paragraphs. By presenting history as evidence-based interpretation, this investigation shows students that history is not a finished story and offers a detective case to solve: *Who fired the first shot at Lexington Green?*[1] Students refer to conflicting primary sources as they construct their responses. They learn a key strategy for analyzing and questioning historical sources: sourcing. The writing process in this investigation reiterates the concept of interpretation by prompting students to develop an evidence-based position in response to the historical question and primary sources. Introductory and concluding paragraphs give partial expression to their interpretation for students who may be experiencing argument writing for the first time. It's a foundation we'll build upon in future investigations that introduce students to more complex aspects of historical reading, thinking, and writing.

If you're familiar with history education research or teaching materials, the content in this investigation will look familiar. This historical question and the primary sources used to guide it were developed as part of the Amherst Project on American History in the 1960s and adapted by Sam Wineburg in his seminal work on identifying expert and novice ways of historical reading and thinking. Wineburg, Martin, and Monte-Sano also feature this historical question, the sources used here, and other sources in their 2011 book *Reading Like a Historian: Teaching Literacy in Middle and High School Classrooms.* We chose Lexington Green because it is an excellent way to introduce students to historical reading practices and the concept of studying history by inquiring into controversies of the past. In addition, it is generally covered early on in the U.S. history curriculum. We added new literacy scaffolds and incorporated this controversy as the first in a series of six modules designed to improve students' historical writing.

HISTORICAL BACKGROUND

As Wineburg, Martin, and Monte-Sano point out, what most people remember about the Battle of Lexington Green is "more myth than history."[2] For years, the towns of Lexington and Concord have lobbied to be known as the birthplace of the American Revolution. While many agree that the battle led to the death of eight militiamen and wounding of ten, with no British dead, the question of who fired the first shot remains. Another question is whether the initial shot or the subsequent skirmish at Concord should be considered the advent of the American Revolution.

Popular Lore

Popular versions are rife with inaccuracies. Henry Wadsworth Longfellow's 1860 poem, "Paul Revere's Ride," is no exception. Longfellow highlighted Revere's role in warning the colonists that the British Army was marching into the countryside to retrieve stored weapons ("Listen, my children, and you shall hear, of the midnight ride of Paul Revere"), even though riders like Dawes and Prescott played comparable if not greater roles. Historian Jill Lepore argues that the poem isn't really about the American Revolution at all, but rather the Civil War. At the time that Longfellow wrote, tensions were mounting between North and South. Even so, certain phrases remain fixed in our collective memory ("One if by land, and two if by sea") as does the impassioned riding of Paul Revere.[3]

Ralph Waldo Emerson established that Concord was where the American Revolution began when he wrote: "By the rude bridge that arched the flood,/ Their flag to April's breeze unfurled,/Here once the embattled farmers stood/ And fired the shot heard round the world." Emerson wrote "Concord Hymn" for the 1837 dedication of an obelisk that commemorates the Battle of Concord. Emerson had lived with Ezra Ripley, his stepgrandfather and a believer in Concord's role in the Revolution. Perhaps Emerson's version was less than impartial when it came to emphasizing Concord. In fact, historians point out that the lore surrounding Lexington and Concord tends to overshadow what really ignited the Revolution. Later that day, on the "Regulars'" march through the Massachusetts countryside back to Boston, many British soldiers were killed, turning skirmishes into a full-blown conflict that led to the siege of Boston.[4]

A Spark

What we do know is that the Battle of Lexington and Concord was uniquely positioned in historical time, a triggering event that set the American Revolution into motion.[5] This may be the most relevant link between the lesson sequence and the standard K–12 social studies curriculum—as a review of British-colonial relations and the emblem of escalating tensions and fundamental disagreement over governance that led to their divorce.

During the Seven Years' War, intercolonial unity contributed to an emerging and distinct identity among American British colonists. The war's conclusion sent many Indian groups into disarray as they struggled to adapt to the French cession of territory and a British ban on gift-giving. Increasingly, native groups ceded their land in treaties as colonists resisted the Royal Proclamation of 1763 banning them from settling west of the Appalachians. By the time the British sent 10,000 troops to the colonies for protection, the Seven Years' War and its aftermath had contributed to an emerging American identity.[6]

It was at this point that the British levied taxes (e.g., the Sugar Act, Stamp Act, Intolerable Acts) to pay for the Seven Years' War and the protection of the colonies they felt was necessary. These measures angered some colonists who organized resistance (including the Boston Tea Party), but for years most colonists remained loyal to King George and considered themselves British subjects.

When the king ordered General Gage to use military force to quell any rebellion against British authority in the colonies, tensions heightened. The British Regulars' march was intended to seize and destroy a supply of weapons housed in Concord, Massachusetts.[7] But the plan backfired when colonial propaganda in response to the Battle of Lexington and Concord garnered support for the rebel cause. One announcement published in Virginia 10 days later said, "Be it known, that this morning, before break of day, a brigade, consisting of about 1000 or 1200 men . . . found a company of our colony militia in arms, upon whom they fired, without any provocation. . . ."[8] What started as a brawl between British Regulars and local farmers and militia set in motion a series of events (the Second Continental Congress, the Declaration of Independence) that culminated with the colonies' independence from Britain in 1781.

Historians' Views

More recent historiography offers insight into the events at Lexington and Concord. When historian Louis Birnbaum delved into eyewitness testimonies on different sides of the conflict, he found "no awareness of participating in cataclysmic events."[9] Neither colonists, be they Loyalists or rebels, nor the British knew how events would play out. Birnbaum reminds us to think about historical events from the perspective of those involved and to recognize how different the world of the Battle of Lexington and Concord was from ours. Large distances and the time it took to cross them were "largely responsible for the lack of mutual understanding between the colonists in America and those who controlled the British Parliament and made the laws governing the colonies."[10] As a result, colonists' frustrations festered, and the British retained an incomplete understanding of those in America.

Birnbaum gives us a detailed account of the events from April 1–18, 1775, leading up to the conflict at Lexington, grounded in eyewitnesses' perspectives. As Birnbaum's archival work makes clear, the rebels were a well-organized group, ranging from the Sons of Liberty and Dr. Joseph Warren, carefully tracking British troop movements in Boston, to Sam Adams and John Hancock lying low in Lexington, to John Adams at his home in Braintree, to less famous figures who supplied boats or horses that enabled rebels to communicate across the region.

Military expert General John Galvin has tracked the history of the Minutemen and the highly organized system of 40-plus regiments of local militia and Minutemen in place in 1775. Galvin argues that instead of a "farmers' uprising" or "unorganized and leaderless bumpkin militia," those who fought for the colonists were part of a well-structured, relatively efficient force. In terms of military history, then, the Battle of Lexington and Concord was "the culmination and final proving ground of the Massachusetts provincial militia system, as well as the first step in the creation of the Continental Army."[11]

Perhaps most compelling is D. H. Fischer's framing of the events leading up to the American Revolution, which he calls "a series of contingent happenings, shaped by the choices of individual actors within the context of large cultural processes."[12] Fischer focuses his analysis on Paul Revere, who was "much more than merely a midnight messenger,"[13] and General Thomas Gage, commander-in-chief of British forces in the American colonies. Like Birnbaum and Galvin, Fischer moves us away from worshipping mythical heroes who acted alone to appreciating the intricate network of people involved in the events that led up to April 19, 1775. Although they cannot pinpoint who actually fired the first shot, historians recognize that those living in 1775 had no script or story, but were people with interests, concerns, and values living in a particular place and time—all of which influenced the choices they made as history unfolded around them.

LITERACY PRACTICES STUDENTS WILL LEARN

Reading History

Using these texts, Wineburg (1991) found that when historians read, they source a text first (i.e., seek information about who created it, when, and for what purpose).[14] Authentic historical reading takes place in light of such background information. Our project was conducted similarly: asking students to source before continuing with a reading. Often, however, students focused on peripheral aspects without fully understanding the texts. To encourage closer reading and comprehension, we constructed the *IREAD* tool to support literal and disciplinary understanding (see Figure 3.5, Lesson Plan, Day 1). Chapter 2 gave information about each element of the tool. In completing *I*, students identify the overarching argument or position of a text (headnotes contain sufficient information about authors so students can reach conclusions on their own). Moving on to *R*, students explore the main idea of each paragraph, restating it in their own words. When students reconstruct the main ideas in a text, comprehension improves, particularly for students with learning disabilities and struggling readers.[15] Lines in the margins prompt students to paraphrase the main ideas of each paragraph. *IR* supports more basic reading comprehension. In this way we tailored the curriculum to be developmentally appropriate for younger and struggling readers. While making historical analysis accessible to most students may limit historical authenticity, multiple close readings are important for all readers.

> *Teachers Reflect.* "[*IREAD*] makes them write what the author thinks. And that forces them to realize that someone wrote it and that they're a person and they have a perspective and it's not just a bunch of facts or stories."

The fact is, historical sources are not simply a list of details to absorb: They represent people and social exchanges that must be puzzled over in order to yield any meaning. Texts are human creations, which is the basis of sourcing, the historical reading strategy highlighted in Investigation 1 (see Figure 3.6, Lesson Plan, Day 2). When they source, students note the author, his or her motivation or purpose, the type of document (diary, speech, etc.), the audience, and the occasion of the text's creation. Indeed, these aspects of a historical text offer as many clues about the meaning of the text as the literal sentences and paragraphs.

As they model how to source the Barker diary, teachers should explain that it was written by a British officer sent to destroy the colonists' weapons. One could guess that his opinion of events at Lexington Green might differ from the colonists', given that he served the British Army. And, although we think of diaries as personal, official diaries from this period were often used as evidence in trials or investigations of controversial events to determine what happened. It's possible that Barker wrote with the understanding that this information might be used as an official record by others, but perhaps he just wanted to get the events straight in his mind immediately after they happened. Here, we frame sourcing as attention to author, motivation, genre, audience, or occasion for writing.[16] These aspects of historical thinking are

FIGURE 3.1. Modeling Sourcing with Barker's Diary

 Barker's diary

Head Note: Lt. John Barker was part of one group of British soldiers who were sent to destroy weapons the colonists had stored. Here, he describes what happened when British soldiers marched into the town of Lexington on their way to destroy these weapons.

19th. At 2 o'clock in the morning we began our march by wading through a river that came up to our waists. After going a few miles we came to a town called Lexington. We heard there were ★hundreds of people gathered there who planned to go against★ us. At 5 o'clock we arrived and saw a number of people, between 200 and 300, formed in a field called Lexington Green in the middle of the town.

We continued marching, ★keeping prepared against an attack though without intending to attack them ★. On our coming near, they fired one or two shots. As soon as that happened, our men without any orders, rushed in upon them, fired and put them to flight. We regrouped, but with some difficulty because our men were so wild they could hear no orders.

Source: Excerpt adapted from ★Lieutenant John Barker's★ ★diary. ★ He was an officer in the ★British★ army. April 19, 1775.

Comment [1]: (1) Before I start reading I'm going to find out who wrote this and figure out what I can about him/her. Who wrote this will tell me something about what the text might say.

Comment [2]: (4) We heard there were **hundreds** of people **gathered there who planned to oppose us**. [emphasize words in bold]' This wording makes it sound as though the colonists were the aggressors, and that there were many colonists gathered.

Comment [3]: (5) So, I've noticed several phrases here that make the British troops look like the victims and the colonists look like the aggressors. This makes me wonder if the author is trying to make himself and his soldiers look good or if this is really what happened. Is an officer of British troops who killed colonists a reliable source? What would a colonist say? Everyone is going to have a different perspective but I'm thinking I need to compare his story to others to get a better sense of how trustworthy this source is. I am also remembering that this is an official's diary so I'm wondering if he's writing all of this down in this way to make himself and his soldiers look good.

Comment [4]: (2) This tells me that this was written by an officer in the British army. This makes me think that his perspective will be different than an American colonist.

Comment [5]: (3) I also notice that this is a diary of an official. Diaries of officials are often read by others so he may have written with the knowledge that someone else will read it.

Comment [6]: (6) So, now that I've finished reading this text, I notice that I have done 3 things that help me "source" the text. I have (a) noticed the author, (b) identified the type of text, and (c) looked for word choices and phrases that give away the author's point of view.

covered in step *E* of *IREAD* (see Figure 3.1 for the kind of commentary and annotation a teacher would model to make sourcing explicit for students learning to read historically).

In the second document (Figure 3.2),[17] Minutemen tell their story in a sworn statement before justices of the peace in Lexington, Massachusetts. One might expect the colonists to make a case against the British in order to deflect blame for the battle that sparked the Revolutionary War. It's notable that so many men tell the same story, although they may have used the intervening 6 days to collude about events. Still, a sworn statement required taking an oath on the Bible, something people took seriously. Then again, this testimony took place before local officials who may have been partial to the cause.

FIGURE 3.2. Coaching Students to Source the Minutemen's Statement

 Minutemen's statement

Head Note: Many colonists rebelled against British control by forming small groups of soldiers (also known as Minutemen). In this testimony, a group of minutemen told their story about who was to blame for starting the Battle of Lexington Green.

★We Nathaniel Mulliken, Philip Russell (followed by the names of 32★ other men present on Lexington Green on April 19, 1775)...All of lawful age, and inhabitants of Lexington, do ★testify and declare ★, that on April 19th, at about 1 or 2 am, we were told that there were British soldiers marching from Boston towards Concord.

Comment [7]: Who are the people who submitted this statement (see attribution for clue)? What point of view or interests might the authors have regarding the events they describe? How might they portray the events at Lexington?

We were ordered to meet at the field at the center of town on Lexington Green, where we were told by our captain to go back home, but to be ready to come back when we heard the beat of the drum. We further testify and declare that about 5 o'clock in the morning, hearing our drumbeat, we returned, and soon ★found a large body of troops marching towards us ★.

Comment [8]: What kind of statement is this? Who did they testify before (see attribution)? What does this indicate about its reliability?

At that point, some of our group were making their way toward Lexington Green, and others had reached it. Our men began to leave. ★While our backs were turned★ on the British troops, we were fired on by them, and a number of our men were killed and wounded. To our knowledge, not a gun was fired by any person in our group on the British soldiers before ★they fired on us★. The British continued firing until we had all made our escape.

Comment [9]: What do their word choices tell you about who started the fighting or who was more aggressive? Find one phrase in this paragraph and one in the next that point the finger at one side.

Source: Excerpt adapted from a ★sworn statement★ by ★34 minutemen ★, before three Justices of the Peace. Lexington, April 25, 1775.

Comment [10]: How many people submitted this statement? What had to happen before they could submit this statement?

Word choice signals an author's purpose or motivation. When Barker writes "hundreds of people gathered there who planned to go against us," he frames the colonists as aggressors. Meanwhile, the Minutemen's statement specifies their position ("[we] found a large body of troops marching toward us," "while our backs were turned," "they fired on us"), which places the blame with the British. When comparing sources, students should consider how authors know the things they share and whether they are in a good position to discuss the events they share with accuracy and truthfulness. Given these positions, students must consider what aspects of statements are believable. Taking students through these considerations and questions begins the process of learning to read critically and think historically.

Writing History

This curriculum offers support to develop students' writing: *IREAD* helps students access and evaluate content while the sample essays, planning sheets, and *H2W* build their background knowledge about writing. The emphasis on planning plus composing highlights writing as a process, with guided reflection on students' accomplishments as a way to foster goal-setting and self-monitoring. Using the cognitive apprenticeship model eases the teacher's transition from modeling to less guidance and ultimately student independence. Each investigation plays a role in this comprehensive writing intervention.

In contrast to the writing tasks found in most high school history classrooms (summaries of information, short-answer responses), Investigation 1 orients students to historical writing as argumentative or interpretive exercises.[18] When writing the introduction, students must make a claim in response to the central question, while the conclusion reiterates that claim and highlights the evidence that led up to it (see Figure 3.7, Lesson Plan, Day 3). We use the first investigation to "jumpstart" the writing process with *H2W*. In subsequent investigations, students will learn to plan and write full essays using additional tools. Along with stating a position in the introduction, we ask students to provide relevant historical context and frame their claim as one interpretation of a controversial topic. Students review an event or issue, explain the controversy, and discuss why people disagreed about it. The paragraph concludes with the student's claim.

From the start, our investigations put students in the position of deliberating among multiple interpretations of controversial topics. Students often struggle with how to write an argument as opposed to a summary. By responding to the central question, they can make a simple argumentative claim more naturally, since answering a question requires interpretation (and more than one interpretation is plausible). When students are ready for complex tasks, they can consider how each response (the British or the Minutemen) might be plausible. If they are unsatisfied with an obvious answer, they should be encouraged to propose an alternative interpretation.

Instead of supporting and rebuttal paragraphs in this investigation, students write only an introduction and conclusion. In our work, we noticed that some students had difficulty planning and writing five paragraphs for the first investigation, especially when they had encountered the *IR* steps in *IREAD* for the first time. In this way, students get a more gradual introduction to expectations in the reading and writing activities. We also suggest that forming an introduction and conclusion at this point can be a defensible, albeit emerging historical argument. Younger students and those who struggle with literacy may benefit from setting a goal to write these paragraphs. Thus, introduction + conclusion is a miniature version of the entire essay—it contains key aspects of a full essay, including a claim, but requires less composition at an early point in the year.

The reflection process begins with having students read sample introductory and conclusion paragraphs in response to the same question only *after* they have tried composing their own (reading a sample essay on the same topic could make it difficult for students to grapple with their own response). After putting forth the effort to compose, students are ready to learn from others' attempts. Comparing the samples with the *H2W* and their own paragraphs offers the chance to reflect on the strengths and weaknesses in their work, become aware of the requirements of argument writing, and develop goals for improvement.

> ***Classroom Notes.*** Our goal is to establish that writing is not confined to taking notes, filling in blanks, or reporting details. Instead, students have a voice. They can sort through primary sources and construct their own response.

HOW TO TEACH THIS INVESTIGATION

Each element of the curriculum is introduced in this investigation. On Day 1, students get an overview of the investigation process, learn relevant background and vocabulary, and focus on basic reading comprehension as they begin to use the *IREAD* reading tool. On Day 2, students learn to source historical texts (a key historical reading strategy) and use that information to evaluate a text. On Day 3, students learn how to structure, plan, and compose an introduction and conclusion paragraph. The Essay Response Template found in Appendix A (Figure A.7) can be used as the last page of each student packet; just fill in the blank with the appropriate historical question.

Teaching Principles

This investigation kicks off a series of curriculum modules that pose central historical questions and sources for students to deliberate. By involving students in the controversy, thinking about history becomes part of an evidence-based interpretation. When using only conventional approaches to history, students don't think like historians when faced with primary and secondary sources. One way we introduce developmentally appropriate tasks is by presenting investigations as detective cases to solve, which connects academic work to more familiar ideas. Presenting historical reading and thinking through the *IREAD* foldable is another. While historians don't generally follow steps from a list as they read and analyze historical sources, students must develop complex and integrated ways of thinking; using the tools makes this approach visible and accessible. In this way, *IREAD* offers them small steps on the path to thinking like a historian.

The cognitive apprenticeship process begins with teachers modeling sourcing and annotating texts using *IREAD* and introducing the *H2W* tool and sample essays (Stages 1 and 2: "Preparing students to learn" and "Modeling how to read like a historian"). We have found that teachers interpret modeling in different ways. We see four major tasks as key aspects of modeling that help students: (1) name and explain what is being modeled; (2) show how to model (in this case, annotate a projected document so that everyone can see what you do when you source using *IREAD*); (3) show how you think when you use the strategy you are modeling—make your reasoning visible to students by thinking aloud; and (4) recap by noting the strategy you just modeled and the key things you did or thought as you used that strategy. Too often, the knowledge that teachers want to share is left implicit in a lesson; these steps offer students a strategy that they can try themselves. (The comments in Figure 3.1 represent the kinds of things a teacher might say as she or he models how to source the Barker diary.)

Once teachers have made sourcing explicit, students are given a chance to source the second document (using questions to prompt students or redirect them to the foldable). Figure 3.2 offers examples of questions teachers can use to give students guided practice with *E* and reinforce the sourcing reading strategy. By using cognitive apprenticeship, teachers can offer a mix of direct instruction and practice to help their students learn complex literacy strategies.

> *Classroom Notes.* It's important to actively model reading the first document and share your thinking, rather than trying to elicit information from students who haven't yet been exposed to historical reading.

Things to Keep in Mind

If your students have not been exposed to the concept of history as the interpretation and analysis of primary sources, you may want to seed these ideas with familiar content (see the Food Fight Mystery in Appendix B). Teaching history as inquiry also requires paying attention to classroom culture and structures. Consider your classroom: How is it set up? Do students work individually, in pairs, or with a group? Who does most of the talking? With the exception of the teacher modeling in parts of Investigations 1–3, these lessons ask students to make sense of the content and develop interpretations on their own. To do this, students take an active role, interacting with one another and processing different ideas. Teachers must adjust their role accordingly, starting with more active modeling and explicit instruction, and then shifting to facilitating and coaching. By having students work in pairs or small groups, they can learn from one another and gain independence without completely floundering. Debriefing sessions give teachers a way to check in on student work, reinforce good thinking, and address misconceptions or confusion. An important part of these investigations is listening to students and responding to their ideas in ways that support growth.

HOW MIGHT STUDENTS RESPOND? STUDENT WRITING AND TEACHER FEEDBACK

For Investigation 1, we ask students to draft only the introduction and conclusion paragraphs of an essay. By limiting writing, teachers can focus on how well students understand the controversy and its historical relevance, their ability to use historical thinking to make inferences about documents, and their ability to draw a conclusion. Because these skills are new to students, they may stumble using them for the first time.

In our samples, neither Tamia nor Aaron struggled with this idea (for more on each student, see Chapter 1). Both students were able to distinguish the authors of the documents as historical actors with different perspectives and motives. Tamia (Figure 3.3) recognized that different perspectives may lead to different accounts, that people cannot be certain of the truth, and even suggested that conflicting accounts may be motivated by the desire to direct blame at the opposing side. However, in her concluding paragraph she struggles with reconciling these opposing views and seems to simply pick a side without using documents to support her conclusion. Aaron (Figure 3.4) made similar inferences about the authors in the introduction and then used the dates of the documents to infer which account was more reliable. While this inference may be merely

> **Classroom Notes.** Reading students' essays—either Tamia's and Aaron's or their own—helped teachers prepare for each investigation by alerting them to the kinds of support students might need.

FIGURE 3.3. Tamia's Essay for Investigation 1

On April 19, 1775 there was an conflict between the british and colonists. Because there are to different paspectives we don't know who fired first because they don't want to get in trouble. People disagree because like I said in the perspectives and they also have to different opinions. The person who fired the first shot is the British.

On the day of April 19, 1775 the British shot first because they don't like the colonists. The British were marching for 3 hrs in the first document The colonies fired first document I agree because they did fire first

Praise: "I like how you distinguish the authors' perspectives!"

Praise: "True—The best that we can do is use historical evidence to reconstruct what happened."

Polish: "You argue both sides here. Which is your answer to the historical question?"

Polish: "How do the documents support your answer?"

Goal: "For next time, use evidence from the documents to support your conclusion."

FIGURE 3.4. Aaron's Essay for Investigation 1

> On April 19, 1775 the British faught the Minutemen at Lexington Green. The controversy toys is that each side says the other fired first. People disagreed with the controversy because who ever fired the first shot would be responsible for the revolutionary war. I belive that the Minutemen fired first because I found Barkers diary more reliable.
>
> I belive the minutemen fired first because their statement is less reliable because it was written to days after the event which gave them time to get their lie to together. I trust barker's diary because it was written the day the event happend. I doubt the that minutemans statement because their statement was 6 days old. When all of the facts on both sides are considered I trust barker's diary more.

CAP *(margin note next to first paragraph)*

CAP *(margin note next to second paragraph)*

Praise: "Right. This would help explain why we have two different accounts."

Praise: "Good detective work! I like how you are using the dates to think about the evidence in the documents."

Polish: "I see what you mean but also wonder if you can think of any reason why writing on the same day might raise doubts about Barker's account?"

Goal: "Sharpen your arguments by thinking about how your reader might disagree."

conjecture, it shows that he was thinking about both the content and the context of the documents.

LESSON PLANS AND MATERIALS

Teachers and students will need to have the following: Lesson plans (Figures 3.5–3.7), Investigation 1 packet (clipboard with overview, Barker diary, Minutemen's testimony—see Figure 3.8), Additional materials for this investigation (background cards—see Figure 3.9), Disciplinary literacy tools (*IREAD, H2W,* sample essays, and essay prompt sheet—see Appendix A), film clip, and overhead projection capacity (to model annotating and to compare the sample essays with *H2W*).

FIGURE 3.5. Lesson Plan, Day 1: Background Knowledge, Reading Comprehension, and Historical Reading

Materials: **Investigation 1 student packets, historical background cards, *IREAD*, *H2W*, Essay prompt sheet, Reflection guide, Sample essays, Projector, Online film clip**

Suggested time: **1 hour per day**

INTRODUCTION

1. Introduce students to the curriculum: They will learn how to be "historical detectives" by investigating issues from six "cases" of American history. They will prepare for the case (by understanding the question and background information), investigate the case (by reading historical sources and thinking about evidence), and write a final judgment (by organizing evidence and writing to share their findings with others).

2. Introduce the controversy and why it is important. Highlight the historical question.

BACKGROUND INFORMATION

3. Watch Chapter 2 of "Blows Must Decide," Season 1, Episode 2 of the PBS film *Liberty! The American Revolution.* See http://www.youtube.com/watch?v=obP5TSKXn-A.

    a. Discuss: (i) How did the British view the colonists? (ii) How did the colonists view the British? (iii) Why did each side want to claim that the other side fired the first shot?

4. Review relevant events (see background cards in the *Additional Materials*). Cut out and create a set of four cards for each group. Ask students to put the cards in chronological order. Then have students decide whether each event was a cause or an effect of the Battle at Lexington Green. Finally, ask students to explain to one another how each event may have caused the Battle of Lexington Green or resulted from it. For a greater challenge, cover the dates on each card. For a lower challenge, label the effects of the Battle at Lexington Green.

HISTORICAL READING: GENERAL READING COMPREHENSION

5. Preview vocabulary (e.g., "put them to *flight,*" or "planned to go against us," in Barker's diary; "colonists," Barker's diary, and "minutemen" in Minutemen's testimony).

6. Overview of reading primary sources and using the *IREAD* foldable (see Appendix A).

    a. Explain to students that we figure out answers to questions in history by looking at documents or artifacts that have been left behind. We will look at primary documents, those created by people in the time we are studying.

    b. Each document will include:

        i.   A "Head Note"—an introduction that gives background and an overview

        ii. A "Source" line or attribution—tells who created the document and when

        iii. The text itself—What the author created that give us clues to the past

    c. *IREAD* gives us a way to investigate these documents—like detectives, we will ask questions and make judgments.

7. Model "*I R*" of "*IREAD*" with Barker document.

8. Guide students as they use *I R* with the Minutemen's document.

9. Debrief: What is making sense about *IREAD* so far? What is confusing?

FIGURE 3.6. Lesson Plan, Day 2: Historical Reading and Thinking

INTRODUCTION

1. Warmup: Ask students to remember the historical question and which side of the controversy that Lt. Barker and the Minutemen were on.

HISTORICAL THINKING AND READING: SOURCING WITH E OF IREAD

2. Model *E* of *IREAD* with Barker diary. Make your thinking visible as you think aloud while reading and using *E*.

3. Guide students as they use *E* of *IREAD* with the Minutemen's testimony.

   a   Give students an opportunity to identify the information for *E* with your guidance (asking questions to prompt students or redirecting them to the foldable). You may consider doing this as a whole class or having students work with a partner/group and then debriefing their work as a whole class.

4.   Evaluate ("Judge") the primary sources based on the following:

   a. *Authors.* In whole class, pairs, or small groups, discuss and share out: Given what you know about who the authors were and what they might have been able to witness or not witness, what are the reasons to trust each author? What are the reasons to doubt each author? Check for understanding of both documents and the concept of sourcing.

   b. *Type of document.* Discuss and share out: Given what they know about the kind of document this is, what are the reasons to trust each author? What are the reasons to doubt each author? Check for understanding of the documents and sourcing.

   c. *Audience.* Discuss and share: Given what they know about the intended audience, what are the reasons to trust each author? What are the reasons to doubt each author? Check for understanding of the documents and sourcing.

   d. Students review annotations on both documents in order to make judgments.

   e. Ask students to write one reason to trust each author and one reason to doubt each author. Write it on the blank line next to *E* on the bottom of each document.

5. Debrief

   a. Think-pair-share: "Based on your judgments of the authors, how does each text help you think about the central question (*Who fired the first shot at Lexington Green?*)? Which text is more helpful or reliable? Why?"

   b. Preview: Tomorrow students are going to write an essay telling their position on this question. When they do, it will be important to share their thinking about the authors' reliability (i.e., the judgments they made about the author).

FIGURE 3.7. Lesson Plan, Day 3: Planning and Historical Writing

INTRODUCTION

1. Review "How to Write Your Essay" or "*H2W*"

   a. Explain that students are going to learn how to write two paragraphs today, using a guide called How to Write Your Essay or *H2W* (see Appendix A, Figures A.1–5). To make this easier, student will write only the introduction and the conclusion today.

   b. Direct students to look at *H2W* and follow along. As you go over each sentence, elicit ideas from the class, making sure they understand where to find information for each element in the introduction.

   c. Continue to review *H2W*, focusing on the conclusion. Students will use the information they discussed yesterday to compare the documents, and explain their argument in response to the central question.

   d. Tell students that they will learn to write five paragraphs later in the year, but that a good basic essay includes an introduction and conclusion.

COMPOSING

2. Ask students to compose their own introduction and conclusion paragraphs.

   a. Direct students to use the documents they annotated, and to follow the *H2W* guide.

   b. Students who are comfortable with writing can use the transition words and phrases on their own.

REFLECTION

3. Show students the sample essays provided (see Appendix A, Figure A.8). Explain the goal of noticing what the student is doing well and what the student could improve.

   a. Review the introduction. Ask students to compare this paragraph with *H2W*, and to decide if it includes all the parts. Discuss how to make the sample better.

   b. Review the conclusion. Ask students to compare this paragraph with *H2W* and decide if it includes all the parts. Discuss how to make the sample better.

4. Wrap up.

   a. Think-pair-share. Ask students to talk about what part of their writing they like most and least.

   b. Explain the Reflection Guide (see Appendix A, Figures A.10 and A.11)—a way of reflecting on writing using a graph that will help focus on the parts of a good essay.

      i. Ask students to check what parts they have included and make notes on the chart about what they will work on next.

   c. Ask students to make one change to their introduction or conclusion based on what they know about writing these paragraphs.

FIGURE 3.8. Materials: Investigation #1 Packet

Name: _____ **Class:** _____ **Date:** _____

INVESTIGATION #1:
WHO FIRED THE FIRST SHOT AT LEXINGTON GREEN?

OVERVIEW:

You are a historical detective trying to uncover who fired the first shot at Lexington Green on April 19, 1775. Was it the British or the colonists? This was the first battle of the Revolutionary War, so whoever is blamed could be responsible for the Revolution. Your clues are historical documents written at the time of the event. Read and discuss as you investigate the event. At the end, you will share your interpretation, or argument, about who fired the first shot in writing. You will also explain clues that led you to this argument.

Good Detectives . . .

...are focused on learning.

...cooperate with their partners and teacher.

...keep others from getting off track.

...think about evaluating and using evidence.

FIGURE 3.8. Materials: Investigation #1 Packet, Continued

Name:_____ Class:_____ Date:_____

I-

Barker's Diary

Head Note: Lt. John Barker was part of one group of British soldiers who were sent to destroy weapons the colonists had stored. Here, he describes what happened when British soldiers marched into the town of Lexington on their way to destroy these weapons.

R-_____

19th. At 2 o'clock in the morning we began our march by wading through a river that came up to our waists. After going a few miles we came to a town called Lexington. We heard there were hundreds of people gathered there who planned to go against us. At 5 o'clock we arrived and saw a number of people, between 200 and 300, formed in a field called Lexington Green in the middle of the town.

R-_____

We continued marching, keeping prepared against an attack though without intending to attack them. On our coming near, they fired one or two shots. As soon as that happened, our men without any orders, rushed in upon them, fired and put them to flight. We regrouped, but with some difficulty because our men were so wild they could hear no orders.

Source: Excerpt adapted from diary of Lieutenant John Barker, an officer in the British army. April 19, 1775.

Timeline of events

Judgments

E_____

A_____

D_____

FIGURE 3.8. Materials: Investigation #1 Packet, Continued

Name:_____ Class:_____ Date:_____

I-

Minutemen's Statement

Head Note: Many colonists rebelled against British control by forming small groups of soldiers (also known as Minutemen). In this testimony, a group of Minutemen told their story about who was to blame for starting the Battle of Lexington Green.

R-_____
_____
_____
_____

We Nathaniel Mulliken, Philip Russell (followed by the names of 32 other men present on Lexington Green on April 19, 1775). . . All of lawful age, and inhabitants of Lexington, do testify and declare, that on April 19th, at about 1 or 2 am, we were told that there were British soldiers marching from Boston towards Concord.

R-_____
_____
_____
_____

We were ordered to meet at the field at the center of town on Lexington Green, where we were told by our captain to go back home, but to be ready to come back when we heard the beat of the drum. We further testify and declare that about 5 o'clock in the morning, hearing our drumbeat, we returned, and soon found a large body of troops marching towards us.

R_____
_____
_____
_____
_____

At that point, some of our group were making their way toward Lexington Green, and others had reached it. Our men began to leave. While our backs were turned on the British troops, we were fired on by them, and a number of our men were killed and wounded. To our knowledge, not a gun was fired by any person in our group on the British soldiers before they fired on us. The British continued firing until we had all made our escape.

Source: Excerpt adapted from a sworn statement by 34 Minutemen, before three Justices of the Peace. Lexington, April 25, 1775.

Judgments

E_____

A_____

D_____

COLONISTS DEVELOP THEIR OWN SOCIETY (1607–1763)

- British oversee settlement of colonies but mostly leave colonists to rule themselves.
- Colonists saw themselves as a society ruled by the people and did not respect authority as much as Europeans.
- Compared to Europe, there were fewer very wealthy people and economic differences between people were not as noticeable.
- 80% of the non-slave population owned property and could vote
- Slaves were 20% of the total population by 1776.

BRITISH TAXATION & AUTHORITY UPSET COLONISTS (1763–1775)

- British colonists fight French colonists in the Ohio River Valley and Canada from 1754-1763 ("French & Indian War" or "Seven Years' War"). Britain wins.
- The war complicates relationships with American Indians.
- Proclamation of 1763 banned colonists from going into land won in war, but colonists resist the proclamation and clash with Indians.
- British put 10,000 troops in colonies for protection of colonists from Indian attacks.
- To pay for the war and protection of the colonists, British levy a series of taxes from 1764 to 1773 (Sugar Act, Stamp Act, Townshend Acts, Tea Act, Intolerable Acts).
- Colonists angry about taxes and British authority. Colonists organize resistance to the British (Boston Tea Party, First Continental Congress).

BRITISH REACT TO COLONIAL RESISTANCE (1775)

- King George ordered British General Gage to use military force to stop challenges to the king's authority in the colonies.
- General Gage sent troops to destroy the colonists' supply of weapons in Concord, Massachusetts.
- On April 19, British troops arrived in Lexington, Massachusetts, on their way to Concord.

COLONISTS REBEL (1775–1781)

- In May 1775, the Second Continental Congress met and appointed George Washington as the commander-in-chief of the colonies.
- In July 1776, the Continental Congress sent the Declaration of Independence to King George.
- The Revolutionary War continues until the colonists win in 1781.

CHAPTER 4

Were Shays and His Followers Rebels or Freedom Fighters?

Overview of Chapter 4

Investigation	Foundational Concepts	Disciplinary Literacy Practices	CCSS Links	C3 Links	Principles of Teaching
Investigation 2: *Were Shays and his followers rebels or freedom fighters?*	Historical argument as frame We learn history by analyzing and questioning historical sources	Contextualize historical sources Compare & evaluate historical sources Write supporting and rebuttal paragraphs	RI.5.6 (p. 14) RI.5.8 (p. 14) RI.5.9 (p. 14) RH.6–12.1 (p. 61) RH.6–12.2 (p. 61) RH.11–12.3 (p. 61) RH.6–12.6 (p. 61) W.5.1a–c (p. 20) W.5.9 (p. 21) WHST.6–12.1b (p. 64) WHST.6–12.9 (p. 66)	D2.His.1.6–8 D2.His.4.6–12 D2.His.6.6–8 D2.His.10.6–8 D2.His.13.6–8 D2.His.16.6–12 D3.2.6–8 D3.4.6–12 D4.1.6–12 D4.4.6–12	Develop students' background knowledge Present developmentally appropriate tasks Cognitive apprenticeship Stages 1 and 2: Prepare students to learn and model how to read and write like a historian

I N THIS INVESTIGATION, we continue to present history as argument by asking students to interpret the actions of Daniel Shays and his followers, notorious rebels who were often cast as a threat to the fledgling republic. Students analyze and question conflicting sources, weighing the merits of a speech by a Shays supporter against a letter from Abigail Adams, who disapproved of Shays. After considering different perspectives, students compose a response to the central question: *Were Shays and his followers rebels or freedom fighters?*

This investigation is a good opportunity to introduce contextualization, since the authors' location and time place them in very different positions with respect to the events they share. As part of the process of reading, inquiry, and analysis, students learn to contextualize primary sources and use information about the historical context of sources to compare and evaluate them. They also continue to work on basic reading comprehension and, because the authors' backgrounds and experience with the new nation contrast, this is also a good investigation for students to practice sourcing (which they learned in Chapter 3).

For argument writing, students learn to support a claim using evidence, refute opposing arguments, and recognize that planning is an important preparation for composing. Teachers model how to plan using the "Planning Your Essay" sheet in conjunction with *H2W* and the sample essays. The investigation introduces the idea that a claim does not stand without evidence to support it, that they must identify and select relevant evidence from primary sources to bolster their arguments. Students also learn that people can interpret evidence differently. Consequently, this investigation introduces them to the concept of rebuttal, considering an alternative perspective and explaining why one interpretation reflects the evidence the best.

HISTORICAL BACKGROUND

Textbooks tell a tidy story of Shays' Rebellion. Often portrayed as a single event, Shays' Rebellion has come to symbolize the plight of farmers after the Revolutionary War. Faced with high taxes and an ongoing economic depression, many lost their land to foreclosure and were imprisoned for failure to pay their debts. A group of Massachusetts farmers fought back, so the story goes, by marching, pitchforks in hand, with Daniel Shays to close courthouses and seize weapons at an armory.

As always, history is not so simple. According to Francis Cogliano, the rebellion was longer than a single day—it spanned many months across 1785, 1786, and 1787—and Shays led only a few of the efforts.[1] Similar protests occurred in Maryland, New Hampshire, Pennsylvania, Vermont, and Virginia. Cogliano also shows the range of activities that took place (submitting a petitions of grievances to local and state governments, closing and taking over courthouses in Massachusetts counties) as well as the disastrous attempt to seize the Springfield arsenal in 1787. Students are told that those involved were farmers, but recent historians cite how well-to-do businessmen and creditors like Shays were also involved, because they were concerned about the financial state of Massachusetts.[2] Whereas Leonard Richards portrays Shays as a reluctant participant, Gary Nash argues that Shays had been involved for much longer.[3] Nor could pitchforks have been the only weapons used by the rebels, many of whom had fought in the Revolutionary War.

Were They Rebels?

Even Shays' contemporaries couldn't agree on the so-called "rebels" and the extent to which they rebelled. Americans of the late 1700s held strong opinions about Daniel Shays and his followers. Many spoke out against the insurgents, including an unknown author whose acrostic poem was published in the *Hampshire Gazette,* published in Northhampton, Massachusetts, in June 1787:

I nsolvent debtors, aiming ne'er to pay:
N otorious gamblers risking all at play.
S editious whigs, who think a man should die,
U nless his sentiments with their' comply.
R evengeful tories, democracy disdain;
G reat Britain, they think ought to rule & reign.
E nlarg'd jail-birds, men with five years pay:—
N ews-men, Court members, servants run away
T he vicious ign'rant herd; for knaves fit tools
S ome may be honest, yet deluded fools.[4]

Many leaders at the time agreed with these sentiments. George Washington, by then a retired Revolutionary War hero, urged the rebels to stop, even before the January 1787 attack on the federal arsenal. In December 1786 he wrote to Henry Knox: "Vigilance in watching, and vigour in acting, is, in my opinion, become indispensably necessary. If the powers are inadequate amend or alter them, but do not let us sink into the lowest state of humiliation and contempt, and become a byword in all the earth."[5] Public opinion did not change after the attack. Benjamin Franklin referred to Shays' Rebellion as "mad attempts to overthrow [the government of Massachusetts]." He explained that these efforts "alone proceed from the wickedness or from the ignorance of a few."[6] In June 1787, John Hancock called the participants "unhappy and deluded offenders" who took "attrocious and traiterous" actions. He argued that if they respected the concept of self-government and understood the need for good government, they would behave in an orderly manner and obey the law.[7]

Historian Carol Sue Humphrey emphasizes the rebels' personal motives: that the prospect of losing their land drove them to close the courts which were ordering the foreclosures.[8] This reflects the notion supported by many at the time that the rebels acted out of self-interest, without regard for the damage they might inflict on the new nation.

Why such outrage? To many, Shays' Rebellion echoed concerns about the viability of the young country and its reputation abroad. By the time the Paris Peace Treaty ended the Revolutionary War in 1783, the United States had been operating under the Articles of Confederation for 2 years. By design, these Articles gave the federal government little power, and few means to intervene in the individual states, or address the suffocating debt many faced after the war. Leaders like Washington were aware that the world was watching, ready to act on any sign of weakness. The fact that the federal government could do nothing to stop the rebellions nor influence the Massachusetts government was embarrassing, and led to fears that the rebellion would crush the new nation. After 8 years of war, no one wanted another conflict, especially between citizens who had fought together to free their land from British control.

Or Were They Freedom Fighters?

Others were more optimistic. In January 1787, Thomas Jefferson argued from Paris that "the people are the only censors of their governors: and even their errors will tend to keep these to the true principles of their institution. . . . The basis of our government being the opinions of the people, the very first object should be to keep that right. . . . Cherish therefore the spirit of our people, and keep alive their attention."[9] In other words, if the United States was truly a government of the people, the people's protest should not be ignored. Later Jefferson argued: "A little rebellion now and then is a good thing. . . . It is medicine necessary for the sound health of government."[10] He differed from many peers in embracing the people's voice as a means of checking the government's power. To some extent, his position was borne out: The year after the rebellion, Massachusetts elected a new legislature that declared a moratorium on debts, and greatly reduced taxes. Yet, at the time, the future of the country was uncertain and the participants in these events did not know what was to come.

National Park Service historian Richard Colton agrees with Jefferson. He argues that Shays and his men believed they were fighting *for* the new nation to ensure its health. He wrote that Shays' group was "not outside the system—it was the system. . . . They were not rebels, but rather, Regulators of a government that required correction."[11] In fact, the participants in this movement called themselves "Regulators," a term that came to mean fighting abusive governmental power. Many had fought the elitist tyranny associated with British rule, but found that after the war, their circumstances had only worsened.

Historians agree that crushing debt and economic depression led to dissent, but differ in their interpretation of people's reactions at the time. While Humphrey emphasizes their selfish motives, Richards argues that Massachusetts farmers had been meeting and writing petitions for more than a year when the state legislature adjourned in July 1786 without addressing their grievances. Cogliano's research clarifies the grievances: In Hampshire County, a third of the men had been sued for debt between 1784 and 1786, and in Worcester County, 93 of 103 men in custody in 1785 were jailed for debt. Amidst high taxation, the government took actions that undermined families' ability to pay their debts. Meanwhile, the elite ruling class in Boston was far removed from such realities, which made them seem more like British royalty than fellow countrymen.

Richards argues that once the legislature recessed, the farmers, many of them Revolutionary War heroes, made a plan to close the courthouses—not to avoid foreclosure and imprisonment, but to gain the attention of the state government. Other historians contend that their goal was to keep from being imprisoned.[12] When the state tried to form a militia in response, many sympathized with the farmers and refused to join. However, in January 1787, at least two militias clashed with Regulators at the Springfield Armory, where four men died. Eventually Shays was captured and exiled; 18 others received death sentences and 2 were actually hanged.

By the spring of 1787 when the rebellion finally fizzled out, delegates to the Constitutional Convention were starting to rewrite the dysfunctional Articles of Confederation. Although the Convention was planned before Shays' attack, 8 of the 12 appointed their delegates during the height of Shays' Rebellion.[13] They carried their reactions to the Convention; as they shaped the new nation, the rebellion was a recent memory. Colton calls these events the "last battle" in the American Revolution, as the new nation struggled to figure out the meaning of democracy.[14]

Whom to Believe?

Were the protestors simply trying to lower the taxes and punishments of those in debt? Or were they acting for the good of the state in trying to rid Massachusetts of elitist practices? In his testimony after confronting Daniel Shays at the Springfield Armory, Colonel Buffington says he told Shays: "I am here, in defense of that country you are endeavoring to destroy" and that Shays replied: "If you are in defense of this country, we are both defending the same cause."[15] Perhaps both sides felt they were acting on behalf of the nation, but had different interpretations of what it meant to serve their country. We use the terms *rebels* and *freedom fighters* to characterize these competing interpretations of Shays and his followers. In this investigation, students use contrasting sources to develop their own argument about this important event in U.S. history.

LITERACY PRACTICES STUDENTS WILL LEARN

Reading History

While continuing to emphasize literal comprehension of texts and sourcing, this investigation extends historical reading practices to contextualization. As students continue to source (guided by *E* in *IREAD*—see Appendix A), the first text they see is a speech by Daniel Gray, "Chairman of a Committee for the above purpose."[16] After reading for literal comprehension (guided by *IR* of *IREAD*), students should recognize that this is a speech in support of those protesting the government that outlines their complaints.

> *Classroom Notes.* We don't ask students to choose one text over another as right or wrong, nor replace the textbook. Instead, we want students to see how each text can be both helpful and limited in developing an interpretation about Shays and his followers.

The attribution also explains that Gray was a part of a unit of armed soldiers addressing townspeople about the issues—he was not only a sympathizer; he was an actual part of the movement.

Now students will begin to learn how to contextualize a historical text (see Figure 4.9, Lesson Plan, Day 2). Teachers model the process by projecting the document, annotating clues about its context while sharing their thoughts aloud (see Figure 4.1). The attribution tells us where the speech was given and when (Gray was addressing townspeople in Hampshire, Massachusetts, where the protests occurred). What was Gray up to? Was he trying to explain his position and rally support for it? Pointing out the date of December 7, 1786, shows that Gray's speech occurred in the midst of these activities. As a class, or using the textbook, the speech can be placed on a timeline of events. Gray's speech came late in the 2nd year of protests but before the explosive events at Springfield. Beyond the attribution, teachers can model ways to identify information about life in 1786, the concerns, interests, or beliefs people had. Certain phrases provide clues: "little money right now," "harsh rules for collecting debts," "foreign debt," "government will not allow people to petition the court," "unlimited power to Justices of the Peace," and so on. Figure 4.1 shows sample annotations to Gray's speech, focusing on general reading comprehension (*IR*), sourcing (*E*), and contextualization (*A*).

> **Teachers Reflect.** "I saw the importance of building background knowledge. And I began to see that kids really have no concept of time and place, where things belong, what's happening to make a person feel this way. . . . It wasn't just like one day a star fell out of the sky . . . this was something that happened in time that caused this, this, this. Kids needed to see that . . . to be able to get the controversy, conflict and . . . understand what the author's trying to say about it."

Reading historically means that no one text should be considered absolutely trustworthy, but each is a clue to a larger story. Abigail Adams' letter to Jefferson stands in stark contrast to Gray's speech. Identifying her as the author links her to John Adams and the Founding Fathers' vested interest in the success of the new nation. She was also a member, at least by association, of the ruling class and might have opposed anyone who challenged it. Neither she nor anyone else knew if the nation would persevere or not. Adams' wording reveals her purpose and beliefs ("the men are ignorant, restless criminals . . . this mob of rebels wants to weaken the foundation of our country"). Contextualizing this source also lends insight: Adams wrote from London, and was not a direct eyewitness. However, she was from Massachusetts ("my home state") and might have understood the situation better than we know. Given her association with the leaders of the time, she likely had a more complete view than Daniel Gray of the challenges facing the new nation. Although the letter was written after the attempted takeover of the Springfield Armory, given the speed with which news traveled overseas, Adams would not have heard about it. Yet she could hardly have been more negative.

Sourcing and contextualization aren't just about noting an author's name or when a text was written. The point is to use this information to draw inferences about different texts, their authors, and an event itself with respect to a historical question. To encourage students to make inferences, *IREAD* prompts them to make judgments based on information they've annotated. In the early investigations, the judgment box at the bottom of a text cues students to make inferences based on their reading and analysis. Ideally, students will weigh each text before considering them as a whole.

FIGURE 4.1. Sample Annotations for Gray's Speech

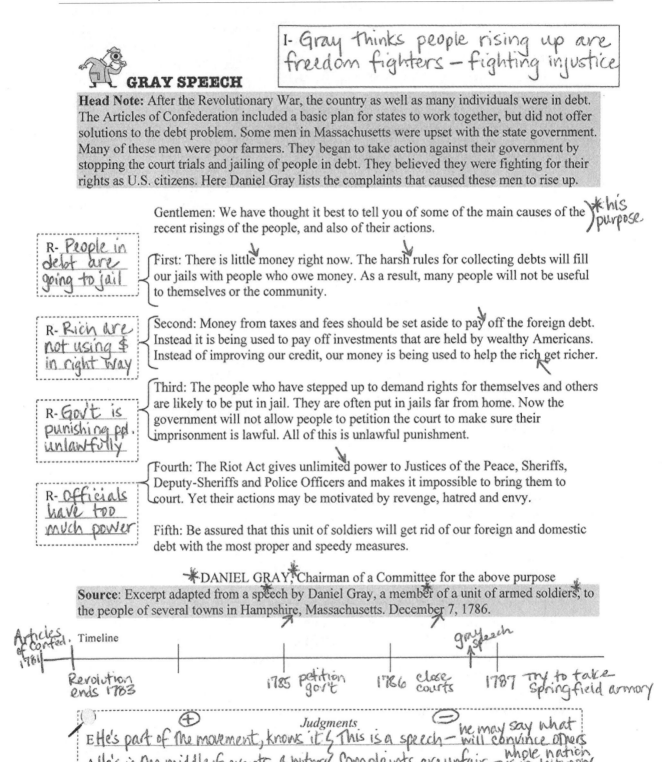

GRAY SPEECH

I- Gray thinks people rising up are freedom fighters – fighting injustice

Head Note: After the Revolutionary War, the country as well as many individuals were in debt. The Articles of Confederation included a basic plan for states to work together, but did not offer solutions to the debt problem. Some men in Massachusetts were upset with the state government. Many of these men were poor farmers. They began to take action against their government by stopping the court trials and jailing of people in debt. They believed they were fighting for their rights as U.S. citizens. Here Daniel Gray lists the complaints that caused these men to rise up.

Gentlemen: We have thought it best to tell you of some of the main causes of the recent risings of the people, and also of their actions.   *his purpose

R- People in debt are going to jail

First: There is little money right now. The harsh rules for collecting debts will fill our jails with people who owe money. As a result, many people will not be useful to themselves or the community.

R- Rich are not using $ in right way

Second: Money from taxes and fees should be set aside to pay off the foreign debt. Instead it is being used to pay off investments that are held by wealthy Americans. Instead of improving our credit, our money is being used to help the rich get richer.

R- Gov't is punishing ppl. unlawfully

Third: The people who have stepped up to demand rights for themselves and others are likely to be put in jail. They are often put in jails far from home. Now the government will not allow people to petition the court to make sure their imprisonment is lawful. All of this is unlawful punishment.

R- Officials have too much power

Fourth: The Riot Act gives unlimited power to Justices of the Peace, Sheriffs, Deputy-Sheriffs and Police Officers and makes it impossible to bring them to court. Yet their actions may be motivated by revenge, hatred and envy.

Fifth: Be assured that this unit of soldiers will get rid of our foreign and domestic debt with the most proper and speedy measures.

*DANIEL GRAY, Chairman of a Committee for the above purpose

Source: Excerpt adapted from a speech by Daniel Gray, a member of a unit of armed soldiers, to the people of several towns in Hampshire, Massachusetts. December 7, 1786.

Articles of Confed. 1781

Timeline

gray speech

Revolution ends 1783

1785 petition gov't

1786 close courts

1787 Try to take Springfield armory

Judgments

⊕

⊖

E He's part of the movement, knows it | This is a speech – he may say what will convince others

A He's in the middle of events, a witness | Complaints are unfair – whole nation is in debt now

D

When it comes to sourcing, students are prompted to write down their reasons for trusting and doubting each author. In contextualizing, we ask students to consider the time, place, and details of life before answering a prompt (e.g., "Given what else was going on at this time/place, the author's argument does/does not make sense because . . . ").

Writing History

Now that students have had a chance to warm up with simpler writing (the introductory paragraph in Investigation 1/Chapter 3), we introduce the heart of the argument essay—planning and composing the supporting and rebuttal paragraphs. A standard five-paragraph essay contains three paragraphs that support the thesis of the essay by elaborating on the claim and providing evidence. It's a format often used in secondary English/Language Arts classes, but in an argument essay, the third supporting paragraph typically contains a rebuttal against the opposing view. This addition to the text structure is made explicit for students in the *H2W* tool.

> *Classroom Notes.* Students understand that they have to answer a good argument when they disagree with someone. Leverage that understanding to help them grasp the purpose of rebuttal.

While the purpose and structure of rebuttals are clear to most adults, they can confuse a beginning writer. Students will often simply switch sides in the rebuttal paragraph, citing the opposing argument without trying to refute it. A reason for this lies in how students approach the writing process. Often they compose without a plan, putting thoughts to paper without considering their audience. While most expository writing requires planning and revision, argument writing asks the writer to anticipate and then respond to opposing viewpoints. Most of us, including students, naturally voice opposition in conversation when responding to someone who disagrees with our view, but when writing a rebuttal, the opposing side has to be inferred, which is challenging for novices.

This investigation leverages students' intuitive understanding of rebuttal by making clear how to recognize and respond to counterclaims in planning an essay. In every investigation, students will read documents presenting different sides of an issue, identify and weigh evidence in each one, and then form judgments about the evidence in order to plan their argument.

Arguing for the strength of evidence is important in all three middle paragraphs of the text structure. When students write about history, they must use disciplinary thinking to select and evaluate historical evidence. As they read and annotate while considering the source and context (*E* and *A* of *IREAD*), they must take a stand on a historical question. The first time students plan and write their middle paragraphs, they may struggle with making judgments about good evidence or grasping the purpose of rebuttal.

Planning. Planning essays is an important part of the writing process. Because students and teachers often have little experience with planning, material from this investigation is designed to help teachers think through the planning process and how to model it. Figure 4.2 gives an explanation of what to say as you model how to plan with the planning graphic sheet. The comments shared in Figure 4.2 show how to guide students in understanding the "big picture," using documents to prepare for composing. Figures 4.3 and 4.4 illustrate a sample completed plan using a blank planning graphic organizer and documents on Shays' Rebellion. The completed plans derive from the first sample essay on Shays' Rebellion (see Appendix A, Figure A.9); that is, the plan represented in Figure 4.3, Figure 4.4, and Figure 4.5 would prepare someone to produce the first sample essay.

We share annotated documents that have now been highlighted for the purpose of planning, to show how easy it is to to record quotes and judgments that may be included in an argument (note Q1, J1, etc.). Based on tips from teachers, we've found that colored markers work well for showing the relationship between quotes and judgments as well (e.g., marking Q1 and J1 the same color to signal they belong in the same paragraph). Teachers will want to go through the process before trying this in front of students for the first time—try it with the second sample essay for practice, or using a different set of documents to create your own argument.

> *Classroom Notes.* Walk students through the sample essays (see Appendix A, Figures A.8 and A.9). With prompting, they can identify each element of the text structure in the sample essays, contrast the two essays' use of evidence, and even suggest improvements.

HOW TO TEACH THIS INVESTIGATION

What's New in This Investigation?

In Investigation 2, students will learn to contextualize primary sources and practice sourcing as they read. Students will become familiar with the expectations for supporting and rebuttal paragraphs (via a "text structure" and examples of other students' writing). Last, students will learn to plan and then compose these parts of an essay. The main goal is to consider the controversy and develop an interpretation based on the evidence.

The 1st day will introduce the controversy, relevant background knowledge, basic comprehension, and historical reading. The 2nd day will emphasize historical reading and evaluative thinking about sources. The 3rd day will use the text structure and sample essays to help students understand how to write supporting and rebuttal paragraphs. This last day will end with the students composing their own paragraphs.

Teaching Principles

Teachers continue with Stages 1 and 2 of the cognitive apprenticeship model of instruction ("Prepare students to learn" and "Model how to read and

FIGURE 4.2. Sample Explanation of How to Use the Planning Your Essay Sheet

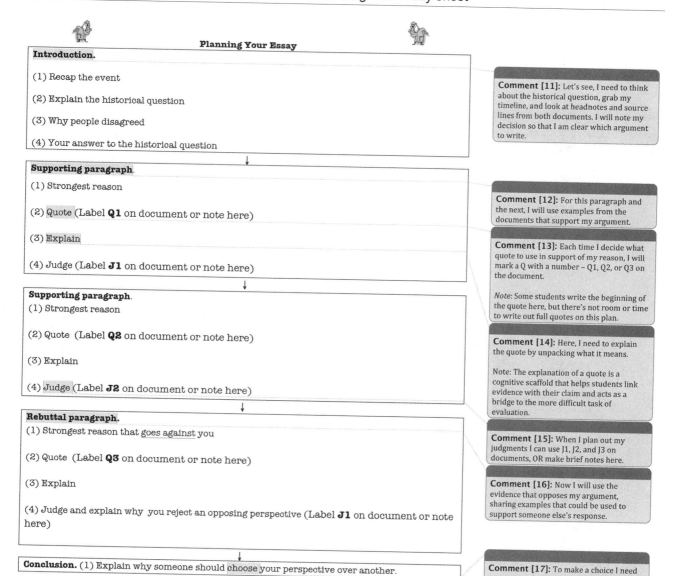

Planning Your Essay

Introduction.

(1) Recap the event

(2) Explain the historical question

(3) Why people disagreed

(4) Your answer to the historical question

> Comment [11]: Let's see, I need to think about the historical question, grab my timeline, and look at headnotes and source lines from both documents. I will note my decision so that I am clear which argument to write.

Supporting paragraph.

(1) Strongest reason

(2) Quote (Label **Q1** on document or note here)

(3) Explain

(4) Judge (Label **J1** on document or note here)

> Comment [12]: For this paragraph and the next, I will use examples from the documents that support my argument.

> Comment [13]: Each time I decide what quote to use in support of my reason, I will mark a Q with a number – Q1, Q2, or Q3 on the document.

> Note: Some students write the beginning of the quote here, but there's not room or time to write out full quotes on this plan.

Supporting paragraph.

(1) Strongest reason

(2) Quote (Label **Q2** on document or note here)

(3) Explain

(4) Judge (Label **J2** on document or note here)

> Comment [14]: Here, I need to explain the quote by unpacking what it means.

> Note: The explanation of a quote is a cognitive scaffold that helps students link evidence with their claim and acts as a bridge to the more difficult task of evaluation.

Rebuttal paragraph.

(1) Strongest reason that goes against you

(2) Quote (Label **Q3** on document or note here)

(3) Explain

(4) Judge and explain why you reject an opposing perspective (Label **J1** on document or note here)

> Comment [15]: When I plan out my judgments I can use J1, J2, and J3 on documents, OR make brief notes here.

> Comment [16]: Now I will use the evidence that opposes my argument, sharing examples that could be used to support someone else's response.

Conclusion. (1) Explain why someone should choose your perspective over another.

> Comment [17]: To make a choice I need to compare the evidence. I should try to find a reason that rebuts the opposing position,

write like a historian"). As teachers scaffold the thinking process and literacy practices, modeling their thinking and guiding students using questions and *IREAD*, Planning Your Essay, and *H2W* tools, it's important to point out key segments that offer insight into the historical context. As the teacher reads aloud a contextual clue such as when a document was created, she should annotate that element for students (see Figure 4.2). Teachers will need a way to project annotations as a visual guide.

When students hear teachers think aloud about key segments of the text, they start to realize they don't have to know everything in order to process a text and identify important questions. The comments provided in the examples suggest ways that teachers can share the thoughts and questions that go through their heads as they read key segments of the text (such comments

FIGURE 4.3. Sample Plan

Planning Your Essay

Introduction.
(1) Recap the event   Shays' Rebellion, Mass., late 1780s

(2) Explain the historical question   men interfere w/ courts → soldiers stop...

(3) Why people disagreed ⎨ → gov't has a right to send people → jail
                         → Daniel Shays' actions patriotic?

(4) Your answer to the historical question   Freedom Fighter

↓

Supporting paragraph.
(1) Strongest reason   Gray's speech has many reasons why farmers began to rebel against gov't

(2) Quote   (see document)

(3) Explain   Gov't seems like England was during Revolution

(4) Judge (see document)

↓

Supporting paragraph.
(1) Strongest reason   Shays and his men were protesting unfair taxes

(2) Quote (see document)

(3) Explain   nation was not using $ to pay off debt

(4) Judge (see judgments)

↓

Rebuttal paragraph.
(1) Strongest reason that goes against you   Abigail Adams thinks they are rebels

(2) Quote (see document)

(3) Explain   Adams is worried that any unrest will hurt America

(4) Judge and explain why you reject an opposing perspective   Adams is wrong about Shays' thinking – he wants to use taxes to pay debt.

↓

Conclusion. (1) Explain why someone should choose your perspective over another.
unfair punishment / unlawful reasons / disagree w/ gov't vs. stirring up trouble → End unjust laws so America is a better place

FIGURE 4.4. Gray Speech with Planning Annotations

GRAY SPEECH

[handwritten annotation, boxed:] I- Gray thinks people rising up are freedom fighters — fighting injustice

Head Note: After the Revolutionary War, the country as well as many individuals were in debt. The Articles of Confederation included a basic plan for states to work together, but did not offer solutions to the debt problem. Some men in Massachusetts were upset with the state government. Many of these men were poor farmers. They began to take action against their government by stopping the court trials and jailing of people in debt. They believed they were fighting for their rights as U.S. citizens. Here Daniel Gray lists the complaints that caused these men to rise up.

Gentlemen: We have thought it best to tell you of some of the main causes of the recent risings of the people, and also of their actions. *[handwritten:] ✱ his purpose*

[handwritten annotation, boxed:] R- People in debt are going to jail

First: There is little money right now. The harsh rules for collecting debts will fill our jails with people who owe money. As a result, many people will not be useful to themselves or the community.

[handwritten annotation, boxed:] R- Rich are not using $ in right way

Second: Money from taxes and fees should be set aside to pay off the foreign debt. *[handwritten: J3]* Instead it is being used to pay off investments that are held by wealthy Americans. Instead of improving our credit, our money is being used to help the rich get richer. *[handwritten: Q2]*

[handwritten annotation, boxed:] R- Gov't is punishing ppl. unlawfully

Third: The people who have stepped up to demand rights for themselves and others are likely to be put in jail. They are often put in jails far from home. Now the government will not allow people to petition the court to make sure their imprisonment is lawful. All of this is unlawful punishment. *[handwritten: Q1, J1]*

[handwritten annotation, boxed:] R- Officials have too much power

Fourth: The Riot Act gives unlimited power to Justices of the Peace, Sheriffs, Deputy-Sheriffs and Police Officers and makes it impossible to bring them to court. Yet their actions may be motivated by revenge, hatred and envy.

Fifth: Be assured that this unit of soldiers will get rid of our foreign and domestic debt with the most proper and speedy measures.

✱DANIEL GRAY, Chairman of a Committee for the above purpose

Source: Excerpt adapted from a speech by Daniel Gray, a member of a unit of armed soldiers, to the people of several towns in Hampshire, Massachusetts. December 7, 1786.

[handwritten timeline:]
Articles of Confed. 1781

Timeline

Revolution ends 1783

1785 petition gov't

1786 close courts

gray speech

1787 Try to take Springfield armory

[handwritten judgments box:]
⊕ Judgments ⊖

E He's part of the movement, knows it ⎨ This is a speech — he may say what will convince others

A He's in the middle of events, a witness ⎨ Complaints are unfair — whole nation is in debt now

D

J2

[handwritten note cloud:] Note: Mark up documents for your plan as you decide how to use documents. Colors can help students see relationships between quotes and judgments.

FIGURE 4.5. Adams Letter with Planning Annotations

> I- Adams thinks people Rising up are rebels who were destroying the nation.

ADAMS LETTER

Head Note: On January 25, 1787 the men who were involved in Shays' Rebellion tried to take the weapons stored at the armory in Springfield, Massachusetts. They wanted to change the new government in the U.S. When Abigail Adams wrote to Thomas Jefferson she was in London, and did not yet know about this event. In this letter, she writes about the court mobbings that took place throughout 1786 in efforts to stop trials and prevent debtors from being put in jail. These events eventually led to the creation of a new Constitution that could better solve these problems.

London January 29th 1787

My Dear Sir:

> R- Mobs have shut down Courts + hurt the nation.

With regard to the Riots in my home state, which you asked me about: I wish I could say that people have exaggerated them. It is true, Sir, that they have gone on to such a degree that the Courts have been shut down in several counties. The men are ignorant, restless criminals, without conscience or morals. They have led other men under false ideas that could only have been imagined. Instead of that honest spirit which makes a people watchful over their Liberties and alert in the defense of them, this mob of rebels wants to weaken the foundation of our country, and destroy the whole fabric of our nation.   Q3

> R- Rebels have not been careful with their money.

These people are few in number, when compared to the more sensible and thoughtful majority. I cannot help hoping that they will end up helping the state, by leading to an investigation of the causes of these riots. Luxury and wasteful spending of money both in furniture and dress had spread to all of our countrymen and women. This led people to build up debts that they were unable to pay off. Vanity was becoming a more powerful principal than patriotism. The lower classes were unable to pay taxes, even though they owned property. Those who had money were afraid to lend it for fear that the government would take more money from them.

Though late in the month, I hope you will not find it out of season to offer my best wishes for the health, long life and prosperity of yourself and family, or to assure you of the sincere esteem and friendship with which I am Yours,

A. Adams

Source: Excerpt adapted from a letter written by Abigail Adams to Thomas Jefferson on January 29, 1787.

⊕ | *Judgments* | ⊖

E As wife of Founder, she may have the good of the U.S. in mind. | She is not one of the "rebels" so she is an outsider & may not understand.

A She is from the state, all of this is happening in so she probably knows about events from locals! | She is in London, removed from the events. She hasn't witnessed the events & may not know whole story.

P

are illustrative only, not prescriptive). Once teachers model, think aloud, and show students how to contextualize the Gray speech, students will have the chance to try it out on their own, using the Adams letter. Reviewing background knowledge will help students make connections between the texts and their historical context. As they work in pairs or small groups, students can find support as they practice new reading and thinking practices. The same type of modeling applies when teachers show students how to plan an essay.

Teachers offer developmentally appropriate tasks in this investigation by using the *H2W* tool with sample essays; this can help clarify students' expectations for writing arguments. Most students don't walk into the classroom knowing how to write an argument, so the *H2W* tool offers a visual representation of each paragraph (see the full explanation of this tool in Chapter 2). As they read expectations for a supporting paragraph, teachers should think aloud to identify the corresponding examples in the sample essay. Students can practice doing the same with the next supporting paragraph, linking excerpts of sample essays to features of argument essays outlined in *H2W*. After reviewing the rebuttal paragraph, students can identify ways to improve the sample essay. Teachers should model how to plan, using the blank graphic organizer version of *H2W*, so that students can learn to plan their own supporting and rebuttal paragraphs.

Then, as students compose, they can focus on only the supporting and rebuttal paragraphs rather than an entire essay. Such supports also make the task of composition more accessible for struggling readers.

Things to Keep in Mind

Since students come to the investigation with a range of skills, teachers may need to adapt the lesson. Some students will write one supporting paragraph, while others should be encouraged to try their hand at the entire essay. For more advanced students, extend their work by integrating primary sources found in the Web links of the Historical Background. Students can refer to the original versions of the sources adapted for this investigation (see endnote 16, this chapter). Deliberating among a number of different accounts gives students more evidence to draw on as they formulate their interpretations.

As students are gaining fundamental aspects of thinking historically and writing arguments, teachers may not see much immediate progress. Since their essays may not resemble the sample essays, students will need to set realistic goals that take their developing skills into account. This kind of work is fairly difficult; positive reinforcement will help students persist. Beyond modeling and guided practice, let students share their ideas in discussion. One of the most important ways to help students improve is allowing students time to write their own supporting and rebuttal paragraphs.

FIGURE 4.6. Tamia's Essay for Investigation 2

The freedom fighters was daniel shay, and his men because the people in charge was being unfair they was recieving unlawful punishments. They were going against or close down innocents. Because maybe people came their and they fought back so we can say for example: if me and lindsey got in an arguement and was about to fight but I was like I'm not about to fight and people heard to me but we still fought she messed with me so I'm an freedom fighter.

Polish: "Why does Gray consider these punishments "unfair"? Please explain."

Praise: "I see you worked from the documents to answer the Historical Question!"

Polish: "Look at the text that you underlined and starred in Gray's speech. Can you find a quote that supports this point?"

Goal: "Nice job meeting your goal from Investigation 1! Next time, be sure to include quotes and explanations to support your reasons. Try writing a rebuttal paragraph, too. Let's discuss ways to save time for planning and writing as you work."

HOW MIGHT STUDENTS RESPOND?
STUDENT WRITING AND TEACHER FEEDBACK

In Investigation 2, students encounter supporting and rebuttal paragraphs for the first time. Using the *H2W* tool, they need to identify reasons on each side of the controversy, support those reasons with quotes from the documents, explain how the quotes support their point, and evaluate the evidence to draw a conclusion. Explaining quotes and rebutting opposing arguments are the most challenging aspects for novice writers.

In our sample essays, Tamia (Figure 4.6) makes some important advances in Investigation 2. This time she takes a clear stand and presents a reason that has some internal logic. Although she doesn't follow the format of *H2W*, she does respond to its prompts. She works from the documents to cite a reason in support of her conclusion, paraphrases the Gray article ("unjust punishments"), and explains her reasoning in the form of an analogy. While the analogy elucidates her *own* reasoning—that one is justified to fight back when attacked—it does little to explain Gray's reasons for calling the punishments unjust. She also skips the rebuttal paragraph, which was a common accommodation for struggling writers.

Aaron (Figure 4.7) also shows good progress. He offers multiple reasons to support his conclusion and he clearly benefits from the *H2W* format. He also

FIGURE 4.7. Aaron's Essay for Investigation 2

Abigail Adams was very well connected an example of the men being rebels is when she says "Courts have been shut down in several counties. They are also rebels because they tried to steal weapons. These Quotes and facts are reliable because she was married to Jhon adams. / Another strong reason they were rebels is because she wrote to thomas Jefferson "They are ignorant, restless, criminals with no consensus or morals. She knew this because she was well connected. This was reliable because she had no reason to lie to thomas Jefferson. One this may be wrong is because Abigail Adams was far from the event. One reason they could have been freedom fighters is because "their money was being used to help the rich get richer." This is reliable because Daniel Gray was very associated with the event.

Praise: "I like how you've use the entire document (headnote, text and source note) to make your argument."

Polish: "What do you mean by 'well connected?' How does it strengthen Abigail Adam's account?"

Praise: "You represent the opposing side well by including a quote and explanation."

Polish: "How might you respond to these opposing arguments?"

Goal: "For your rebuttal paragraph, try to respond to opposing arguments so that readers can see that your conclusion is still valid."

draws on the complete document (headnote, text, and source note) to craft his essay. Though he puts everything into a single paragraph, he integrates reasons, quotes, explanations, and evaluations effectively for his first reason, and to some extent for his second. There is still room for improvement. First, Aaron could clarify how Abigail Adams is "well connected" in his evaluation of the documents. Second, although he presents an opposing view in this essay ("Adams was far from this event"), he doesn't try to rebut it in a way that restores the strength of his argument.

LESSON PLANS AND MATERIALS

Teachers and students will need to have the following: Lesson plans (Figures 4.8–4.10), Investigation 2 packet (clipboard with overview, Gray Speech, Adams Letter, adapted Planning Your Essay graphic organizer—Figure 4.11), Additional Materials for This Investigation (timeline—Figure 4.12), Disciplinary Literacy tools (*IREAD, H2W,* sample essays, and essay prompt response sheet—see Appendix A), Shays film, and overhead projection capacity (to model annotating and planning and to show links between the sample essays and text structure).

FIGURE 4.8. Lesson Plan, Day 1: Background Knowledge, Reading Comprehension, and Historical Reading

Materials: **Investigation 2 student packets, historical timeline, *IREAD*, Planning Your Essay adapted for this investigation, *H2W*, Projector, Online film clip**

Suggested time: **1 hour per day**

INTRODUCTION

1. Warmup. Connect prior knowledge or personal experiences to content or themes in this particular investigation (i.e., "Did you ever do anything you thought was good that others thought was bad?").

2. Introduce the Shays' Rebellion controversy and historical question, and review the investigative process students will use (e.g., prepare for the case, investigate both sides, and write a final judgment).

BACKGROUND INFORMATION

3. Watch Part 2 of 5 (0:00–8:40) of *Shays' Rebellion: America's First Civil War* (presented by the History Channel in 2006, R. J. Cutler, director), periodically stopping to discuss the following questions.

   a. What were people like Daniel Shays concerned about after the Revolutionary War?

   b. Review: What were the weaknesses of the Articles of Confederation?

   c. What were government leaders in Massachusetts and the United States concerned about after the Revolutionary War?

   d. What different ways of protesting did Shays and his followers use to make their voices heard?

4. Cut up the rectangles from the timeline (Figure 4.12). Have students explain how each is a cause or effect of Shays' Rebellion and arrange them chronologically.

HISTORICAL READING: GENERAL READING COMPREHENSION

5. Preview vocabulary, if necessary (see Appendix B for an example).

6. Model *I* and *R* of *IREAD* with Gray's speech.

7. Guide students as they use *I* and *R* with the Adams letter.

HISTORICAL THINKING AND READING: SOURCING WITH *E* OF *IREAD*

8. Model *E* of *IREAD* with the Gray speech.

9. Guide students as they use *E* of *IREAD* with Adams' letter.

10. Debrief: What is/is not making sense about *IREAD* so far?

FIGURE 4.9. Lesson Plan, Day 2: Historical Reading and Thinking

INTRODUCTION

1. Set the purpose. Remind students that they will investigate both sides of the case by annotating sources and judging the author's reliability and the context.

2. Review the historical question and identify which side of the controversy Gray and Adams were on.

HISTORICAL THINKING AND READING: SOURCING WITH *E* OF *IREAD*

3. Students will discuss their annotations to make a judgment and consider the four questions below to make a judgment about the author's reliability.
   a. Who were the authors of each document?
   b. What kind of document is each document?
   c. Who is the audience for each document?
   d. Based on what you've noticed about each author, which main ideas are made more convincing or less convincing? Why?

4. At the bottom of the page, have students write one reason to trust the author or one reason to doubt the author.

HISTORICAL THINKING AND READING: CONTEXTUALIZING WITH *A* OF *IREAD*

5. Introduce *A* of *IREAD* and explain why it's important to notice historical context.

6. Model *A* of *IREAD* with the Gray speech, putting major historical events and the document dates on a timeline.

7. Guide students as they use *A* of *IREAD* with Adams' letter:
   a. Give students a chance to identify contextual information.
   b. Where necessary, instruct students to identify the location, date of the document, and any events described in the document to put them on the timeline you created.

8. Students review their *A* annotations on both documents and discuss:
   a. What do you notice about the locations, dates, and historical events surrounding each document?
   b. Does one document seem more convincing than the other? Why?
   c. Does noticing the location, dates, and major historical events make any of the *main ideas* more convincing or less convincing?

9. Students respond to the "Judge" part of *A* and write down a note in the margin to summarize their judgment of each document or a main idea in each document based on their analysis of the historical context.

10. Debrief: Using judgments about the author and context, students discuss and respond to the historical question: *Were Shays and his followers rebels or freedom fighters?*

FIGURE 4.10. Lesson Plan, Day 3: Planning and Historical Writing

INTRODUCTION

1. Set the purpose. Explain that students will learn to structure an effective response to the central historical question.
2. First, review what each body paragraph is supposed to do in the *H2W*.
3. Compare the supporting paragraphs on the *H2W* with those in the sample essay.
   a. Ask students to find elements from *H2W* in the 1st and 2nd supporting paragraphs in the sample essay.
   b. Ask students for suggestions on how to make these paragraphs better.
4. Compare the rebuttal paragraph on *H2W* with that in the sample essays (see 3a and 3b above).

PLANNING AND COMPOSING

5. Go over the Planning Sheet ("Planning Your Essay"). Point out where students can note their supporting reasons, evidence, judgments, and rebuttal while planning (this will become the structure of their essay).
6. Model how to plan by projecting a blank plan, writing in your ideas, and thinking aloud to share your decisionmaking as you select and organize content for your essay.
   a. First, show your deliberation about the historical question and how you decide what claim to make. The claim becomes the main focus of the essay.
   b. Next, model how you think about and select reasons that support your claim as well as supporting quotations or other evidence. Show students how you can number evidence on the documents for use in your essay (Q1, Q2, etc.) or write a brief reference to particular quotations on the planning sheet.
   c. For each piece of evidence cited, model how you might make a brief note to help you explain the evidence in your essay and evaluate its credibility. Show students how you can number judgments on the documents instead of writing notes on the plan sheet (J1, J2, etc.).
   d. Reinforce the main purpose of planning throughout your modeling—to organize and prepare to write an evidence-based argument that will convince others.
7. Give students practice with planning by having them work in pairs or groups to plan an essay with an opposing claim (i.e., one you did *not* just model). Alternately, students can plan an essay with the same claim but try to select different evidence and judgments.
8. Support students as they begin composing supporting and rebuttal paragraphs:
   a. Remind students to use their annotated texts, the planning sheet, and *H2W*.
   b. Everyone should try to write at least one supporting and one rebuttal paragraph. If students have time and are comfortable with the activity, they can write two supporting paragraphs and one rebuttal paragraph.

REFLECTION

9. Distribute the Reflection Guide (see Appendix A) and ask students to evaluate their work. Then ask them to switch with a peer to get feedback from someone else.
10. As a class, look at and celebrate one or two good papers.
11. Ask students to decide on one thing to improve the next time they work on an investigation. Have them make a note of it in their Reflection Guide.

FIGURE 4.11. Materials: Investigation #2 Packet

Name: _____ **Class:** _____ **Date:** _____

INVESTIGATION #2:
WERE DANIEL SHAYS AND HIS MEN REBELS OR FREEDOM FIGHTERS?

You are a historical detective trying to decide if Daniel Shays and his men were rebels or freedom fighters when they mobbed courthouses and tried to capture weapons in 1786–1787. Many of these men fought for independence in the Revolutionary War. So, why would they turn around and fight against the government of their new, independent nation so soon after the Revolution?

Take out your pens and get ready to investigate!

FIGURE 4.11. Materials: Investigation #2 Packet, Continued

Name:_____ Class:____ Date:_____

I-

Gray Speech

Head Note: After the Revolutionary War, the country as well as many individuals were in debt. The Articles of Confederation included a basic plan for states to work together, but did not offer solutions to the debt problem. Some men in Massachusetts were upset with the state government. Many of these men were poor farmers. They began to take action against their government by stopping the court trials and jailing of people in debt. They believed they were fighting for their rights as U.S. citizens. Here Daniel Gray lists the complaints that caused these men to rise up.

Gentlemen: We have thought it best to tell you of some of the main causes of the recent risings of the people, and also of their actions.

R-_____

First: There is little money right now. The harsh rules for collecting debts will fill our jails with people who owe money. As a result, many people will not be useful to themselves or the community.

R-_____

Second: Money from taxes and fees should be set aside to pay off the foreign debt. Instead it is being used to pay off investments that are held by wealthy Americans. Instead of improving our credit, our money is being used to help the rich get richer.

R-_____

Third: The people who have stepped up to demand rights for themselves and others are likely to be put in jail. They are often put in jails far from home. Now the government will not allow people to petition the court to make sure their imprisonment is lawful. All of this is unlawful punishment.

R-_____

Fourth: The Riot Act gives unlimited power to Justices of the Peace, Sheriffs, Deputy-Sheriffs and Police Officers and makes it impossible to bring them to court. Yet their actions may be motivated by revenge, hatred and envy.

Fifth: Be assured that this unit of soldiers will get rid of our foreign and domestic debt with the most proper and speedy measures.

DANIEL GRAY, Chairman of a Committee for the above purpose

Source: Excerpt adapted from a speech by Daniel Gray, a member of a unit of armed soldiers, to the people of several towns in Hampshire, Massachusetts. December 7, 1786.

Timeline

Judgments

E_____
A_____
D_____

FIGURE 4.11. Materials: Investigation #2 Packet, Continued

Name:_____ Class:____ Date:_____

I-

Adams Letter

Head Note: On January 25, 1787 the men who were involved in Shays' Rebellion tried to take the weapons stored at the armory in Springfield, Massachusetts. They wanted to change the new government in the U.S. When Abigail Adams wrote to Thomas Jefferson she was in London, and did not yet know about this event. In this letter, she writes about the court mobbings that took place throughout 1786 in efforts to stop trials and prevent debtors from being put in jail. These events eventually led to the creation of a new Constitution that could better solve these problems.

London January 29th 1787

My Dear Sir:

R-_____

With regard to the Riots in my home state, which you asked me about: I wish I could say that people have exaggerated them. It is true, Sir, that they have gone on to such a degree that the Courts have been shut down in several counties. The men are ignorant, restless criminals, without conscience or morals. They have led other men under false ideas that could only have been imagined. Instead of that honest spirit which makes a people watchful over their Liberties and alert in the defense of them, this mob of rebels wants to weaken the foundation of our country, and destroy the whole fabric of our nation.

R-_____

These people are few in number, when compared to the more sensible and thoughtful majority. I cannot help hoping that they will end up helping the state, by leading to an investigation of the causes of these riots. Luxury and wasteful spending of money both in furniture and dress had spread to all of our countrymen and women. This led people to build up debts that they were unable to pay off. Vanity was becoming a more powerful principal than patriotism. The lower classes were unable to pay taxes, even though they owned property. Those who had money were afraid to lend it for fear that the government would take more money from them.

Though late in the month, I hope you will not find it out of season to offer my best wishes for the health, long life and prosperity of yourself and family, or to assure you of the sincere esteem and friendship with which I am Yours,

A. Adams

Source: Excerpt adapted from a letter written by Abigail Adams to Thomas Jefferson on January 29, 1787.

Judgments

E_____

A_____

D_____

FIGURE 4.11. Materials: Investigation #2 Packet, Continued

Name:_____ Class:_____ Date:_____

Planning Your Essay

Introduction. *You did a great job on the introduction last time. This time let's focus on only the supporting and rebuttal paragraphs. What side are you on? Circle your answer.

REBELS or FREEDOM FIGHTERS

↓

Supporting paragraph.

(1) Strongest reason

(2) Quote (Label **Q1** on document or note here)

(3) Explain

(4) Judge (Label **J1** on document or note here)

↓

Supporting paragraph.
(1) Strongest reason

(2) Quote (Label **Q1** on document or note here)

(3) Explain

(4) Judge (Label **J1** on document or note here)

↓

Rebuttal paragraph.
(1) Strongest reason that <u>goes against</u> you

(2) Quote (Label **Q3** on document or note here)

(3) Explain

(4) Judge and explain why you reject an opposing perspective (Label **J3** on document or note here).

↓

Conclusion. *Stay tuned for the next investigation when we bring back the introduction and conclusion.

FIGURE 4.12. Additional Materials for This Investigation: Timeline

Timeline of Relevant Events and Issues

AMERICAN REVOLUTION
-Debt from spending $ on war effort
-Soldiers fought vs. tyranny & unfair taxes
-MA farmers borrowed $ to produce more crops
-Leaders emerged such as Washington, Adams, Franklin

ECONOMIC INSTABILITY
-*U.S. Gov't:* bankrupt, national currency worthless
-*State Gov'ts:* owed $ borrowed to fight Revolution, state currency worthless, increased taxes to pay state debt
-*MA farmers:* don't sell as many crops after War, protest state taxes; in 1785- people put in prison for not paying debt; in 1786- 2,000 face foreclosure, mob courthouses to close courts; in 1787- try to take Springfield arsenal in January

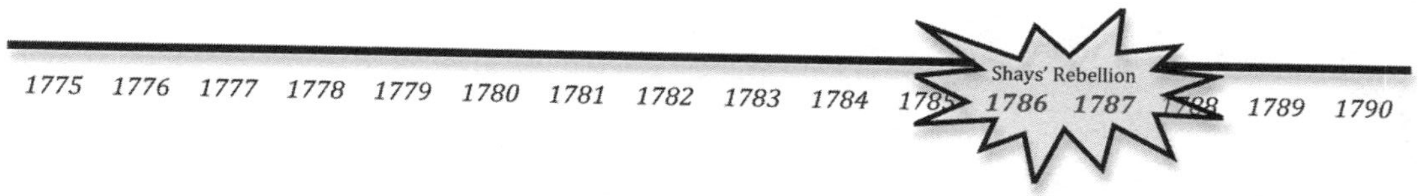

ARTICLES OF CONFEDERATION
-Weak central gov't; most power in states' hands
-Difficult for U.S. Gov't to raise $
-Concern that rebellion might spread
-Concern that U.S. looks weak/cannot function

NEW CONSTITUTION
-Constitutional Convention opens spring 1787
-12 of 13 states ratify in 1789; last in 1790
-George Washington comes out of retirement, elected President 1789

Shays' Rebellion

1775 1776 1777 1778 1779 1780 1781 1782 1783 1784 1785 1786 1787 1788 1789 1790

Did the Alien and Sedition Acts Violate the U.S. Constitution?

Investigation	Foundational Concepts	Disciplinary Literacy Practices	CCSS Links	C3 Links	Principles of Teaching
Investigation 3: *Did the Alien and Sedition Acts violate the U.S. Constitution?*	Historical argument, or interpretation, as foundational frame We learn history by analyzing and questioning historical sources and artifacts	Consider authors' claims and evidence Compare and evaluate historical sources Plan an essay	RI.5.6 (p. 14) RI.5.8 (p. 14) RI.5.9 (p. 14) RH.6-12.1 (p. 61) RH.6-12.2 (p.61) RH.11-12.3 (p.61) RH.6-12.6 (p.61) RH.6-12.8 (p.61) W.5.1a-d (p.20) W.5.9b (p.21) WHST.6-12.1a, b, e (p. 64) WHST.6-12.9 (p. 66)	D2.His.1.6-8 D2.His.4.6-12 D2.His.6.6-8 D2.His.10.6-8 D2.His.13.6-8 D2.His.16.6-12 D3.2.6-8 D3.4.6-12 D4.1.6-12 D4.4.6-12	Develop students' background knowledge Present developmentally appropriate representations of content: Text edited for struggling readers Cognitive apprenticeship Stage 3: Support students' practice

Overview of Chapter 5

IN THIS INVESTIGATION, students make an argument about the constitutionality of the 1798 Alien and Sedition Acts by analyzing and questioning opinion pieces written at the time, and comparing the Acts to the U.S. Constitution and Bill of Rights. Thomas Jefferson and Massachusetts legislators took opposite positions on this issue and used specific examples to support their ideas. Students will learn to evaluate claims and evidence presented by authors as another way (along with sourcing and contextualizing) to compare and evaluate historical sources.

Now familiar with the major components of argument writing, students will plan and compose an entire essay. Planning becomes a key step in producing organized, reasoned, and evidence-based writing. The goal is to write an argument that is based on evidence in response to the central historical question.

HISTORICAL BACKGROUND

Investigation 3 highlights such enduring themes in U.S. history as the balance of power between state and federal governments, the political party system, strict versus loose interpretations of the Constitution, the rights of citizens, and the extent of civil liberties in the face of perceived threats to national security. It focuses on the Alien and Sedition Acts of the late 1790s which involved a number of issues—the uncertainty of a fledgling republic, increased power of the federal government (the National Bank, the Whiskey Rebellion), the influence of the French Revolution (the XYZ Affair), the process of nullifying laws,[1] and heated debates between Federalist and Democratic-Republican leaders (Jefferson, Madison, Hamilton, Adams, et al.)—that shaped the new nation's direction (for teachers who want to spend more time on these, we provide separate resources at notes 2–3).

In 1798, anticipating war with France, President John Adams signed into law the Alien Enemies Act, the Alien (Friends) Act, the Sedition Act, and the Naturalization Act.[2] Together, these are typically referred to collectively as the Alien and Sedition Acts in U.S. history textbooks and assessments. These laws increased residency requirements for new citizens; made it possible to arrest, imprison, or deport aliens during time of war; gave the president the power to deport aliens; and made it illegal to write, speak, or publish anything negative about the government.[3] Most historians believe that the acts show an increasing divide between political parties; passed by a Federalist-controlled Congress, the Acts targeted newspaper editors in the Democratic-Republican party, which was favored by new citizens affected by the Naturalization Act.[4] Facing war with France, Federalists felt the Acts were necessary for national security, the common good, and preservation of the United States.[5] Some called the conflict "the Quasi-War." Though some historians claim national security concerns motivated the Alien Enemies Act and Alien (Friends) Act,[6] Democratic-Republicans were concerned that they violated First Amendment rights and established an excessive role for the federal government.[7] Such an opposition eventually led to the demise of the Federalist Party in the 1800 elections.

Constitutionality

The debate over constitutionality centered on the Sedition Act, which placed limits on the untested First Amendment. Although the framers of the Constitution and the Bill of Rights included freedom of speech and the press, what these freedoms actually protected was still unclear, since the Federalists and Democratic-Republicans interpreted them differently. The Federalists drew on Sir William Blackstone, who believed that, according to English common law, free speech did not cover any statements that diminished respect for the government (even if true) or lies.[8] The Federalists expanded on this position by accepting truth as a defense against sedition, and requiring proof that the defendant sought to undermine the government. A letter from Jefferson to Madison shows that Democratic-Republicans saw the Sedition Act as violating rights laid out in the First Amendment. Alan Taylor argues that the Democratic Republicans never articulated their interpretation until forced to by the Sedition Act. The result was a broader interpretation of free speech that is more aligned with the notions we hold today.[9]

Party Differences

Competing views of the Sedition Act must be understood within the framework of each party's interpretation of the Constitution. Democratic-Republicans held a strict interpretation that any powers not specifically enumerated by the Constitution should be reserved for the states. Federalists preferred a strong central government and felt that, although not specifically laid out for the federal government, certain powers could be implied. Other debates focused on federal powers beyond those mentioned in the Constitution, and how such powers and their limits could be determined. Historians largely agree that the Virginia and Kentucky Resolutions laid the groundwork for the justification for Southern secession in the Civil War, but differ over the meaning of the acts in the history of civil liberties. For example, John Miller argued that the Democratic-Republicans didn't necessarily oppose restriction of the press but felt the states were the more appropriate body of government to decide this.[10] Over 50 years later, Jack Lynch (2007) points out that Thomas Jefferson wasn't opposed to regulating speech, but believed that only the states had the authority to do so. While both parties may have believed in restricting civil liberties, they differed as to the extent.

Historians' Views

Historians also differ over whether the Sedition Act was an isolated incident or one of many threats to civil liberty. Historians like Miller and James Morton Smith tend to see the United States as a libertarian nation firmly rooted in civil liberties by the late 1790s, and consider the Sedition Act an aberration of the Federalists, who turned to ideas about seditious libel in English common law. Other historians argue that at the time the Bill of Rights was drafted, the Framers didn't conceive of civil liberties with so much clarity but were still grounded in English common law and a more authoritarian concept of government. Instead, they believe that libertarian thought in the United States evolved over time.[11]

Of course, historians' conceptions of civil liberties have also changed over time. At present the United States has come down on the side of free speech and freedom of the press. Historians' views of these Acts and similar laws have been overwhelmingly negative. Ironically, the very same Acts provoked a greater defense and definition of speech and press freedoms than had existed before.[12] According to Lynch, the Federalists caused "an almost fundamentalist belief in the freedom of speech"—the exact opposite of their intention.[13]

Supporting Students

To understand this investigation, students will need to draw on three areas of knowledge: the U.S. Constitution and the Bill of Rights; the Alien and Sedition Acts and what led to their passage; and Federalist and Democratic-Republican disagreements over government. Students will learn background information about each on the first day of the lesson (see Figure 5.4, Lesson Plan, Day 1). Without a grounding in historical context, students may accept the central question at face value and respond without any understanding of the controversy. When this happens, students can offer simplified arguments that misinterpret the question, dodge the evidence, or rest on personal opinion.

Patrick Rael suggests using "givens" to improve questions, and encourage responses based on historical understanding by highlighting significant historical context (e.g., "Given that the country's relationship with France was tense, were the Alien and Sedition Acts constitutional?").[14] We use cards about the Constitution and Bill of Rights, a timeline of events related to the question, film clips highlighting different views of the Acts, and an explanation of key differences between the parties to ground students in the topic and help them understand its significance. Such steps will put students in a better position to write a historical argument.

LITERACY PRACTICES STUDENTS WILL LEARN

Reading History

Students will focus on literal comprehension and historical reading [15] strategies in Investigation 3 (see Figure 5.4, Lesson Plan, Day 1 and Figure 5.5, Lesson Plan, Day 2). This time they will likely be ready to practice sourcing on their own. Given the difficulty many students have learning to contextualize historical documents,[16] we suggest that teachers model how to contextualize the Kentucky Resolutions and then guide students through contextualizing the Massachusetts legislature's response (see Figure 5.1 for an annotated document).

Sourcing. As they source, students will note that Thomas Jefferson, co-author of the Declaration of Independence some 20 years earlier, also wrote the

Kentucky Resolutions. They may be interested to know that James Madison, often called the Father of the U.S. Constitution, wrote the Virginia Resolutions opposing the Acts. In reply, the Massachusetts Legislature, among others, drafted a response to the Kentucky and Virginia Resolutions supporting the Acts. What's significant is that Massachusetts was home to President John Adams. Armed with this information, teachers can help students navigate the political alliances of 1798, which indicate the authors' positions: Democratic-Republicans like Jefferson and Madison opposed the Alien and Sedition Acts, while Federalists Adams and Hamilton supported them.

Contextualization. Identifying key people, events, and concerns of the time is an important part of contextualization. Given the amount of background knowledge needed for this investigation, segmenting time and using a timeline with students is essential. In this and other investigations, we segment time in order to highlight the events and issues most relevant to this particular question. Whenever we offer timelines to support students' historical thinking, we are not simply creating chronologies; instead, we select events to include and omit for the purpose of the particular inquiry. Where a timeline begins and ends (how we segment time) can change the inquiry, so teachers may want to consider how they plan to segment time for each investigation.

Students note dates and issues of the day in order to place authors and their statements within a context (see Figure 5.5, Lesson Plan, Day 2). When Adams signed the acts into law in July 1798, he had taken office only a year earlier, following George Washington. Thomas Jefferson wrote the Kentucky Resolution in October 1798, and the Massachusetts Legislature responded a few months later, in February 1799. Although these authors were not using the fast-paced abbreviated text of today's electronic communication, they were engaged in a personal, albeit handwritten, conversation with one another.

Teachers can help students connect writers and their affiliations with the major interests and concerns of their parties. Democratic-Republicans generally supported strong state government, a strict interpretation of the U.S. Constitution, the right of citizens to publicly protest if they disagree with their government, and the idea that political power rests with the people. Federalists tended to advocate for a strong central government, a looser interpretation of the Constitution, and wealthy and educated leaders. They felt voting was a citizen's most important responsibility, and that any protest might weaken the new nation. Thus, students should understand that any discussion of the Alien and Sedition Acts isn't only about these particular laws, but about the role of the Constitution (only a decade old at the time) in governing the new nation.

Another relevant aspect of the Alien and Sedition Acts involves America's relationship with France. The French Revolution started in 1789 and led to rocky relations with the United States. Democratic-Republicans wanted to support the French people in their quest for freedom, but Federalists tended to be pro-British. Their differences were exacerbated when France and Britain went to war in 1793, causing difficulties for American merchant ships. France suspended commercial relations with the United States and did not pursue diplomatic efforts, but rather insisted on bribes before engaging in negotiations (the XYZ Affair). Many Americans worried that war with France was immi-

FIGURE 5.1. Sample Annotations for the Kentucky Resolutions

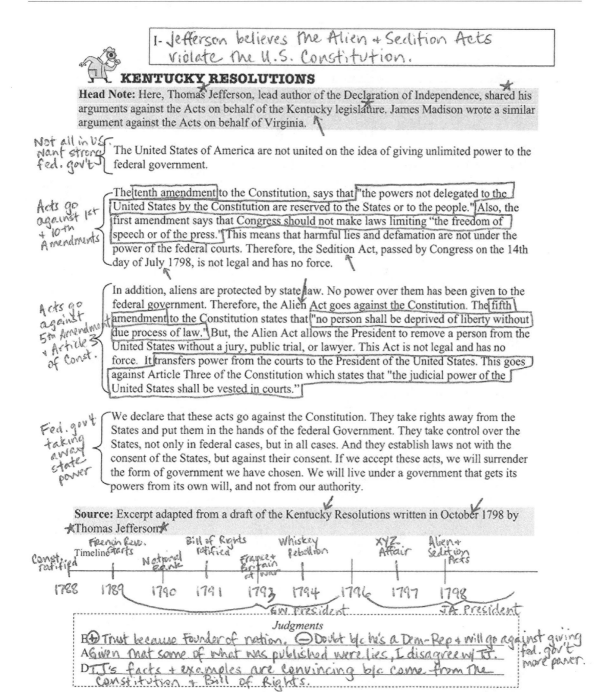

nent. Set against these tensions, one can see why the Alien and Sedition Acts may have been passed to ensure the security of the new nation.

Authors' Evidence. Here, teachers introduce students to the last step in *IREAD*, and the final reading component of this curriculum: determining the quality of evidence that is provided by authors to support their arguments (see

Figure 5.5, Lesson Plan, Day 2). While not exclusive to history, this aspect of reading encourages students to take a critical eye to text rather than tacitly accepting the statements of others.[17] Not all historical sources are arguments (e.g., tax records), but we include argumentative sources for strategic reasons. Research suggests that exposing students to texts with explicit argumentative structure leads to better recall and structuring of arguments.[18] By focusing on authors' evidence, students may look more deeply at the context of these sources, since authors are rooted in the periods from which they write.

The Kentucky Resolutions and Massachusetts' response are great examples of authors building convincing arguments based on solid evidence. Both sources quote the Constitution and the Bill of Rights, which gives students the chance to review important content. In modeling *D*, teachers can point out where Jefferson quotes the Tenth Amendment to assert the Democratic-Republican stance (any powers not specifically cited in the Constitution are reserved for the states). Jefferson also quotes the First Amendment to explain why Congress does not have the right to limit freedoms specified in the Bill of Rights.

In the following paragraph, he cites the Fifth Amendment and Article 3 of the Constitution to attack the Alien Act on the grounds that it gives the president powers delegated by the Constitution to the judiciary branch, and overlooks due process in allowing the president to remove someone single-handedly. In the last sentence, Jefferson refers to a fundamental Democratic-Republican belief that the power of the federal government should derive from the will and consent of the people, not the whim of government authorities.

The Federalist position stated in the Massachusetts response highlights the view that branches of the federal government have powers implied by the Constitution, whether or not they're spelled out. (Teachers should guide students to the third paragraph to consider this evidence.) Because Article I, Section 8 gives Congress the power to "provide for the Common defence [*sic*] and general Welfare of the United States," the Federalists assume that actions like the Alien and Sedition Acts are covered by the "necessary and proper" clause (also in Article I, Section 8), affirming the right of Congress to create laws that fulfill its duties.

The Massachusetts response quotes the Acts ("'dangerous to the public safety'") and cites what was going on at the time ("threatened with invasion by the French") to argue that a nation under threat needed Congress to protect it. The second paragraph highlights differences in interpreting the First Amendment. For the Massachusetts legislators, the Sedition Act doesn't violate the First Amendment, since lies are not protected. In other words, they interpret the Amendment differently, saying that the Sedition Act will actually protect proper use of speech and the press. This point may be difficult for students to grasp, since they will be more familiar with Jefferson's interpretation of the First Amendment.

After modeling *D* (using the Kentucky Resolutions), teachers can coach students on the examples, quotes, and references the legislators used to support their argument. Applying *D* to these historical sources not only gives students the chance to gain knowledge about the controversy, but a chance to weigh good evidence in each argument.

Students may draw different conclusions about historical sources. They may trust the Massachusetts document because it was written by elected officials, yet have doubts because the legislators were Federalist and partisan in their thinking. Some students could conclude that the response makes sense, given a fear of war with France. Other students may decide that the facts and examples are less convincing since the United States wasn't at war with anyone at the time.

Writing History

Some teachers bemoan students' tendency to make claims without supporting them or include evidence that has nothing to do with the claim, or write incoherent statements. Now that students have been given the main components of argument writing—claims, evidence, explanation, analysis, rebuttal—Investigation 3 shows students how to live up to these expectations by supporting them as they plan their essays (see Figure 5.6, Lesson Plan, Day 3). Students ready to plan on their own can use the "Planning Your Essay" organizing sheet (see Figure 5.2 for a sample plan); others may need the process modeled again.

Either way, planning starts with deliberating about the evidence and constructing an evidence-based position in response to the central historical question. This will become the claim, and the main focus of the essay. When teaching how to write historical arguments, teachers should direct students to begin with the question and the sources, rather than the claim. Ideally, students should choose a position best supported by the evidence; an iterative process of moving back and forth between question and sources is part of historical thinking. While argument writing can lead students to decide on a claim before choosing examples to support it,[19] such an approach undermines historical thinking. We encourage students to consider the evidence as they construct interpretations and explain what led them to make their claims. Discussion and deliberation help students process the evidence and figure out a claim that is consistent with the weight of the evidence (see Chapter 7 for a discussion structure you can use here).

> *Classroom Notes.* Prompts such as "What does this piece of evidence tell you?", "How does the evidence you selected support your claim?", or "What do the authors write that relate to your claim?" help students use relevant evidence to support their claim.

Once students construct a claim, they will need to identify reasons and select relevant evidence that led them to their claim. We want students to see that there's a logical path between claim, reasons, and evidence. Reasons might include general ideas supporting a claim (e.g., "truthful speech is protected by the Constitution"), while evidence could be quotes or examples that illustrate the idea and support the claim (e.g., "Massachusetts legislators interpreted the First Amendment differently than we do today").

FIGURE 5.2. Sample Plan for an Argument that The Alien and Sedition Acts Did Not Violate the Constitution

Planning Your Essay

Introduction.

(1) Recap the event Alien and Sedition Acts were passed in reaction to events between England and France & America

(2) Explain the historical question What is the best interpretation of the Constitution?

(3) Why people disagreed DR and Federalists disagreed on how to govern the nation

(4) Your answer to the historical question AS. acts do NOT violate C...

↓

Supporting paragraph.

(1) Strongest reason Freedom of speech protected if truthful

see Mass Response:
(2) Quote (Label **Q1** on document or note here) " the amendment is a safety measure ... not its abuse "

(3) Explain the press must be responsible in what it publishes

(4) Judge (Label **J1** on document or note here) bc threats by French gov't = reasonable to worry about harmful lies

↓

Supporting paragraph.

(1) Strongest reason Federal gov't must protect nation

(2) Quote (Label **Q1** on document or note here) "Congress shall have the power to make all laws... necessary... its powers "

(3) Explain Article 1 Constitution gives Congress power to declare war

(4) Judge (Label **J1** on document or note here) makes sense- Federalists did not trust citizens

↓

Rebuttal paragraph.

(1) Strongest reason that goes against you Dem Rep.s believe acts go against the Const.

(2) Quote (Label **Q3** on document or note here) from Jefferson, "We declare that these acts go against the Constitution "

(3) Explain Alien and Sedition Acts take rights of states away when using a strict interpretation of the Const.

(4) Judge and explain why you reject an opposing perspective (Label **J3** on document or note here). Jefferson is pro-French but is wrong not to worry

↓

Conclusion. (1) Explain why someone should choose your perspective over another.

America was facing danger from abroad, so these acts did not violate the Constitution

Once students start to look at supporting claims with evidence, they sometimes spend more time finding a quote or example than making sure there's a good fit between their evidence and their claim. Carefully reading and annotating sources will help them select evidence, but students may still need to be prompted to consider the relevance and credibility of the sources. Ultimately, students should recognize that the *quality* of evidence—its relevance, specificity, and credibility—is more important than the ability to insert a quotation. In argument writing, good evidence aligns with the claim.

> *Teachers Reflect.* "They would restate what the person is saying in their own words. And I would say, 'That's good that you're saying what it means to you, but you're not really taking the next step. You're just comprehending—you want to also say okay, why do you believe that.' I don't think they were really questioning themselves in their evaluation."

Historical writing requires additional demands on evidence use: students must go beyond logical reasoning to historical thinking. This curriculum pushes students to critique evidence rather than automatically accept the texts they read. *IREAD* scaffolds this practice: As students plan and compose their essays, they return to their "judgments" to select and frame evidence, paying attention to its limits and strengths as artifacts that can shed light on the historical question.

We want students to ask themselves, "Given authors' positions and context, what can (or can't) they tell me that has bearing on the historical question?" Asking questions like the ones in *IREAD* are initial steps toward evaluating the usefulness of evidence in responding to a historical question. By considering authors' perspectives, historical context, and the strength of their arguments, students gain concrete ways to analyze and critique sources. A quotation may be logically connected to the claim but wholly unreliable as evidence given the question under consideration: The use of evidence in historical writing thus involves attention to reliability, how it informs the historical question, and its connection to the claim. We remind students to include judgment of the evidence in planning and composing their answers—not just as a step in the reading process, but as an essential part of writing historical essays.

HOW TO TEACH THIS INVESTIGATION

What's New in This Investigation?

In Investigation 3, students learn that some authors make arguments and try to convince others using facts, examples, or quotations (D of *IREAD*). This evidence may come from documents (the U.S. Constitution) or specific events (the French Revolution). Students also learn to plan and compose an entire essay. Planning involves deliberating about the evidence, constructing a claim in response to the question, selecting specific and relevant evidence to support the claim, and forming judgments about the evidence they include. Thinking through these elements will help students incorporate good evidence and produce more coherent essays.

On Day 1, students learn relevant background knowledge and practice basic comprehension and sourcing (*IRE* of *IREAD*). On Day 2, teachers model *A* and *D* with the Kentucky Resolutions and give students practice with the Massachusetts response. On Day 3, students plan and compose an entire essay, then reflect on their progress.

Teaching Principles

This chapter presents two approaches to developmentally appropriate representations of content we use throughout the curriculum: graphic supports for annotations and adapting historical sources. The annotation process is scaffolded so that over time, the supporting graphics found in the margins will disappear. This helps students to internalize the aspects of historical reading embedded in *IREAD* and independently practice them. Advanced students can try their hand at the original (see note 15) or a less modified version, and will likely not need graphic supports to guide their annotation.

> *Classroom Notes.* Students will vary in terms of willingness to plan and compose an entire essay. It is more important to save time after each investigation to reflect on the quality of student writing than to allow the maximum writing time with no time for reflection.

In adapting sources for each investigation, we use the same principles suggested by Wineburg and Martin: focusing, simplification, and presentation.[20] The original Kentucky Resolutions were pages of tiny print arranged in two columns. Old-fashioned spelling was changed to follow modern conventions (e.g., an S looks like an S rather than an F). We simplified vocabulary and sentence structure, and even modified complex sentences (thus, "An audacious and unprincipled spirit of falsehood and abuse had been too long unremittingly exerted" becomes "A daring and dishonest spirit of lies and abuse has been allowed for too long").

For each primary source, the headnote gives an overview of the source along with pertinent information. An attribution (the source line at the bottom) makes clear who created the document, when, where, and the genre (letter, speech, etc.). We used a minimum of 12-point type, limited the length of each document to two-thirds of a page, and left ample margins to ensure that the page didn't look too crowded or overwhelming. We made similar adaptations for all sources in this curriculum, and share our thinking in case teachers want to try this on their own.

Teachers continue with Stages 2 to 3 of the cognitive apprenticeship model of instruction ("Model how to read and write like a historian" and "Support students' practices") to help students identify and learn historical reading and writing practices. Since learning to contextualize has proven difficult, we suggest that teachers model the contextualization strategy embedded in *A* with the first document in this investigation. The investigation introduces the concept of critiquing evidence used to bolster authors' arguments. For this reason, we suggest modeling *D* with the first document.

As students plan an entire essay for the first time, teachers can work collaboratively with students to support their planning, reminding students of the purpose and steps involved in planning, and highlighting supports for students as they work. Guide students to work as a class or in small groups to use the documents, *H2W*, and the Planning Your Essay graphic organizer when deciding on quotes and judgments, choosing the strongest evidence and judgments rather than accepting any response from the group. Depending on their needs, students may choose their own quotes, reasons, and judgments. Others who find planning confusing can follow a plan you generate with the class to gain a firmer grasp of the process. Either way, you will need to check and give feedback on the reasons they think are strong and the judgments they make.

Things to Keep in Mind

This investigation encourages independence in working on reading comprehension and sourcing (*IRE* of *IREAD*), and scaffolding contextualizing and critiquing arguments (*AD* of *IREAD*). Organizing students into groups or pairs will ease the transition to working on their own, so that students can help one another. Pacing independent work, such as giving groups 4 minutes per step of *IREAD* before prompting them to move on, will keep the class together and on track. As a class, go over any challenges faced by the groups. As you model *A* and *D*, think aloud as you read, contextualize, and critique evidence used by authors in their arguments. Annotate, using some form of projection system, so that students can see your thinking.

> *Classroom Notes.* Planning should *not* involve writing out the entire essay. We made this mistake one year and found that students missed the experience of organizing their thinking—the key benefit of planning—and were less motivated when composing their essays.

If some students would benefit from a discussion, give them time to deliberate on the historical question before they begin planning. You can use the Structured Academic Controversy model found in Appendix B, Figure B.2, and referred to in Chapter 7 or have a less formal discussion. As a class, you can debrief everyone's ideas.

On the 3rd day, the planning focus should be on organizing thoughts and evidence to support the central claim. As you guide students' planning, emphasize how brief notes and marking up the documents are more helpful than trying to write everything out. When it's time to compose, students can choose a plan that argues the position they agree with most. This is the first time we ask students to write an entire essay, so they may need encouragement. If students are struggling, encourage them to write one supporting paragraph rather than two. Help students pace themselves by giving regular reminders of the amount of time they will have.

HOW MIGHT STUDENTS RESPOND?
STUDENT WRITING AND TEACHER FEEDBACK

In Investigation 3, students write a complete essay for the first time. This is an opportunity to put all the pieces together while refining support and rebuttal paragraphs. It's also a new challenge. Some students have difficulty completing the essay, while others can struggle with sections where they demonstrated success during the first two investigations. Setbacks such as these are a common part of the learning process and can be addressed through supportive and formative feedback. Teachers should also take note that the historical question for this investigation is more challenging as it asks students to consider the aims of the Constitution.

Tamia was absent for Investigation 3, so we have no sample essay from her. Because each investigation is designed to introduce a new set of practices (particularly in Investigations 1–4) and support student independence, her absence provides an opportunity for us to suggest ideas that help students catch up when they miss an investigation. For example, Tamia's teacher could tell her to look at the finished work of two students who are close in ability—or maybe a bit above her level, but not so advanced that she can't relate. She could take notes on a blank investigation about what she learned from looking at peers' work, maybe even find kids who wrote from opposing points of view.

It may be that Tamia had no work for this investigation because she was reluctant or resistant to try the work. Or she may have simply missed class for 3 days. Either way, her teacher should leave some supports in place to help build her confidence. She might continue writing at the paragraph level, rather than completing an entire essay, or continue working in small groups. If there isn't time to have Tamia do additional work to catch up, her teacher might pair Tamia up with a partner in the next investigation, so she has someone to co-plan with.

Aaron (Figure 5.3) holds his ground and even makes some progress in Investigation 3. On the conceptual level, he continues to show an understanding of the role that reasons, quotes, explanations, and evaluations play in a strong supporting paragraph and hits the mark with his first supporting reason. In addition, perhaps because the authors of both documents are legislators, he acknowledges that authors with dissenting opinions have similar credentials. This could be an important step away from picking one author or document as the "correct" account.

Such an insight presents the perfect opportunity for Aaron to think about other ways to evaluate documents, especially given the focus on facts and examples in this investigation. And again, while he presents an opposing view, he does not attempt to rebut it. As a result, Aaron's goals after this investigation remain the same. It is not unusual for students to take more than one investigation to make forward progress. Students sometimes need to see the same feedback several times before they show a breakthrough in their thinking and writing.

FIGURE 5.3. Aaron's Essay for Investigation 3

In 1798 the ailien and sedition acts were made. We wanted to find out if the violated the constitution or not. People disagreed because some thought if violated the const. and some did not. In my opinion I think they do violate the constitution. I think It violates the constitution for 2 main reasons. First, in thomas Jeffersons Kentucky resulutions he says "congress can make no law limiting freedom of speech or of the press. that shows the acts did violate the constitution because they limited what could be printed. I belive this is reliable because legislators like thomas Jefferson are required to be familiar with the law. Second, I think it violates the constitution because legislators wrote the document that says so. Another quote I found was "dangerous to public safety". This shows that if the public was uninformed it could be dangerous. I also belive this because it was written by legislators. The strongest reason why it did not violate the constitution is because it was protecting the pulic. the same quote "dangerous to public safety" can be used to show that something were to much for the public to handle so those acts were protecting them. I also think this is reliable because it was written by legislators. In conclusion, I think the ailien and sedition acts of 1798 did violate the constitution.

Praise: "I like your choice of quote here. It supports your conclusion well."

Praise: "You make a good point here—the authors of both documents know about the Constitution."

Polish: "How might you use the authors' choice of facts and examples to evaluate their arguments? Why would someone disagree with this reason?"

Goal: "For your rebuttal paragraph, remember to respond to opposing arguments so that readers understand why you disagree."

LESSON PLANS AND MATERIALS

Teachers and students will need the following: Lesson plans (Figures 5.4–5.6), Investigation 3 packet (clipboard with overview, Kentucky Resolution, Massachusetts Response found after the lesson plans found in Figure 5.7), Additional materials for this investigation (Constitution and Bill of Rights background cards, Figure 5.8), Disciplinary literacy tools (*IREAD*, Planning Your Essay graphic organizer, *H2W*, and essay prompt sheet in Appendix A), two film clips, and overhead projection capacity (to model annotating sources and share plans).

FIGURE 5.4. Lesson Plan, Day 1: Background Knowledge, Reading Comprehension, and Historical Reading

Materials: Investigation 3 student packets, *IREAD*, Planning Your Essay, *H2W*, Essay prompt sheet, Reflection Guide, Projector, Online film clip. *Suggested time:* **1 hour per day**

INTRODUCTION

1. Warmup: Should the federal government have the right to arrest someone because they come from a country that supports terrorism or because they've written something negative about our country? Think-pair-share.

2. Introduce the historical question for this investigation and connect it to the warmup. (e.g., Americans debated similar issues in 1798. The Alien Acts gave the federal government the right to imprison or deport immigrants. The Sedition Act made it illegal to say, write, or publish anything negative about the government or its leaders, etc.).

3. Review the purpose of the investigation (to write an evidence-based argument responding to the question) and the detective process students will use to achieve this goal (prepare for the case, investigate the case, write the final judgment).

BACKGROUND INFORMATION

4. The U.S. Constitution and Bill of Rights. In groups, read aloud and discuss the Background Cards in Figure 5.8:
   a. Which excerpts come from the Bill of Rights? From the Constitution?
   b. Which document—Bill of Rights or Constitution—defends an individual's rights?
   c. Which document spells out the rights and responsibilities of the government?
   d. Do any of these cards change your response to the warmup? If so, how?

5. The Alien and Sedition Acts
   a. What were the Acts? Read page 1 of the packet and your textbook for background on what led to the Acts.
   b. Discuss: What were the Alien and Sedition Acts? What led Congress to pass them?
   c. Perceptions of the acts. Go over the major differences between Democratic-Republicans and Federalists (textbooks can help with this) and watch the excerpt of the HBO miniseries *John Adams*, in which Adams and Jefferson discuss and disagree about the Alien and Sedition Acts (Part VI: Unnecessary War).
   d. Discuss: Why did John Adams support the acts? Why did Thomas Jefferson oppose them?

HISTORICAL READING: GENERAL READING COMPREHENSION

6. Preview vocabulary, if necessary (see Appendix B).

7. Guide students as they use *IRE* with the Kentucky Resolutions. Then have them practice *IRE* with the Massachusetts response in pairs (circulate and coach, if necessary).

8. Debrief: Have a different pair share annotations for each letter (this does not need to be exhaustive) and write annotations on the overhead (as long as they're correct).
   a. Discuss and clarify any points of confusion—either mistakes in using *IREAD* or misunderstanding of the documents.

9. Judge the authors' reliability (*E*): Discuss reasons to trust and to doubt the authors. Ask each student to write a reason to trust and another to doubt each author.

FIGURE 5.5. Lesson Plan, Day 2: Historical Reading and Thinking

INTRODUCTION

1. Ask students to recall the historical question and which side of the controversy Massachusetts and Kentucky were on. Explain that they will continue to investigate both sides of the case by annotating with attention to context and evidence.

HISTORICAL THINKING AND READING: CONTEXTUALIZING WITH *A* OF *IREAD*

2. Review *A* of *IREAD* and explain the purpose of noticing historical context.
3. Model *A* of *IREAD* with the Kentucky Resolutions, including segmenting time by selecting major historical events to include on a timeline as well as the documents' dates. Also, note the places where each was written.
4. Guide students as they use *A* of *IREAD* with the Massachusetts Response and identify contextual information (as a whole class or in pairs followed by debriefing).
   a. Where necessary, instruct students to identify the location, date of the document, and any additional events described in the document and ask them to put them on the timeline you created.
5. Students review their *A* annotations on both documents in order to make judgments about the influence of historical events and issues surrounding the documents. Discuss:
   a. Does noticing the location, dates, and major historical events make any of the main ideas more or less convincing?
   b. Does anything about historical events at the time make one side more convincing?
6. Judge the influence of context. Students write a note in the margin to summarize their judgment of each document based on their analysis of the historical context.

HISTORICAL THINKING AND READING: ANALYZING AUTHORS' ARGUMENTS WITH *D* OF *IREAD*

7. Explain *D* of *IREAD* and the purpose of considering an author's facts and examples.
8. Model *D* of *IREAD* with the Kentucky Resolutions. Highlight references to events, concerns from the time period, or historical documents.
9. Guide students as they use *D* of *IREAD* with the Massachusetts document in pairs or the whole class. Where necessary, instruct the students to identify where authors refer to events, concerns from the time, or historical documents as evidence to support a point.
10. Students review their *D* annotations for both documents and discuss:
    a. Do the examples from specific texts make one argument more convincing?
    b. Do the facts about specific events make one argument more convincing?
    c. In what ways do the authors disagree in their interpretation of these outside texts or events? Why do they seem to disagree?
11. Judge the authors' facts and examples. Students write a note in the margin to summarize their judgments of each document based on the quality of authors' facts and examples.

FIGURE 5.6. Lesson Plan, Day 3: Planning and Historical Writing

INTRODUCTION

1. Prepare for the planning process: Students read through all of their annotations and consider how they will respond to the central historical question. Share (e.g., thumbs-up for yes, thumbs-down for no) and discuss briefly.

2. Review the purpose of the investigation (to write an argument responding to the question that is supported by evidence).

PLANNING

3. Help students plan an entire essay with the Planning Sheet by planning together. This will involve prompting students with questions and gathering their ideas for each section of the plan. (Note: Be ready to share your own ideas if necessary.)

    a. Decide on a claim you will make for your class plan.

    b. Review key ideas about the controversy that you will include in your introduction and note them on the plan (project this group plan as you create it together).

    c. Supporting paragraphs:

        i. Ask students to share a strong main idea that supports the claim. Have them explain why it is a strong idea. Note it on the group plan.

        ii. Select evidence from the documents to support this idea and number it on the document (e.g., "Q1") or note a reference to it on the plan.

        iii. Discuss the credibility of the evidence selected and a judgment to include in your essay (write "J1" on the document or note the idea on the plan).

        iv. Repeat this process for a second supporting paragraph.

    d. Rebuttal paragraph: Look for a main idea that supports an opposing point of view. Select a quotation that shares this opposing view. Then, identify a judgment of the authors, context, or facts/examples that will reject this main idea or evidence. The rebuttal should reject the opposing side.

4. If time, ask students to work in pairs to create their own plan (or a plan for a different claim in response to the historical question).

COMPOSING

5. Ask students to compose their own essays using the plan they agree with most. Tell them they'll share their essays after composing.

6. Highlight the supports students have as they compose their essays: the documents they annotated, the *H2W* guide for writing their essay, transition words and phrases (on the back of *H2W*), and the plan they created on the Planning Your Essay sheet.

REFLECTION

7. Ask students to pair up with someone who wrote a different argument than they did.

    a. Students can share essays to see how another student interpreted the same issue differently.

    b. Direct students to consider how a classmate's essay met our writing goals and fill out their classmate's Reflection Guide (Appendix A) for this essay.

8. Students switch papers so they can review their own and a partner's assessment.

    a. Ask students if they agree with their partner's assessment. If not, allow them to make changes to the Reflection Guide.

    b. Ask each student to write down at least one goal for improvement for their next essay (in the "I am working on" column).

FIGURE 5.7. Materials: Investigation #3 Packet

Name: _____ Class: _____ Date: _____

INVESTIGATION #3:
DID THE ALIEN AND SEDITION ACTS VIOLATE THE U.S. CONSTITUTION?

You are a historical detective trying to decide if the Alien and Sedition Acts of 1798 violated the U.S. Constitution.

The Federalist-controlled Congress passed the Alien and Sedition Acts while John Adams was President. Federalists and Democratic Republicans had different opinions about the amount of power states and federal government should have. They also disagreed about how much the French Revolution threatened the stability of their new nation. They shared their disagreements about different leaders and issues in public newspapers. Democratic Republicans strongly objected to the Alien and Sedition Acts, but Federalists supported them.

Did these Acts violate the U.S. Constitution?

FIGURE 5.7. Materials: Investigation #3 Packet, Continued

Name:_____ Class:____ Date:_____

I-

Kentucky Resolutions

Head Note: Here, Thomas Jefferson, lead author of the Declaration of Independence, shared his arguments against the Acts on behalf of the Kentucky legislature. James Madison wrote a similar argument against the Acts on behalf of Virginia.

The United States of America are not united on the idea of giving unlimited power to the federal government.

The tenth amendment to the Constitution, says that "the powers not delegated to the United States by the Constitution are reserved to the States or to the people." Also, the first amendment says that Congress should not make laws limiting "the freedom of speech or of the press." This means that harmful lies and defamation are not under the power of the federal courts. Therefore, the Sedition Act, passed by Congress on the 14th day of July 1798, is not legal and has no force.

In addition, aliens are protected by state law. No power over them has been given to the federal government. Therefore, the Alien Act goes against the Constitution. The fifth amendment to the Constitution states that "no person shall be deprived of liberty without due process of law." But, the Alien Act allows the President to remove a person from the United States without a jury, public trial, or lawyer. This Act is not legal and has no force. It transfers power from the courts to the President of the United States. This goes against Article Three of the Constitution which states that "the judicial power of the United States shall be vested in courts."

We declare that these acts go against the Constitution. They take rights away from the States and put them in the hands of the federal Government. They take control over the States, not only in federal cases, but in all cases. And they establish laws not with the consent of the States, but against their consent. If we accept these acts, we will surrender the form of government we have chosen. We will live under a government that gets its powers from its own will, and not from our authority.

Source: Excerpt adapted from a draft of the Kentucky Resolutions written in October 1798 by Thomas Jefferson.

Timeline

Judgments

E_____

A_____

D_____

FIGURE 5.7. Materials: Investigation #3 Packet, Continued

Name:_____ Class:____ Date:_____

 Massachusetts' Response

Head Note: Here, legislators from Massachusetts respond to the Virginia and Kentucky Resolutions by arguing in support of the Alien and Sedition Acts.

We consider the Alien and Sedition Acts constitutional, appropriate, and necessary. Aliens have temporary rights, which should be taken away whenever they become "dangerous to the public safety" or are found guilty of treason against the government. Congress has a duty to defend the nation. When Congress passed the Alien Act, we were threatened with invasion by the French. Thousands of aliens were ready to cooperate in an attack. The removal of aliens is a common practice when preparing for war. The law, therefore, was just and necessary.

The first amendment says that Congress cannot make laws reducing the "freedom of speech or of the press." The Sedition Act does not take away these freedoms. The true liberty of speech and the press is the liberty to say and publish the truth. This is different than the reckless use of speech and writing to spread lies and damage people's reputations. The amendment is a safety measure for the reasonable use of the press, not its abuse. This right is not violated, but approved and set up by the recent act of Congress.

The federal government has the power and the duty to defend against war. It has the right to keep rebellions under control and protect each state from attack. The Constitution specifically grants these powers to the federal government in Article I, Section 8. It says that Congress shall have the power to make all laws that are "necessary and proper for carrying out its powers."

The Alien and Sedition Acts are justified by the Constitution. These Acts are wise and necessary. A spirit of lies and abuse has been allowed for too long. This spirit has been leading public opinion astray. It has threatened to undermine and destroy the whole fabric of government.

Source: Excerpt adapted from the Massachusetts legislators' response to the Virginia and Kentucky Resolutions. February 9, 1799.

Judgments

E_____

A_____

D_____

FIGURE 5.8. Additional Materials for This Investigation: Background Cards

NOTE CARDS OF RELEVANT BACKGROUND INFORMATION

First Amendment: The right to petition the government and peaceably assemble as well as freedom of speech, freedom of press, and freedom of religion.	**Article I** outlines the powers of the Legislative Branch (Congress). This includes the Senate and House of Representatives. Members of Congress are elected from the states. Congressmen and -women suggest bills and can declare war, provide for the common defense, and make other decisions.
Fifth Amendment: Citizens' lives, freedom, and property cannot be taken away from them without due process of law.	**Article II** outlines the powers of the Executive Branch, including the president. The president is the commander-in-chief of the armed forces. He can make treaties with other nations. He chooses judges and other government officials.
Tenth Amendment: The powers that are not given to the federal government in the Constitution are set aside for the state governments or the people of the United States.	**Article III** outlines the powers of the Judicial Branch, including the Supreme Court. The Supreme Court includes men and women who are judges that hear cases about laws and problems in the nation. They also define what the crime of treason is.

What Path Offered the Best Chance of Survival for the Cherokee in the Early 1800s: Staying in Their Original Territory or Removal to the West?

Overview of Chapter 6

Investigation	Foundational Concepts	Disciplinary Literacy Practices	CCSS Links	C3 Links	Principles of Teaching
Investigation 4: *What path offered the best chance of survival for the Cherokee in the early 1800s: staying in their original territory or removal to the West?*	Reading, thinking, and writing are interconnected activities in studying history	Discussing and evaluating evidence Planning and composing a full essay	RI.5.6 (p. 14) RI.5.8 (p. 14) RI.5.9 (p. 14) RH.6–12.1 (p. 61) RH.6–12.2 (p. 61) RH.11–2.3 (p. 61) RH.6–12.6 (p. 61) RH.6–12.8 (p. 61) W.5.1a–d (p. 20) W.5.9b (p. 21) WHST.6–12.1a-e (p. 64) WHST.6–12.4 (p. 66) WHST.6-12.9 (p. 66)	D2.His.1.6–8 D2.His.4.6-12 D2.His.6.6-8 D2.His.10.6–8 D2.His.13.6–8 D2.His.16.6–12 D3.2.6–8 D3.4.6–12 D4.1.6–12 D4.4.6–12	Pose central historical questions that have multiple possible answers and present historical sources to investigate Develop students' background knowledge Present developmentally appropriate tasks Cognitive apprenticeship Stage 3 and 4: support students' practice and provide additional, more challenging forms of practice

INVESTIGATION 4 PRESENTS a different kind of question, not necessarily the kind that historians ask, but rather, a policy debate that the Cherokee faced in the early 1800s: *What path offered the best chance of survival for the Cherokee in the early 1800s: staying in their original territory or removal to the West?* Students analyze and question a letter and pamphlet from Cherokee leaders on opposite sides of the debate. We purposefully avoided using one Cherokee source and one from a U.S. government official to stop students from automatically taking one side or the other. Instead, we selected sources that demonstrate the complexity of historical debates (that there are often no clear-cut answers). The example shows that the Cherokee were not a united, homogenous group.

To approach this issue with some degree of historical fidelity, students need to put themselves in the position of the Cherokee of the early 1800s and recognize that the Cherokee didn't know how the story would unfold at the time they made the decision. Investigation 4 pushes students to make an argument grounded in historical context rather than current biases. To make a good historical argument, students must leave aside their knowledge of the Trail of Tears or abuses by the federal government, and consider what information the Cherokee had as well as their belief system and values. The question is not whether the Cherokee had a right to the land but which path would allow the Cherokee nation to thrive, given what else was happening at the time.

More than previous lessons, Investigation 4 highlights the interconnectedness of reading, thinking, and writing in the study of history. Now that students have learned major strategies for reading and writing, they can put them all together. As students go from background knowledge to reading and historical thinking and then planning and composing, they will see that all these activities are related; each day contributes to the final goal of producing an evidence-based argument in response to a historical question. Reading and historical thinking guide students to an interpretation best supported by the evidence, which becomes the basis for their written argument.

As students annotate the Cherokee Letter and the Boudinot Pamphlet, they engage in prewriting. When students plan their essay, they reread primary sources and reconsider the evidence in light of the question—they read critically. In thinking about the central question and practicing literacy strategies, they begin to realize that each strategy is not an end in itself, but part of a process leading to an evidence-based argument.

In terms of disciplinary literacy, Investigation 4 emphasizes evaluating evidence rather than accepting texts at face value, along with the practice of planning and composing a full essay. One note: We sometimes see a dip in student success at this juncture, when students are asked to master a large amount of literacy and historical thinking content. Starting around Investigation 4 or 5, students begin to integrate strategies more easily, since the reduced content lets them practice what they've learned.

HISTORICAL BACKGROUND

When the Cherokee first came in contact with Europeans, they were one of the largest confederations of towns in what is now Georgia. In the late 1600s, the Cherokee allied with English settlers against other indigenous groups who allied with other colonial powers such as France and Spain. These relationships changed by the mid-1700s, as the Cherokee clashed with the growing numbers of English settlers moving into the Appalachian highlands. In 1768, White encroachment forced the Cherokee to cede a large tract of land on the upper Tennessee River in the Treaty of Hard Labor. During the Revolutionary War, the Cherokee briefly sided with the British in order to protect their land holdings, but eventually established official peace with the Americans.

By the 1830s, the Cherokee had assimilated many White norms. In 1827 the Cherokee in Georgia created their own written constitution. A year later they published a newspaper, the *Cherokee Phoenix*, in Cherokee and English. Missionaries' efforts to spread Christianity and establish schools proved successful. Some Cherokee leaders, including Chief John Ross, wore European clothes and lived a European lifestyle.[1] Some even owned plantations and slaves.[2] By assimilating, American Indians hoped to be accepted and respected by Whites so that they could retain their land. But was such assimilation enough to resist White encroachment and removal?

As president, Thomas Jefferson encouraged assimilation. In his first Annual Message to Congress in 1801, he reported that "the continued efforts to introduce among them the implements and the practice of husbandry, and of the household arts, have not been without success."[3] Jefferson continued to share progress with assimilation in his 1807 and 1808 Messages to Congress. In 1808 he implied that the end goal of assimilation might be citizenship: "one of the two great divisions of the Cherokee Nation have now under consideration to solicit the citizenship of the United States, and to be identified with us in laws and government in such progressive manner as we shall think best."[4] This approach was often motivated by the notion that American Indians were savages who needed to be civilized and would benefit from exposure to "superior" American society. But Jefferson, and those who shared his view, could not keep up with White settlement. Some historians have argued that assimilation efforts were simply a preparation for integrating American Indians once their land was taken away. Historian Ronald Satz points out, "Civilizing the Indians for their assimilation into American society never took precedence over pushing them outside the area of white settlement; it merely justified it."[5]

Even Jefferson supported removal when assimilation seemed untenable. The Cherokee had direct experience with this side of U.S. federal Indian policy. Theda Perdue has found evidence of division over removal in the early 1800s, when leader Black Fox leaned toward Jefferson's offer to cede land in exchange for territory in the West.[6] Most Cherokee opposed the idea, and removed Black Fox from power until the disagreement passed. Cherokee women were largely excluded from tribal politics, especially since the adoption of Anglo American political structures. Yet they spoke out against ceding land to the U.S. government and removal in three separate petitions to the male-dominated National

Council.[7] Nevertheless, a large contingent of Cherokee moved to what is now Arkansas in 1817 and 1819, later known as the Western Cherokee. Despite their voluntary agreement, they were forced even farther west in 1828.[8] Just as it was never clear whether American Indians could assimilate enough, it was unclear whether they could ever move far enough west.

Federal Policies

These questions did not trouble Andrew Jackson, who became president in 1828. Jackson had been a military leader during violent conflicts with the Creek in 1812–1814 and the Seminole in 1817–1818. At the end of hostilities in 1814, the U.S. government seized 22 million acres of land from the Creek, a strong message to tribes considering aggressive action. The Seminole waged three wars with settlers before the United States paid those who remained to move west.[9] After the defeat of the Sac and Fox, President Jackson made an example of their leader Black Hawk, imprisoning him and then sending him from town to town to show "the strength of the white people."[10] The federal government sent a clear message that fighting spelled ruin.

As his treatment of Black Hawk showed, Andrew Jackson used his presidency to intensify federal efforts to move American Indians west, a position evident in his first Annual Message to Congress in 1829: "I informed the Indians inhabiting parts of Georgia and Alabama that their attempt to establish an independent government would not be countenanced by the Executive of the United States, and advised them to emigrate beyond the Mississippi or submit to the laws of those States." Here, Jackson played the role of the benevolent leader concerned with the well-being of tribes whose territory have been surrounded by the states. If they remained, they would be ruined by encroaching White settlements and unable to retain their ways.

Using this logic, Jackson proposed setting aside land for American Indians to preserve their way of life and self-rule with little intervention from the federal government. Their removal would open up land to White settlement, including slavery and cotton cultivation in the South. Jackson framed this as a choice for Indian tribes: Move and enjoy self-determination or remain and follow the laws of the states surrounding them.[11] Anthony Wallace writes that Jackson never publicly spoke of removing American Indians by force, but by 1835 removal no longer seemed voluntary.[12]

The safety and well-being of tribes, national security, and land acquisition were all used to justify federal Indian policy.[13] Whatever the justification, expansionism clearly motivated state and federal government policies. To Wallace, the Cherokees' success at assimilation was threatening to Whites because the Cherokee produced so much cotton that they were able to sell the excess for a profit. Their embrace of agriculture meant that they were no longer willing to cede land. David Wishart states a similar economic view, estimating that a large number of Cherokee households in the East produced a surplus of food. He suggests that their agricultural success may have made their land even more attractive to Whites.[14] While the Cherokee constitution asserted that their nation was sovereign, and therefore independent of Georgia state laws, the Georgians wanted the fertile Cherokee land for agriculture and the metal and mineral deposits found there.

Divisions Within the Cherokee Nation

Divisions within the Cherokee complicated their response to the pressure to move west in the 1830s. Perdue argues that as they established their own system of government and tried to manage negotiations with federal authorities, power had become concentrated in the hands of a Cherokee elite, with fewer people in charge compared with the traditional tribal governance. These leaders amassed economic power as the recipients of bribes and trade to maintain White-Cherokee relationships. Perdue identifies significant social divisions that emerged with these political and economic changes: Cherokee who opposed the centralization of power and wealth were seen as "common Indians," or middle-class, while those with economic and political power comprised the elite within Cherokee society. Many of the elite came from mixed heritage due to contact with White traders. Twelve signers of the Cherokee constitution whom Perdue could locate owned 355 slaves, and most received previous reservations from the United States. These 12 "farmed an acreage four times the average for Cherokee heads of households and produced five times as much corn and six times as much wheat as other Cherokees."[15]

According to Perdue, the Cherokee who wanted entrée into the elite eventually signed the 1835 Treaty of New Echota with the U.S. government. The federal government had successfully worked with tribal factions or opposition leaders to get what they wanted, and they actively developed a relationship with this rising Cherokee middle class.[16] This alternative group, known as the Treaty Party, was led by Major Ridge, John Ridge, and Elias Boudinot. When the national Cherokee council refused to sign a removal treaty, the U.S. government worked with the Treaty Party instead. About 100 members of the Treaty Party met in New Echota to sign the agreement ceding Cherokee land in the East in exchange for land in the West. Other Cherokee boycotted the meeting in protest, though federal negotiators warned that silence would be interpreted as consent. As Robert Remini explains, "The numbers represented only the merest fraction of the Nation. A vast majority—perhaps fifteen-sixteenths of the entire population—presumably opposed it and showed their opposition by staying away."[17] Perdue notes that "the treaty party insisted that its only concern was for the masses, who were 'so completely blinded as not to see the destruction which awaits them.'"[18] Through this fraudulent process, Jackson got the treaty he wanted. The Senate ratified the treaty in 1836, at which point the Cherokee had 2 years to move west. The anti-removal Cherokee continued to protest the treaty and resist removal while the federal government adhered to the Treaty of New Echota.

Prior to this, the Cherokee had worked within the U.S. federal government to assure their future by challenging state laws. When a new law asserted Georgia's sovereignty over the Cherokee, they brought their case to the U.S. Supreme Court (*Cherokee Nation v. Georgia*). On March 18, 1831, the Court decided that the Cherokee were not a sovereign nation, but neither were they subject to Georgian laws. Instead, the Court ruled that the Cherokee were "domestic dependent nations." This phrase perplexed federal Indian policymakers and indigenous peoples for years to come. In response, Georgia passed a law requiring White men to obtain a license from the state before they could enter Indian country. When two men were jailed as a consequence, the Cherokee appeal made it to the U.S. Supreme Court (*Worcester v. Georgia*). The Supreme Court ruled that the Cherokee were a separate nation and declared that Georgian laws dealing with the Cherokee were unconstitutional.

Although favorable to the Cherokee, this ruling had no impact since Georgia and the State Superior Court did not respond to the decision. Without a response, the Supreme Court couldn't issue an order of compliance. Meanwhile, Jackson worked behind the scenes for the release of the two trespassers. In the end the ruling was not enforced because, as Remini argues, there was nothing to enforce.[19] The Cherokee tactics had failed, resulting in the tragic eviction that became known as the Trail of Tears.

LITERACY PRACTICES STUDENTS WILL LEARN

By this point students should realize that each part of the 3-day lesson will lead to writing an evidence-based argument essay, using annotated documents, plans, and *H2W* (including transition words) as they compose their essays. Gathering all of these supports together highlights the integration of reading, analysis, planning, and composing. Previous investigations laid the foundation for the key literacy practices in Investigation 4 that support historical argument writing: evaluating evidence and planning and composing a full essay.

Reading History

Investigations 1–3 showed students how to source, contextualize, and critique authors' arguments. In Investigation 4 students apply the information and subtext they uncover in primary sources.[20] The important question to ask is: Why is this information important and what impact might an author or audience have had on the sources? To help students use the information they identify from primary sources, and to compare and contrast sources, time is set aside on Day 2 to closely examine and consider the sources

Teachers Reflect. "I think I challenged kids' thinking and questioned them in terms of how they reached their conclusions. . . . 'Why' became a constant response to everything they had to say— 'What made you think that? What got you there?'"

(see Figure 6.7, Lesson Plan, Day 2). This concept is embodied in the words *judge* in *IREAD* and *judgment* in *H2W*, signaling that students should think historically, instead of amassing and acceping information uncritically.

We ask students to evaluate the sources after reading so that they can corroborate the sources (consider them in light of each other). Corroboration is the third aspect of historical reading identified by Wineburg in his work with historians and high school students.[21] Whether historians specialized in ancient Japan or colonial America, he found that they typically checked sources against one another to figure out whether details were credible. (A simple way to check if students are corroborating is to see if they flip back and forth between primary sources.)

Students will notice that both authors are Cherokee. However, the authors of the "Cherokee Letter" (Figure 6.1) represented the Cherokee nation; they are addressing Congress about staying on their original territory, a position supported by Chief John Ross. Elias Boudinot's pamphlet (Figure 6.2) puts forth a minority position. As editor of the *Cherokee Phoenix*, Boudinot originally backed Ross. However, by 1832, he began to change his position. When the Cherokee National Council and Chief John Ross would not allow Boudinot to publish alternate views or question the official policy to remain on their land, Boudinot left his job as editor of the *Phoenix*. He joined the breakaway group that signed the Treaty of New Echota, ceding their territory in Georgia for lands west. The Treaty Party comprised a small group of Cherokee who were not authorized by the Cherokee government to negotiate treaties; most Cherokee supported John Ross's leadership as chief and the official position against removal.

Although Boudinot's pamphlet seems to reflect our modern understanding of the issue, the Cherokee letter more likely captures the actual sentiments of most Cherokee of the early 1800s in this region. Relegated to the margins of society, Boudinot may not be respected as a reliable source, a circumstance which ironically gives him a better vantage point to report from outside the mainstream Cherokee view.

As students contextualize, they see how the dates of each source relate to contemporaneous events. The Cherokee Letter came first, after the tribe tried to demonstrate their "civilized nature" (creating a constitution, publishing a newspaper, studying Christianity). By this time Georgia had passed laws that allowed them to take Cherokee land. Boudinot's pamphlet was written after Congress passed the Indian Removal Act, which gave President Jackson authority to negotiate removal treaties with American Indians. In *Worcester v. Georgia*, the Supreme Court ruled the Cherokee were a separate nation and couldn't be governed by state law, while the Creek nation in Alabama signed a treaty certifying that the Creek owned their land but would allow Whites to settle on it.

Boudinot also wrote after the 1831 *Cherokee Nation v. Georgia* decision, which ruled that as a domestic dependent nation, the Cherokee did not have to follow state laws. Even though Boudinot clearly had the advantage of seeing events unfold, the *Phoenix* continued to advocate its anti-removal position until it folded in 1834. Despite these events, the official Cherokee position of 1832 was no different from when the Cherokee Letter was sent to Congress. *Worcester v. Georgia* was a promising ruling for the Cherokee; they may not have believed that Jackson would ignore a Supreme Court decision, despite his negative attitude toward American Indians.

Considering an author's "facts and examples" is another way to compare documents. While the pamphlet cites a number of examples, these warnings didn't necessarily apply to the Cherokee's situation at the time. Boudinot implores the nation to consider the fate of the Creek tribe who lost 22 million

FIGURE 6.1. Sample Annotated Cherokee Letter

Judgments:

(E) + authors selected as reps. of Cherokee to U.S. Congress -- may be closer to what most believed.

(A) + Cherokee tried to assimilate (Constitution, Christianity) so U.S. may want to encourage that

(D) - Treaties with U.S. Gov't have been cancelled

J3- cancelled

Name:_____ Mod:____ Date:_____

The authors believe the Cherokee should stay in their original territory.

Cherokee letter

Head Note: By the 1820s, the Cherokee had adopted White ways in the hopes that the U.S. government would allow them to stay where they were (e.g., they developed their own alphabet, created their own constitution, established churches and newspapers). In this letter to the U.S. Congress, representatives of the Cherokee nation explain why they prefer to stay where they are.

To the honorable Senate and House of Representatives of the United States of America:

GA trying to push Cherokee out. They want to stay.

We are troubled by some of your people. Our neighbor, the state of Georgia, is pushing us to give up our belongings for her benefit. If we do not leave the country and go to the western wild lands, we are told that we will have to follow the laws of the state. We dearly love our country. We owe it to you and to ourselves to explain why we think the country is ours, and why we wish to remain in peace where we are.

This land has been heirs for a long time.

Our fathers passed down this land to us. They possessed this land since before people can remember. It was a gift from our common father in heaven. When the white man came to the shores of America, they found our ancestors in peaceful possession of this land. Our fathers gave it to us as their children. We have taken care of this land respectfully. It contains the ashes of our fathers.

We have the right to this land.

In addition, treaties made at various times give us the faith and promise of the United States (even though these treaties have been canceled over and over again). These treaties recognize our rights as a separate people. These treaties guarantee that our rights will be protected. If we just lived here but didn't own this land, why would the U.S. need our permission to take our lands? The answer is obvious. These governments perfectly understood our right to the land and our right to self-government.

J-Q3

This land has always been ours.

The first European settlers found our forefathers fully in control of this land and ruling over it independently. Since we have never given up this land to others, we do solemnly protest being forced to leave it.

This land is who we are. Our future is tied to this land.

We are attached to our land. It is our fathers' gift. It is the land of our origin and the land of our intellectual birth. We cannot agree to give it up for a far inferior land. The Cherokee's existence and future happiness are at stake. If you take away our liberty and country, you will cause our nation to fall apart and be humiliated. You will slow down or even stop our progress in becoming civilized and in learning the Christian religion. We believe that such an act would be extremely harsh.

You represent a good, intelligent and Christian nation. We ask you to make the right decision.

Source: Excerpt adapted from a letter written by representatives of the Cherokee nation to the U.S. Congress in December 1829.

Before Removal Act

1814 — Creek Nation. Partly defeated. lose 22 million acres.

1827 — Cherokee create own Constitution.

1828 — Georgia passes state laws allowing them to take Cherokee land.

1830 — Indian Removal Act.

1832 — Worcester v. Georgia. + Creek treaty with U.S. 9 allows white on their land. End uplifting land.

FIGURE 6.2. Sample Annotated Boudinot Pamphlet

Name:_____ Mod:____ Date:_____

[handwritten box: The author believes the Cherokee should move West.]

Boudinot pamphlet

Head Note: By the 1830's, Elias Boudinot supported Indian Removal, but Chief John Ross did not. Boudinot was fired from his job as editor of the *Phoenix*, a Cherokee newspaper, because of his beliefs. He became an active member of the "Treaty Party," a group of Cherokee who supported making a treaty with the U.S. that would give their nation land further west. In this pamphlet, Boudinot shares his reasons for supporting removal.

The Cherokee people face a crisis of the greatest importance. Every person must seriously think about and discuss the present condition and future of the Nation.

[margin note: Cherokee will not live successfully if surrounded by/governed by whites]

We believe that our people cannot exist in the middle of a white population. Here, they will be ruled by laws that they did not help make and which they do not understand. The State's control over the Cherokee Government will stop their progress. It will also completely destroy everything like civilization among them. Finally, this control will force them into poverty and misery. This belief is based on the sad experience of the Cherokees in the last two years and upon the history of other Indian nations. *[Q1]*

[margin note: Cherokee won't be able to rule themselves in existing territory controlled by state.]

Think about the progress of the States' power in this country. This progress includes the division and settlement of the lands, the organization of counties, and the formation of county seats and Courthouses. At the same time, the President and the Congress of the United States have repeatedly refused to get involved and support us. We believe that this nation cannot be re-established in its present location. Therefore, we ask this question: Is it better to stay here, surrounded by these embarrassments, or to look for a country where we may enjoy our own laws?

[margin note: stay → ruin]

Even though we love the land of our fathers, we believe that moving will be far better than giving in to the laws of the States. If we stay we will witness the ruin of the Cherokee people.

[margin note: Will not regain rights if they stay]

We believe that most of the Cherokees would prefer removal if they knew the truth. The truth is that they will not be able regain their rights as a separate community. The only choices left to them is to be surrounded by white people and follow the white man's laws or to remove to another country.

[margin note: Creek experience = warning]

We must think about the fate of our poor brothers, the Creeks. Their experience is enough warning to all those who want the Cherokees to stay and follow the laws of the States. *[Q2]*

Source: Excerpt adapted from resolutions written by a member of the Cherokee nation, Elias Boudinot on October 2, 1832. Published in a pamphlet in 1837.

[handwritten:]
Judgments:
E − Boudinot is not representative of Cherokee Nation. He was fired by Chief; minority view?
J2= A + Boudinot writes in 1832 − later than Letter & after Indian Removal Act so may know more
J1= D + Notes specific events (Creeks, state gov't power) that reveal gov't attitude toward American Indians

10

acres of land to the United States. While persuasive, the comparison isn't completely fair since the Creek began this conflict by attacking settlers and, unlike the Cherokee, signed an 1832 treaty allowing settlers on their land. The Cherokee Letter refers to treaties with the U.S. government as evidence of their right to self-government and recognition as an independent nation, while in the next breath, acknowledges that treaties had been repeatedly broken.

By reading these documents with a critical, comparative eye, students should find reasons to trust and doubt both sources, since no one source will ever be all good or all bad and neither was written with the intention of having people in the present debate their merits.

To fully address this question, history detectives need to hear from outside the Cherokee nation in Georgia. What did Georgia leaders think about the Cherokee? What views did the U.S. government, from Supreme Court justices, to the president and Congress, hold? What were the interests of people in the region? Teachers can expand this investigation by including more voices and helping students grasp the larger historical context that surrounded this conversation.

Writing History

In Investigation 4, students will plan and compose an entire five-paragraph essay. Figure 6.3 offers a sample plan (in combination with the annotated documents in Figure 6.1 and Figure 6.2) for the argument that removal was the best decision for the Cherokee. When composing, students are challenged with integrating all the literacy practices learned so far. Teachers can play the role of cheerleader by recognizing the difficulty of the investigation, praising student efforts, and supporting

> *Classroom Notes.* Students can set a goal to write four paragraphs in 2 days the first time they work on their own, but should try to create a plan for five paragraphs in case they are able to accomplish more.

their work. And, once students are ready to compose an essay, they should be given a solid 30 to 40-minute block of time in which to write.

Whether students complete their essays or not, teachers should reserve time for reflection during the last day of the investigation (see Appendix A, Reflection Guide), a habit that will become ingrained as investigations continue. Reflection supports students' metacognition, or awareness of what goes into good writing (see Chapter 2). It also helps students recognize their audience and purpose as they compose, making the writing process more authentic and compelling for them.[22] Finally, the reflection process we advocate reinforces the interpretive nature of history, that is, that there's often not one right answer.

For students to grasp the concepts of audience and purpose, teachers may need to explain this approach before students compose. Have students exchange essays with someone who took an opposing side of the argument. Students can swap essays and complete their partner's Reflection Guide, then switch papers back and read each other's feedback. They should decide which comments they agree with, and set goals for themselves moving forward. If there's time, have students work on revising their essays. By reflecting on the

FIGURE 6.3. Sample Plan (Combined with Annotated Sources in Figure 6.1 & Figure 6.2)

Planning Your Essay

Introduction.
(1) Recap the event *State of Georgia surrounded Cherokee and challenged their rights to self-rule as independent nation*
(2) Explain the historical question *Cherokee had to decide what was best for their people*
(3) Why people disagreed *Some Cherokee focused on their values and rights but others focused on events in U.S.*
(4) Your answer to the historical question *move west for best chance*

Supporting paragraph.

(1) Strongest reason *State's increased control over land*

(2) Quote (Label **Q1** on document or note here)

(3) Explain *if they stay they will have to follow state laws*

(4) Judge (Label **J1** on document or note here)

Supporting paragraph.

(1) Strongest reason *Other tribes have been treated badly*

(2) Quote (Label **Q1** on document or note here)

(3) Explain *the Creeks lost land to whites*

(4) Judge (Label **J1** on document or note here)

Rebuttal paragraph.

(1) Strongest reason that goes <u>against</u> you *Treaties recognize Cherokee rights to rule themselves and will protect them*

(2) Quote (Label **Q3** on document or note here)

(3) Explain *U.S. gov't made treaties as promises*

(4) Judge and explain why you reject an opposing perspective (Label **J3** on document or note here). *the experience of the Creeks is a rude warning*

Conclusion. (1) Explain why someone should choose your perspective over another.
Boudinot may know more about how native Americans are being treated, even though he is in the minority of Cherokee who think this way

work of a partner as well as their own, students will begin to internalize the components of historical argument writing, recognizing purpose and audience as they write—that it's not just okay when people interpret primary sources and historical questions differently, it's to be expected.

HOW TO TEACH THIS INVESTIGATION

What's New in This Investigation?

This investigation offers students increasing independence when annotating sources, more focus on making judgments, greater attention to the essentials of historical writing, and time for reflection after composing the essay. Day 1 starts with learning background knowledge, reading the first primary source, and historical thinking; on Day 2, students concentrate on the second primary source, historical thinking, and planning; Day 3 emphasizes composition and reflection. Aside from evaluating evidence ("making judgments"), students read, analyze, and annotate with greater independence, thinking through and applying *IREAD* on their own. More than any of the preceding investigations, this lesson plan devotes time to three important aspects of the writing process: planning, composing, and reflection.

Teaching Principles

This investigation reflects Stages 3 and 4 in the cognitive apprenticeship model as teachers help students practice the skills they have learned thus far (i.e., "Support students' practice with reading and planning" and "Provide additional, more challenging forms of practice with composing").[23] Teachers pose a central historical question with multiple possible answers, and students continue to work with historical sources to investigate the question. Investigation 4 highlights the different questions we ask when we study history. The first investigation posed a "whodunit" question ("Who fired the first shot at Lexington Green?") that was concrete and required minimal background knowledge—students had to learn about only one event, though some understanding of events that led up to the American Revolution would be helpful. The next two investigations asked abstract questions of interpretation that called for students to look to the past for answers (e.g., once you learn about Shays and his followers, do you think the label "rebel" or "freedom fighter" is more appropriate?). In this and the remaining investigations, students will grasp questions of policy, looking at the past from the perspective of people at a particular historical juncture.

Policy questions require an immersion in historical context. These questions can pique student interest and prompt debate, setting them up to write a lively argument. However, they don't always foster considered thinking, as students tend to jump into the debate armed with modern perspectives and knowledge rather than a historical perspective. The teacher's role is very important when considering the questions found in Investigations 4–6. As students deliberate, teachers need to point out our present-day biases, and remind them that unlike us, the people who decided these issues didn't know how the story would end. Rather, students must examine concerns and values of a previous time, and the impact that events had on people "back then."

You'll notice that our questions offer two obvious responses. Students who grasp the greater complexity of an issue will offer alternative responses or reconcile a combination of responses (e.g., "It made sense for the Cherokee to stay until 1832, but after that it made more sense to move West because . . ."). Few historical questions are as dichotomous as the question setup suggests; time constraints prevented us from asking the myriad of questions a historian would (e.g., "Why did so many Cherokee want to stay?"). Instead, we deliberately framed questions in an either/or format in order to present developmentally appropriate tasks. In working with struggling middle-schoolers and reviewing the research of others, we realized that interpreting history and making an argument are slippery concepts. Since open-ended "why" questions get students to ponder what's being asked, but offer no clues for how to frame a response, students tend to fall back on their default mechanism of reporting information.

Instead, closed either/or questions will lead students toward posing an argument; as they respond directly to the prompt, the prompt itself gives them the language to make a claim. Presenting questions like this is developmentally appropriate for the age and skill range of our population. Once students get a foothold in historical reading, thinking, and writing, they'll be able to advance to more complex, exploratory, and difficult questions (e.g., "Why did the boycott of Montgomery's buses succeed?").

Things to Keep in Mind

During this investigation, students will complete their annotations in pairs or groups (or even on their own). Since they are still developing the practices they need to analyze primary sources, it is important to review their annotation.

Before you debrief, decide which annotations or aspects of the primary source are important given the historical question. Avoid generating too many annotations when debriefing. Instead, strategically identify three or four important annotations per *IREAD* step (leave space for students to spot things you missed). Write the most important annotations onto the source and project as you write, so that those struggling will have a visual guide. If students don't share annotations you think are important to notice, share them.

> ***Classroom Notes.*** We recommend that teachers annotate the sources, consider a response to the central question, and plan and compose an essay to support students' efforts. This will highlight the assignment's challenges and help teachers meet their students' needs.

As students gain greater independence, differentiation will help teachers work with academically diverse students. The original sources and additional sources on this topic[24] are available for students ready for more challenging reading. Some students may be able to handle their own Structured Academic Controversy discussion (see Chapter 7, Figure 7.10), while others will need direct guidance in using the modified documents. In this investigation, teachers function more as coaches, since there's little explicit modeling for the whole class. That doesn't mean that your job is finished. Teachers have a crucial but different role to play in this investigation, circulating around the room as they check on student thinking and progress.

Pay attention to what students are annotating—what are they getting out of their reading? What ideas and evidence appear in their plans and essays? During planning, consider that students may be confused by working with annotated documents for new purposes such as selecting and organizing ideas. Attend to their thinking and build where possible. Teachers may interrupt class to discuss and clarify something they notice different students struggling with. They can ask students to share work that offers a solution to challenges faced by others, or discuss how students could solve it together. Think back to the previous investigation to anticipate what students will need. What might you say to an individual student as you circulate during each section of the lesson (reading, judging, planning, composing, and reflecting)?

Use the Reflection Guide and other types of reflection so students become aware of their writing, and set goals for future essays. Teachers can have students share their essays within and across classes (e.g., show the students in your first class the papers that were written by students in your second class and give Post-its so they can offer praise and an idea for polish).

HOW MIGHT STUDENTS RESPOND? STUDENT WRITING AND TEACHER FEEDBACK

With Investigation 4, students have the opportunity to practice forms of historical thinking they have learned in previous investigations. In particular, they have opportunities to make judgments about sources, context, and facts and examples in order to take a stand on the historical question. Remember that students may have trouble with the historical question in this investigation. Many will apply their personal values to the historical question, rather than the perspectives of the authors and the quality of their arguments.

As we saw in Investigation 1, Tamia's writing (Figure 6.4) can be hard to follow at times. Overall, the parts of her essay do not hold together well, as she selects a quote that advocates for Cherokee removal, but argues that the Cherokee should stay. She follows with a reason that focuses on hiding gold, which has a historical basis but is never explicitly addressed in the documents. Nonetheless, Tamia addresses the historical context and takes a stand. She even uses a quote for the first time. Although space limitations preclude our ability to show Tamia's annotations on the documents, we were able to see that she successfully summarized the main points of each document as well as offered a judgment that made sense. Because she missed the previous investigation, where students were prompted to use our planning sheet for the first time, she may have needed more prompting and support to use this tool. This underscores the need to follow up with Tamia to help her with the planning process.

Aaron (Figure 6.5) shows progress on several fronts in this investigation (after showing limited progress on the last). His essay structure is fully devel-

FIGURE 6.4. Tamia's Essay for Investigation 4

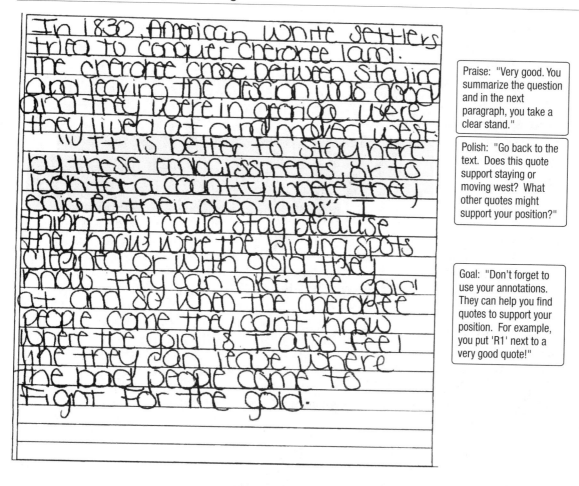

Praise: "Very good. You summarize the question and in the next paragraph, you take a clear stand."

Polish: "Go back to the text. Does this quote support staying or moving west? What other quotes might support your position?"

Goal: "Don't forget to use your annotations. They can help you find quotes to support your position. For example, you put 'R1' next to a very good quote!"

oped, and he effectively explains the reasons behind his two supporting paragraphs and rebuttal. Most importantly, he responds to opposing side arguments for the first time, both by questioning the motives of the Cherokee representatives and by citing Boudinot's use of facts and examples in the conclusion paragraph. While he continues to rely on the credibility of the authors to make judgments, he is beginning to branch out into other kinds of evaluation.

LESSON PLANS AND MATERIALS

Teachers and students will need the following: Lesson Plans (Figures 6.6–6.8), Investigation 4 packet (clipboard with overview, timeline, Cherokee letter, Boudinot pamphlet found after the lesson plans in Figure 6.9), Disciplinary Literacy tools (*IREAD*, Planning Your Essay graphic organizer, *H2W*, Essay Response Template, and Reflection Guide in Appendix A), film clip, and overhead projection capacity (to share and review annotations and plans).

FIGURE 6.5. Aaron's Essay for Investigation 4

The cherokee had to decide if they wanted to stay on their land or remove to the west. The historical question was weather the cherokee should leave oR stay. People disagreed because some belived the indians should leave, but others like Ellias Boudinot thought it would be best if they left. I think the cherokee should have left their land. I think the strongest reason the cherokee should have left is because they knew what happend to the creeks. A quote from the Boudinot pamplet says "we must think of the fate of our poor brothers, the creeks." This shows that Boudinot does not want what happend to the creeks to happen to his people, the cherokee. This is belivable to me because Boudinot had the best intrest of his people in mind. The second strongest reason

The second strongest reason I belive the cherokee should have left is because, In a new land they would be able to govern themselves. A quote from the Boudinot pamplet that supports this idea says "Is it better to stay here, surronded by these embarasments, or to look for a country where we may enjoy our own laws. This is basically asking all cherokee people do they want to be someone else's property for the rest of eternity Or, do they want to branch out and govern themselves. I find this belivable because boudinot uses very convincing facts & examples

¶ —New Paragraph

● It may also be argued that the cherokee should have stayed because this has been their land for hundreds of years and they should not just up and leave. A quote from the cherokee letter to congress says "We are attached to our land. It is our fathers' gift. It is the land of our origin and the land of our intellectuall birth." This shows how attached the cherokee are to their land & why they don't want to leave it. This letter is somewhat belivable because it was written to congress.

When all of the facts on both sides are considered, I think the cherokee should have left for the survival of their nation. I doubt document 1 because, it was written by the cherokee & they would say anything to keep their land. I trust document 2 more because, it used conving facts and examples & Ellias Boudinot had the best intrest of his people in mind. Keeping these facts in mind I would trust document 2.

Polish: "Is the case of the Creeks a fair comparison? If so, explain why. Look at the date of each document. How might you use this information to evaluate the documents?"

Praise: "I like how you have selected quotes and explained your ideas in this essay."

Polish: "What makes Boudinot's choice of facts persuasive? Please explain."

Goal: Consider using context to evaluate the documents (e.g., look at when each document was written.) Be sure to explain your evaluations to make them stronger.

Materials: **Investigation 4 student packets, *IREAD*, Planning Your Essay graphic organizer, *H2W*, Essay prompt sheet, Reflection Guide, Projector, Online film clip**

Suggested time: **1 hour per day**

INTRODUCTION

1. Warmup: If you had to move away from home, what would you bring with you?

2. Introduce the historical question for this investigation and connect it to the warmup (e.g., in the 1830s the Cherokee faced the possibility of moving. The difference is that their ancestors had lived on their land for thousands of years). Point out the source for each document so students can see both authors were Cherokee but disagreed about the best course of action.

3. Review the purpose of the investigation (i.e., to write an evidence-based argument in response to the question) and the detective process students will use to achieve this goal (prepare for the case, investigate the case, write the final judgment).

BACKGROUND INFORMATION

4. Overview: Read page 1 of the student packet for an overview and preview vocabulary your students may not know (removal, assimilation, self-government).

5. View PBS video about the Indian Removal Act and *Worcester v. Georgia*. See Section 4 (fourth yellow dot on the bottom of the screen): "I Ask You, Shall Red Men Live?" in *We Shall Remain, Episode 3: Trail of Tears.* (9:50) http://www.pbs.org/wgbh/amex/weshallremain/the_films/episode_3_trailer.

   a. Discuss: Would the Indian Removal Act make you want to stay or go? Would the Supreme Court decisions make you want to stay or go?

6. Review and discuss the events on the timeline (page 2 of student packet). Use the questions below to prompt students about the events on the timeline as well as their meaning.

   a. For the events of 1814 & 1827: Why would the Cherokee take these actions after the Creek's experience?

   b. For 1828: What does this event tell you about Georgia at this time?

   c. For 1830, 1831, & 1832: What do these events tell you about the U.S. government?

   d. For 1832: Why do you think this happened after the Supreme Court decisions?

READING COMPREHENSION AND HISTORICAL READING & THINKING

7. Set goals for using *IREAD* so that students can become more independent. Students should aim to spend 10 minutes completing *IR* and 10 minutes completing *EAD* with the Cherokee Letter with time to debrief after. Use a timer to give reminders and help students pace themselves.

8. Prompt students to complete *IR* with the Cherokee Letter in pairs or small groups. Circulate to check for understanding. Then, debrief and share annotations.

9. Prompt students to complete *EAD* with the Cherokee Letter in pairs or small groups. Circulate to check for understanding. Debrief and share annotations.

10. Discuss: Do students think the Cherokee representatives made a good argument in their letter? How is this letter useful given the historical question? To what extent is it trustworthy or reliable? Ask students to explain and support their responses.

FIGURE 6.7. Lesson Plan, Day 2: Historical Reading & Thinking and Planning

INTRODUCTION

1. Ask students to recall the historical question and which side of the controversy the Cherokee representatives and Elias Boudinot were on. Remind them to continue to investigate both sides by annotating and judging documents.

READING COMPREHENSION AND HISTORICAL READING & THINKING

2. Prompt students to complete *IR* with the Boudinot Pamphlet in pairs or small groups. Circulate to check for understanding. Then debrief and share annotations.

3. Prompt students to complete *EAD* with the Boudinot Pamphlet in pairs or small groups. Circulate to check for understanding. Debrief and share annotations.

4. Now that students have considered both sources, they should discuss and evaluate the primary sources in pairs or as a whole class.

   a. Judge the reliability of the authors (*E*): Discuss reasons to trust and doubt each author. Remind students to consider the authors, the kinds of document, and the audience or occasion for which they were written.

   b. Judge the influence of historical context (*A*): Discuss ways the authors do and don't make sense given what else was going on at this time and in this region. Remind students to look at their timeline to see when the documents were written as they make judgments.

   c. Judge the quality of authors' facts and examples (*D*): Discuss whether the authors' facts and examples are convincing. Remind students to look at the authors' choices of quotations or references to historical events.

5. Wrap up by having students write 2–3 judgments of each source. Students should recognize that every source has its own strengths and weaknesses when it comes to answering a historical question (rather than deciding that one source is "right" and the other is "wrong").

PLANNING ESSAYS

6. Transition: What response to the central historical question does the evidence best support? Think-pair-share.

7. Review the goal: To convince someone with a different perspective of your argument. Remind students that they will share and reflect on their essays tomorrow after they compose.

8. Plan essays using the Planning Your Essay graphic organizer in Appendix A.

   a. Make notes for the introduction and the conclusion on the plan sheet. Look at the background and timeline to plan the introduction.

   b. Select and organize ideas for the body paragraphs. Students can mark Q1 and J1 on the documents for the first supporting paragraph, and mark Q2 and J2 for the second supporting paragraph. They can mark Q3 and J3 on a document to show material they plan to use for the rebuttal. If students prefer, they can write brief notes on the planning sheet instead of using this numbering system.

   c. Choose transitions from the "Helpful Phrases" on the back of the *H2W* to introduce judgments and introductory sentences for each paragraph.

FIGURE 6.8. Lesson Plan, Day 3: Planning and Historical Writing

INTRODUCTION

1. Warmup: What response to the central historical question is best supported by the evidence? What evidence do you think is convincing?

2. Remind students of the primary goals: to persuade someone with a different opinion that your argument is strongest by using convincing evidence and explaining that evidence.

COMPOSING

3. Give students 5 minutes to finish planning their essay, if necessary.

4. Students compose their own essay on the Essay Prompt Sheet (see Appendix A) and additional lined paper, if needed.

    a. Highlight student supports for composing the essay: the plan they created, the documents they annotated, the *H2W* guide for writing their essay, and the transition words and phrases (on the back of *H2W*).

    b. Using a timer, give students the entire class excerpt for the last 10 minutes to compose. Prompt students to move onto the next paragraph every 8–10 minutes so that they learn to pace themselves.

    c. Circulate around the room as students work. Show students how to find content in their documents, how to use their plan to write sentences, and how to use the *H2W* guide and transition phrases.

        i. Look for students who are struggling and offer support:

            A. Ask students how they will respond to the central question.

            B. Ask students to explain which evidence they will use and how it supports their argument.

            C. Show students transition phrases that may be useful for each paragraph.

            D. Suggest that students move on to the next paragraph if they're spending too much time on one paragraph.

    d. Students may need encouragement. Reinforce effort with participation points or praise. If students are struggling, encourage them to write one supporting paragraph instead of two.

REFLECTION

Be sure to save the last 10 minutes for reflection, even if students haven't completed their essays.

5. Students should exchange essays with someone who chose a different argument.

    a. Have them consider how someone could interpret the same issues differently.

    b. As they react to each other's essay in terms of meeting the writing goal, ask them to complete their partner's Reflection Guide based on that essay (see Appendix A).

6. Have students switch to their own paper and consider their partner's assessment.

    a. Ask students if they agree. If not, let them make changes to the Reflection Guide.

    b. Based on this information, ask students to identify a goal for improvement in subsequent essays (in the "I am working on" column).

FIGURE 6.9. Materials: Investigation 4 Packet

Name: _____ Class: _____ Date: _____

INVESTIGATION #4:

WHAT PATH OFFERED THE BEST CHANCE OF SURVIVAL FOR THE CHEROKEE IN THE EARLY 1800s: STAYING IN THEIR ORIGINAL TERRITORY OR REMOVAL TO THE WEST?

As White settlements expanded West, they threatened to take over Cherokee land in the Southeastern United States. The Cherokee were faced with a decision—to relocate to another land set aside for them by the U.S. government or to stay where they were. Many Cherokee wanted to stay because their families had lived on the land for 10,000 years—it was their land, not the U.S. government's land. But some feared that the Cherokee would be surrounded by U.S. territory and forced to follow U.S. laws.

The U.S. government sent mixed messages about removal. In 1830, the "Indian Removal Act" gave President Andrew Jackson the right to negotiate removal treaties with Indian tribes. On the other hand, in 1831, the Supreme Court ruled that the Cherokee had the right to rule themselves.

Here you will read two points of view from the debate over what was best for the Cherokees at this time.

What do you think?

FIGURE 6.9. Materials: Investigation 4 Packet, Continued

Name:_____ Class:_____ Date:_____

Background: Write any conclusions you make about these events on the left side of the timeline.

1814: The U.S. military defeats part of the Creek Nation. The Creek lose 22 million acres of land in Georgia and Alabama.

1827: The Cherokee Nation creates its own written Constitution. One year later, the Cherokee publish their own newspaper, the *Cherokee Phoenix,* in Cherokee and English.

1828: The state of Georgia passes laws that allow them to take Cherokee land.

1830: Congress passes the *Indian Removal Act.* The Act gives President Jackson the right to negotiate removal treaties with Indian nations.

1831: The Supreme Court rules that the Cherokee are a "domestic dependent nation" (*Cherokee Nation v. Georgia*).

March 1832: The Supreme Court rules that the Cherokee are a separate nation and have the right to rule themselves. Georgia's laws cannot rule the Cherokee (*Worcester v. Georgia*).

March 1832: The Creek Nation in Alabama signs a treaty with the U.S. to allow white settlers on their land. The treaty says that the Creek own the land, but many lose their land to settlers.

FIGURE 6.9. Materials: Investigation 4 Packet, Continued

Name:_____ Class:____ Date:_____

 ## Cherokee Letter

Head Note: By the 1820s, the Cherokee had adopted White ways in the hopes that the U.S. government would allow them to stay where they were (e.g., they developed their own alphabet, created their own constitution, established churches and newspapers). In this letter to the U.S. Congress, representatives of the Cherokee nation explain why they prefer to stay where they are.

To the honorable Senate and House of Representatives of the United States of America:

We are troubled by some of your people. Our neighbor, the state of Georgia, is pushing us to give up our belongings for her benefit. If we do not leave the country and go to the western wild lands, we are told that we will have to follow the laws of the state. We dearly love our country. We owe it to you and to ourselves to explain why we think the country is ours, and why we wish to remain in peace where we are.

Our fathers passed down this land to us. They possessed this land since before people can remember. It was a gift from our common father in heaven. When the white man came to the shores of America, they found our ancestors in peaceful possession of this land. Our fathers gave it to us as their children. We have taken care of this land respectfully. It contains the ashes of our fathers.

In addition, treaties made at various times give us the faith and promise of the United States (even though these treaties have been canceled over and over again). These treaties recognize our rights as a separate people. These treaties guarantee that our rights will be protected. If we just lived here but didn't own this land, why would the U.S. need our permission to take our lands? The answer is obvious. These governments perfectly understood our right to the land and our right to self-government.

The first European settlers found our forefathers fully in control of this land and ruling over it independently. Since we have never given up this land to others, we do solemnly protest being forced to leave it.

We are attached to our land. It is our fathers' gift. It is the land of our origin and the land of our intellectual birth. We cannot agree to give it up for a far inferior land. The Cherokee's existence and future happiness are at stake. If you take away our liberty and country, you will cause our nation to fall apart and be humiliated. You will slow down or even stop our progress in becoming civilized and in learning the Christian religion. We believe that such an act would be extremely harsh.

You represent a good, intelligent and Christian nation. We ask you to make the right decision.

Source: Excerpt adapted from a letter written by representatives of the Cherokee nation to the U.S. Congress in December 1829.

FIGURE 6.9. Materials: Investigation 4 Packet, Continued

Name:_____ Class:____ Date:_____

 Boudinot Pamphlet

Head Note: By the 1830's, Elias Boudinot supported Indian Removal, but Chief John Ross did not. Boudinot was fired from his job as editor of the *Phoenix*, a Cherokee newspaper, because of his beliefs. He became an active member of the "Treaty Party," a group of Cherokee who supported making a treaty with the U.S. that would give their nation land further west. In this pamphlet, Boudinot shares his reasons for supporting removal.

The Cherokee people face a crisis of the greatest importance. Every person must seriously think about and discuss the present condition and future of the Nation.

We believe that our people cannot exist in the middle of a white population. Here, they will be ruled by laws that they did not help make and which they do not understand. The State's control over the Cherokee Government will stop their progress. It will also completely destroy everything like civilization among them. Finally, this control will force them into poverty and misery. This belief is based on the sad experience of the Cherokees in the last two years and upon the history of other Indian nations.

Think about the progress of the States' power in this country. This progress includes the division and settlement of the lands, the organization of counties, and the formation of county seats and Courthouses. At the same time, the President and the Congress of the United States have repeatedly refused to get involved and support us. We believe that this nation cannot be re-established in its present location. Therefore, we ask this question: Is it better to stay here, surrounded by these embarrassments, or to look for a country where we may enjoy our own laws?

Even though we love the land of our fathers, we believe that moving will be far better than giving in to the laws of the States. If we stay we will witness the ruin of the Cherokee people.

We believe that most of the Cherokees would prefer removal if they knew the truth. The truth is that they will not be able regain their rights as a separate community. The only choices left to them is to be surrounded by white people and follow the white man's laws or to remove to another country.

We must think about the fate of our poor brothers, the Creeks. Their experience is enough warning to all those who want the Cherokees to stay and follow the laws of the States.

Source: Excerpt adapted from resolutions written by a member of the Cherokee nation, Elias Boudinot on October 2, 1832. Published in a pamphlet in 1837.

What Was the Most Effective Way to Free Slaves in the United States Before the Civil War: Nonviolence ("Moral 'Suasion") or More Aggressive Action?

Overview of Chapter 7

Investigation	Foundational Concepts	Disciplinary Literacy Practices	CCSS Links	C3 Links	Principles of Teaching
Investigation 5: *What was the best way to free slaves in the United States before the Civil War: nonviolence ("moral 'suasion") or more aggressive action?*	Reading, thinking, and writing are interconnected activities in studying history	Students set goals to read, analyze, plan, and compose with greater independence	RI.5.6 (p. 14) RI.5.8 (p. 14) RI.5.9 (p. 14) RH.6–12.1 (p. 61) RH.6–12.2 (p. 61) RH.11–12.3 (p. 61) RH.6–12.6 (p. 61) RH.6–12.8 (p. 61) W.5.1a–d (p. 20) W.5.9b (p. 21) WHST.12.1a–e (p. 64) WHST.6–12.4 (p. 66) WHST.6–12.5 (p. 66) WHST.6–12.9 (p.66)	D2.His.1.6–8 D2.His.4.6–12 D2.His.6.6–8 D2.His.10.6–8 D2.His.13.6–8 D2.His.16.6–12 D3.2.6–8 D3.4.6–12 D4.1.6–12 D4.4.6–12	Develop students' background knowledge Adapt the curriculum to students' needs while continually emphasizing disciplinary thinking and writing Cognitive apprenticeship Stage 4, provide additional, more challenging forms of practice

Investigation 5 presents students with conflicting primary sources from two African American abolitionists, William Whipper and Henry Highland Garnet. Students will analyze and question these conflicting sources as they construct an argument in response to the question: *What was the most effective way to free slaves in the United States before the Civil War: nonviolence ("moral 'suasion") or more aggressive action?*[1]

Like Investigation 4, this question requires students to consider a policy issue that confronted people in the past; in this case, the issue was hotly debated in the period before the Civil War. Students must put aside their modern-day perspective to understand the context of the 1830s and 1840s, when these speakers delivered their speeches.

This investigation highlights the interconnected nature of reading, thinking, and writing as students integrate literacy practices and their study of history with greater independence. Initially we framed each literacy practice (composing, planning, reading and analyzing sources, understanding the historical question and background) as separate steps so that they could be made visible to students. We also divided the practices into small steps more attainable for struggling students, and phased them in to avoid overwhelming students (introducing reading comprehension and sourcing first with *IRE*, then adding contextualization with *IREA*, then critiquing authors' arguments with *IREAD*).

Each step and practice is part of a holistic writing process, leading up to the final essay. Rather than moving from one step to the next, advanced writers move between steps as they construct a response to the historical question. For example, reading Whipper's ideas may lead students to rethink the historical question and the ways in which Whipper is or is not a helpful source. As they compose, they may find that something doesn't work in their plan, causing them to reconsider their sources and revise their essays. This is the point when they will begin to transition from using discrete steps to seeing them concurrently as part of a whole set of related practices.

Remind students of the overall goal—producing an evidence-based argument—and how each part of the process contributes to it (see Figure 7.5, Lesson Plan, Day 1). Starting with the final step, composing, teachers can talk students through each aspect of an investigation and how it relates to the overall goal of writing a good essay. This will remind students of their purpose and help them make strategic decisions to achieve this goal. Awareness of the big picture will allow students to set and work toward goals for reading, analysis, planning, and composing with greater independence.

HISTORICAL BACKGROUND

Although the activism of abolitionists would culminate in the formation of the Republican Party and lead to the Civil War, they were a small minority in antebellum America. Even those Americans who opposed extending slavery to the Western territories generally did not support abolition (i.e., abolishing the institution of slavery). Neither was the movement united. Although abolitionists held the common goal of ending slavery, they did not agree on how to do so.

Three key groups—free African Americans, gradualist Quakers, and militant White reformers—debated the best way to achieve their aim. Articles and speeches from the 1800s reveal their conversations, disagreements, and arguments. This investigation focuses on free African Americans in the movement, and the trajectory of abolitionism in America as it changed from a movement targeting Northern White politics and gradual emancipation to one that called for the immediate abolition of slaves and direct action in the South.[2]

Changing Approaches to Abolitionism

At the time of the speeches featured in this investigation, most abolitionists supported one of two approaches: political action and moral 'suasion. Advocating the former were the Quakers, specifically, the Pennsylvania Abolition Society founded in the late 1700s, which Richard Newman explains was "dominated by societal elites" and "advocated gradual abolitionism by means of painstaking legal work and legislative action."[3] This approach entailed working within the existing system by petitioning and offering legal aid to African Americans. For this organization, abolitionism was chiefly in the hands of upper-class Whites, who understood the legal code and subtle lobbying, and used social connections to fund their efforts.

The abolitionist movement that most of us know didn't gain traction until the 1830s. This "second wave" of reform focused on immediate abolition.[4] By delivering speeches, publishing articles and pamphlets, and organizing people, these abolitionists used emotional appeal and vivid descriptions to convince people of their position. Their chief tactics were to publish or report stories of people's horrendous experiences while enslaved, to awaken people to the evils of slavery. The "immediatists" argued that slavery was wrong for moral and religious reasons, and undermined the founding principles of the nation. Also known as "moral 'suasion,"[5] this approach was taken by leaders such as Frederick Douglass and William Lloyd Garrison, who used reason to convince the public (including slaveholders) that abolition was the only rational path forward.[6] Unlike the elitist Pennsylvania Abolition Society, Newman argues that these reformers focused on swaying common citizens and integrating Blacks and women into the movement. Instead of working behind the scenes to influence political and legal changes, "mobilizing the masses . . . became the central abolitionist strategy after 1830."[7]

Black activists in the North played an important role in the abolitionist movement. They got involved in public life and debate by making speeches, circulating pamphlets, submitting petitions, and other forms of direct action. As Stephen Kantrowitz tells us, these free Black men weren't just intent on ending slavery, but also on demanding full and equal citizenship. Tracing the experiences of Black activists in Boston over 60 years, Kantrowitz shows that, for them, the Civil War was not a culminating event. Instead, Boston's Black activists fought to be recognized by Whites as equals more than any other right.[8] While Kantrowitz starts his story at the time this investigation begins, James and Lois Horton go further back in time by chronicling the experiences of Northern Blacks from colonial times until the Civil War, as they transitioned from slavery to freedom. Through individual stories, the Hortons focus on the discrimination faced by Black Northerners, the communities they developed, and how they fought prejudice.[9] As the contrasting views of William Whipper and Henry Highland Garnet attest, this group of activists was anything but homogenous.

Whipper and Garnet in Context

Whipper's speech captures many of the ideas behind moral 'suasion. Chief among them was the role played by religion in laying the foundation for change. Author James Brewer Stewart argues that the early immediatists—in part motivated by the Second Great Awakening—saw themselves as "Christian peacemakers" who could convince slave owners of the error of their ways, and usher in "a redemptive new era of Christian reconciliation and moral harmony."[10] Whipper's abolitionist ideology reflected his experience as a free African American and a successful businessman. He was confident that reason and empathy would sway his listeners. Unfortunately, the abolitionists didn't grasp the enormity of the challenge, and how deeply embedded slavery had become in the political and economic life of the country. For Stewart, this naiveté led to a flurry of activism in the form of speeches and pamphlets.

A Northern backlash against such activism divided the group, something that may be evident in the split vote on Garnet's 1843 address. Garnet called for slaves to rebel, even if their resistance would lead to violence, and raised controversy at the National Negro Convention in Buffalo, New York, where the speech was delivered. Framed as a resolution, Garnet's call fell one vote shy of being adopted by the convention, where balloting revealed how divided the movement truly was.[11] Like Whipper, Garnet was also a free African American. As he encountered resistance to his abolitionist sentiments, his radicalism grew. Historians have framed Garnet's speech as proof that a militant strand of abolitionism was present among Black activists, compared with the more abstract approach of White abolitionists.

In placing Garnet's speech next to those of Gerrit Smith and one by William Lloyd Garrison, Stanley Harrold argues that Garnet was part of an overall movement away from peaceful tactics, not just activism unique to Black abolitionists. Harrold interprets Garrison's address, given just 3 months before Garnet's, as saying that "slaves might wade through their masters' blood if necessary to free themselves."[12] Although the three addresses are similar in many ways, Garrison's and Smith's have remained largely obscure. But together they show a more complete picture of abolitionism. As Harrold explains: "The Addresses are products of changing circumstances, emerging perspectives, abolitionist factionalism, romantic masculinity, biracialism, and a growing willingness to acknowledge the role of slaves in the movement. Taken together, they also reflect declining abolitionist commitment to peaceful persuasion directed at whites and expanding abolitionist involvement in slave escapes."[13] Although not a direct call for violence, addresses like Garnet's reflect a call for involving slaves in their emancipation, focusing on anti-slavery activism in the South, and abandoning conventional tactics. In 1843, however, many were still focused on conventional moral approaches. Even Frederick Douglass spoke out against Garnet's call at the convention in 1843.

Faced with the immovability of the slave system and inflammatory actions such as the murder of abolitionist Elijah Lovejoy,[14] many moral 'suasion immediatists turned to more aggressive resistance. In the 1840s, White immediatists like Wendell Phillips targeted "slavery's northern sources of power," where, according to Stewart, Black immediatists focused their efforts to help slaves escape, fight extremists, and demand citizenship.[15] In the face of such resistance and counterattack, the abolitionist movement continued to shift.[16] When Garnet gave his "Call to Rebellion" to the National Negro Convention in 1843, the group did not sanction his resolution, but 4 years later the delegates adopted a similar statement from Garnet, signaling a move to "register defiance to the slave South" rather than simply pointing out their moral shortcomings.[17] Harrold agrees, pointing out that increasingly the abolitionist movement moved away from trying to influence Northern politics, toward antislavery action in the South. Helping slaves escape and targeting federal slave catchers (once the Fugitive Slave Act was passed in 1850) became primary efforts of the activist wing of the immediatist camp.

Not all immediatists supported this agenda. Elder statesmen like Douglass remained skeptical of aggressive action. But after "Bleeding Kansas," leaders like Garnet and John Brown began to agitate for direct confrontation.[18] This violent undercurrent reached its crisis during John Brown's raid on Harpers Ferry in 1859.

Supporting Students

In order for students to put these speeches in broader context, we have organized key events into an Abolitionism Background Cards activity (see Figure 7.9, Additional Materials, and Figure 7.5, Lesson Plan, Day 1) that convey different strands within the abolitionist movement. Because of the time constraints typical in social studies classrooms, we kept the activity brief, but teachers can embellish it by including events from timelines found at *Digital History* or PBS's *Africans in America* (see note 1). The selected events reflect nonviolent tactics—political action focused on gradual emancipation (e.g., Washington freeing slaves in his will, bans on slavery in the Northern states), and moral 'suasion aimed at immediate abolition (New York Antislavery Society meetings, Douglass' *North Star*), as well as more aggressive action (Denmark Vesey's rebellion and Nat Turner's revolt). Touching on such events will give students an understanding of the range of tactics used by the abolitionist movement, though their impact may require exploration. For example, Turner's rebellion led to his execution as well as the deaths of hundreds of Blacks in the region, many of whom weren't even involved. On the other hand, the rebel-

FIGURE 7.1. One Student's Interpretation of Abolitionist Tactics

> One of 'Henry Garnetts Quotes that stood out to me was "There is not much hope for freedom without shedding blood". This quote is very self explanitory. You cant just sit there and wait for someone to set you free, you have to fight your way out. Well you can wait but it will take years.

lion led the Virginia legislature to consider ending slavery. Using background events and maps on page 2 of the student packet (Figure 7.8) can help situate the abolitionist conversation within the larger events around slavery. Ultimately, we hope students will see the American abolitionists as more than one single movement, but rather, a complex conversation among different groups, all of whom wanted to end slavery through a variety of means.

LITERACY PRACTICES STUDENTS WILL LEARN

Reading History

While this investigation presents an engaging topic for students, it may be hard for them to focus on the 1800s without jumping between different eras, particularly the the civil rights movement of the 1950s and 1960s. If they frame nonviolence from the 1800s in a way more appropriate to 1960, they'll need reminders of the particular historical context of the 19th century. We chose the terms *nonviolence* and *more aggressive action* because the language was helpful to students, but we've seen inaccurate uses of these terms. Students sometimes refer to nonviolence as a passive approach and more aggressive action as violence; such interpretations oversimplify and mischaracterize the different sides of the abolitionist movement (see Figure 7.1). This student equates "just sit[ting] there" with a nonviolent approach, when in fact the different nonviolent approaches involved constant and disciplined activism. In this case, "fight[ing]" isn't confined to violence. In the 19th century, many moral 'suasion tactics were characterized by early abolitionists as being too aggressive. Such historical background can help teachers foster students' engagement along with historical thinking.

When they look at the source lines and headnotes, students will see that both authors were African American abolitionists with different ideas on how to free slaves in the late 1830s and early 1840s.[19] Garnet, born to slave parents in Maryland in 1815, used the Underground Railroad to escape to Pennsylvania and then New York City in 1824. Two years before his address, Garnet was ordained as pastor of a Presbyterian church. William Whipper was born in 1804 in Pennsylvania. His mother was an African American servant who worked for his father, a White lumber merchant. As an adult, he gave lectures and wrote on moral reform and abolition; he also became a successful businessman. Both men advocated immediate rather than gradual abolition and shared their views with fellow African Americans. Garnet spoke to abolitionists at the National Negro Convention in Buffalo (although the speech itself is addressed to slaves), and Whipper published his speech in *The Colored American* (originally called the *Weekly Advocate*), a Northern newspaper read primarily by free Blacks.

To contextualize these sources, students can consult the map and sequence of events related to slavery on page 2 of the student packet, adding the dates of these sources and other abolitionist efforts up to 1843 to the timeline. Students are often drawn to the moral arguments of Whipper's speech and may follow up with their personal opinions. To develop their historical thinking, ask students to think about why this moral argument would have been effective when it was delivered, rather than why it appeals to us now.

Paragraph 4, where Whipper explains that most people believe that slavery is legal and that more people sympathize with slave owners than slaves, is a good place for students to start putting Whipper in context, discussing why his ideas would have made sense at the time. A tendency toward anachronistic thinking also led us to exclude a film clip in this investigation. Most of the films we previewed presented the abolitionist movement from a 20th-century point of view, conflating nonviolence of the 1950s with moral 'suasion, or aggressive action of the 1960s with the moderate activism of the 1840s. Other films focused on the more activist and, at times, militant abolitionism of the 1850s, which would make it difficult for students to ground their analyses in the 1830s and 1840s. Accurate contextualizing can help students see that abolitionism was not one single movement, and how these voices represent two directions of reformers in the North.

It's interesting to consider the writers' "facts and examples." Both use religion to justify their positions. Where Garnet claims slaves have the right to rise up, because slavery "goes against God and His laws," Whipper argues that any form of fighting or war contradicts the Bible. Garnet offers examples from slave rebellions to highlight success of past efforts (though he stops short of including the punishing effects such rebellions had on the slaves and instigators themselves). Whipper claims that nonviolence is morally righteous and the only reasoned approach to change, but doesn't show evidence that this approach worked, which frustrated many who subscribed to moral 'suasion at the time.

In developing this curriculum, it was a constant challenge to find material that would make historical and literacy practices accessible to struggling readers while challenging them to recognize the multifaceted nature of history. Although researchers claim that more than two sources aren't necessary to build arguments,[20] combining two sources with two-sided questions can encourage students to choose one over the other rather than consider how all the evidence bears on a question.

One way to invite more nuanced thinking in helping students construct arguments is to take time for deliberative discussions.[21] We use the Structured Academic Controversy (SAC) model as described by Johnson and Johnson in the 1980s, and taken up by others since. We include directions specific for this investigation in the Additional Materials of this chapter (Figure 7.9).[22] This approach can also be adapted and used for other investigations.

Because students generally enjoy talking in small groups, the SAC model directs them to consider evidence from opposing positions (nonviolent tactics or more aggressive action as the most effective way to free slaves). Once students share ways in which the evidence sheds light on two possible responses to the central question, they come together in groups of four to consider which answer is best supported by the evidence. Instead of one side winning, like in conventional debates, the goal is to reach a consensus. During this phase students often construct complicated responses that answer the question and reflect the evidence. Not only does the SAC model foster close reading, it prepares students for writing by requiring them to construct an evidence-based response. Rather than jump to conclusions or try to fit evidence into some preconceived notion, students must delberate about what the evidence tells them.

Writing History

Teachers often see great gains with this investigation, as lessons from previous investigations start to sink in, and students integrate literacy practices that have been previously introduced. Of course, students' learning in terms of their growth and progress must be kept in mind. As one teacher explained: "There are different goals for different kids. And you might have to do a little bit more, but everybody's going to improve in some way."

As all teachers know, not every student crosses the same finish line at the end of the school year. It's important to consider where students start and to measure their progress, rather than looking only at their last essay. Growth and improvement are realistic goals for all students, and some need more support than others.

> ***Teachers Reflect.*** "Certain students sit down and write two paragraphs—that's a victory right there—and other students can already move beyond that. Be flexible and look more at growth than the final product. Focusing more on what each individual student needed really helped me get better."

Recognize Individual Students' Growth. Step back and review the various aspects of the historical arguments that students have been working on, so that you can consider progress in areas such as:

• Making a claim in response to the question, constructing a clear argument rather than simply summarizing.
• Supporting the argument with evidence.

- Explaining how the evidence supports the argument.
- Judging the quality of the evidence (reliability of authors, time period, or strength of authors' evidence).
- Reconciling multiple perspectives.

In watching Tamia's writing over time, we can see her progress. In Investigation 2 she clearly made a claim, but instead of supporting it with evidence from the primary sources, she used a hypothetical example about herself and a friend. By Investigation 4, Tamia used evidence from primary sources to support her claim. It's a notable step forward (she quotes a source and uses it to support a point), but she needs to work on integrating evidence as well as evaluating it. For Investigation 5, teachers should keep in mind that students like Tamia may need help comprehending and evaluating primary sources, as well as selecting and organizing evidence in advance of writing (Tamia's "Planning Your Essay" sheet shows minimal attention to planning).

> **Classroom Notes.** If students struggle tremendously, pause to share one of the essays that they wrote at the beginning of the year. Point out how far they have come and let them know how proud you are of their effort.

Aaron's Investigation 2 essay shows that he selected reasons and evidence (he integrated quotations) to justify his claim and that he recognized opposing evidence. He still has room to grow in explaining why he judged certain evidence credible or found opposing arguments less compelling. By Investigation 4, Aaron used fuller explanations and judgments in his body paragraphs (though some could be more specific), and explained his rebuttal of the Cherokee Letter in the concluding paragraph. Approaching Investigation 5, Aaron could use some support in offering complete explanations and judgments of evidence, as well as in reconciling multiple perspectives, all relatively new and tentative accomplishments. Acknowledging student improvements honors their growth; identifying areas for improvement helps teachers differentiate the curriculum based on a student's needs.

Address Common Challenges. While students grow at different rates, they face common challenges. At this point in the year, we find that students have difficulty rebutting or reconciling multiple perspectives. They refer to or quote an opposing position without explaining why it may be less convincing than their position and why their position is stronger.

Tamia's Investigation 5 essay and Aaron's Investigation 2 essay exemplify this tendency. After arguing that Shays and his followers were rebels, Aaron cited another way of considering the evidence: "One reason they could have been freedom fighters is because 'their money was being used to help the rich get richer.' This is reliable because Daniel Gray was very associated with the event." Aaron includes opposing evidence but doesn't reconcile it with the evidence he found more convincing. Similarly, in Investigation 5, Tamia recognizes an alternative interpretation and uses a quote to illustrate that position. Then she ends her rebuttal with, "But I don't agree what he says," without

FIGURE 7.2. Sample of a Student's Rebuttal for Investigation 5

> William Whipper has a different point of view. He believes that peaceful tactics should be used to end slavery. He wrote, "let it always be our goal to live in a spirit of unity with each other He used this claim because he believes that people should live in happiness and kill each other. But there is a problem with his thinking because people will always have hate towards another person and no one can stop that. Also this author is unreliable because he was born to a white man and slave mother which means he didn't get treated as harshly as other slaves. Also this author used religion as his support for his arguments, making him unreliable.

explaining why she values one interpretation over another.

A third student wrote a more successful rebuttal for Investigation 5 (see Figure 7.2). Here, the student recognizes a different perspective, shares a quote to illustrate the perspective, and explains why her argument is stronger. This includes evaluation of the primary sources as evidence. This student could have crafted a more nuanced critique. For example, Whipper's background doesn't necessarily make him unreliable, but it would give him a different perspective. Whipper's use of religion to support his arguments doesn't necessarily make him unreliable, either (in this context, religious belief was commonly used by abolitionists to convey moral arguments and to reason with others). Keeping an eye on individual growth as well as common challenges will equip teachers to support students' growing independence.

> **Classroom Notes.** Help students understand that they can use the judgments they've made about opposing side reasons to craft a rebuttal.

HOW TO TEACH THIS INVESTIGATION

What's New in This Investigation?

In Investigation 5, students read and analyze both sources over a shorter period of time. They annotate and judge sources, plan, and compose with greater independence. Instead of spending two-thirds of their time reading and analyzing sources, they evenly split their time between reading and analysis during the first 1.5 days, with planning and composing on the 2nd. Rather than modeling, teachers take the role of coach, circulating around the room to support students as they work with greater independence.

On the 1st day, students review the big picture, revisiting the overall goal for these investigations (writing an evidence-based historical argument) as well as how different aspects of the investigations contribute to that goal. Students review relevant historical background, and read and analyze the speech by Garnet. The 2nd day involves reading and analyzing Whipper's speech, making judgments about both sources, and planning. The 3rd day emphasizes composing and reflection. We hope that teachers will preserve a solid 45–50 minutes of composing time for students, as this focused time has been a key ingredient in student success. At the same time, saving 10 minutes for reflection helps students recognize places for improvement and set goals for their next writing task.

Teaching Principles

At this point, teachers should shift their role to coach rather than director.[23] In order for students to work independently, teachers must allow them to struggle a bit, and take a back seat. This investigation shifts to Stage 4 of the cognitive apprenticeship model ("Provide additional, more challenging forms of practice") in which teachers promote independence while continuing to offer feedback. Some students need more guidance (brief teacher conferences, working with a peer, or perhaps additional modeling) in order to grasp all of the historical and literacy practices embedded in this curriculum. Some teachers are successful working directly with small groups while the rest of the class works more independently. Teachers may need to adapt the curriculum to students'

Classroom Notes. Teachers who were most successful using our curriculum attended carefully to students' ideas as they grappled with primary sources. They noticed students' ideas and asked probing questions to support students' learning.

needs while emphasizing disciplinary thinking and writing. When teacher adaptations echo the goals of the curriculum, they support student progress in writing evidence-based essays.

One way to attend to students' thinking is to circulate around the room and check for student understanding. As they circulate, teachers can see whether students' annotations highlight key aspects of the primary sources and demonstrate basic comprehension. Similarly, teachers can see whether students select relevant evidence and consider its credibility as they plan and compose their essays. If teachers see students struggling, they can ask permission to share the student's work with the class, and talk through how to resolve the challenge together. In this way, teachers can respond to students' needs, continue teaching, and encourage independence.

Attending to students' thinking and checking for understanding requires that teachers think about the sources, annotate them, and consider possible responses to the historical question before class. As one teacher explained,

"Actually going through the process myself was helpful, because I could kind of see what they might think, and what pitfalls it might have. Like you kind of troubleshoot before things came up. Again, really knowing the students and where they're at—without that piece, it becomes a monumental task." To prepare, teachers can think about the following questions:

- What is most important to notice in the primary sources?
- If you had to choose two annotations per letter of *IREAD*, what would you include?
- What might challenge students?
- What could you do or say to support students as they annotate?
- In what ways might students evaluate the sources? What difficulties might they face in evaluating the judgments?
- What kind of guiding questions could we ask to help students make judgments on their own?

Once teachers have thought about the sources and considered how students might interact with them, they can guide them to construct historically accurate interpretations. But first, teachers must make sense of the content and literacy practices for themselves as well as anticipate students' needs. To address issues that students struggle with, we recommend that teachers analyze the documents on their own, draft a written response to the historical question, and then consider the following:

- What challenges do students face when composing or reflecting?
- What could you do or say to support your students as they compose?
- How might you promote an authentic reflection after students compose?

Another way to prepare is to analyze a few students' written work in depth and over time, especially when these students are starting to work independently. Take two student essays from Investigation 2 and 4 and track their progress. Students will be working more independently during this investigation, so having a sense of strengths and weaknesses can help teachers coach during the independent practice periods. What are the strengths and weaknesses in each student's use of evidence and historical writing in Investigation 2 and Investigation 4? What difficulties does each student still face? What is one goal you would set for each student? What might you do or say to help each student achieve that goal?

Things to Keep in Mind

The most consistent observation we heard from teachers about this investigation was that it's hard to achieve a balance between giving support and letting students work independently. Here we share some ideas for managing this transition. Students will have less time to read and analyze each document than they have had previously; at the same time they will have greater independence. Working in pairs or small groups, students can help one another read critically and transition to less teacher direction. As students work, teachers circulate and check for understanding. Once they've taken a pass at the sources, it's important for students to share their annotations so that everyone has access to the content, regardless of how far they have progressed independently. Teachers can limit this time by taking only one or two annotations per letter of *IREAD* (or reinforcing only those that seem most important). Some students have no problem reading and analyzing the primary sources independently at this point. Encourage them to move on to the second document, and be sure to have some additional documents that bear on this question to give them.

> **Classroom Notes.** Adaptations that may support the students who struggle most include: (1) encourage them to write four paragraphs, but make a plan for five; (2) have students work with a more capable (and willing) peer; or (3) negotiate and specify precise goals with students individually before they begin.

To help students plan more independently, remind them of the major steps such as using the timeline and background material to plan their introduction; selecting evidence from primary sources to use in supporting and rebuttal paragraphs; organizing ideas by marking Q1, J1, etc., next to ideas they'll use in their essays; and choosing from the *H2W* "Helpful Phrases" to start their sentences. Prior to composing, students can share their plans—in pairs, with the teacher individually, or with the whole class—and give one another feedback so that they have some support. When students are ready to compose, remind them of the resources they have to help them: annotated primary sources, plans, *H2W*, and "Helpful Phrases." Students shouldn't be staring at a blank sheet of paper without a plan; they should have the student packet and literacy tools on their desks as guides throughout the composing process.

During lessons, students must pace themselves. Teachers can help them by writing the amount of time left on the board and giving oral reminders every 10 minutes of how much time remains. This will help students make active choices about using their time. We have noticed that when teachers did not offer guidance about pacing, students had difficulty managing their time and completing the investigation. It's fine if students don't complete an entire essay; in fact, it's better if students use the last 10 minutes of Day 3 to reflect on the quality of their writing, rather than allowing them no time for reflection. Teachers can motivate students by rewarding hard work and focused effort with grades or other incentives, even if they did not finish planning and composing a five-paragraph essay.

Some teachers helped their students work on their own by repeating the ultimate goal of the investigation: to produce an evidence-based historical argument. This way, students can see how each part of the investigation process is related. They also helped students plan and compose by focusing on the argument they were trying to make—this helped students select quotes and compose their essay with the big picture in mind. All of these teacher moves encouraged students to read, analyze, plan, and compose with purpose.

HOW MIGHT STUDENTS RESPOND?
STUDENT WRITING AND TEACHER FEEDBACK

In this investigation, students continue putting all the pieces together, and should start to show some independence in historical thinking and literacy practices.

Tamia (Figure 7.3) shows remarkable progress in Investigation 5, using *H2W* to elaborate her ideas in an essay. She explains the context and source of the historical controversy, offers reasons and quotes for each side of the issue, and offers an evaluation to support her conclusion. In annotations of the documents, it is clear that she has followed the curriculum, engaging in *IREAD* and planning her essay. In short, she is beginning to use structured reading, thinking, and writing. Tamia does mix up events for this time period (drawing on the

FIGURE 7.3. Tamia's Essay for Investigation 5

> In the 1800s, abonlitionist wanted to stop slavery in the United States. Some people had different perspectives on the best way to free slaves. One opinion was to use peaceful methods like protest or boycott also petition. The other perspective was to use violence or aggressive actions. I believe ~~people should use the~~ aggressive actions or violence because we can fight for our slaves no one deserves to be treated wrong. I said violence is the answer because or reason because in the Garnet speech a reason I said its better to ~~due~~ try to fight and die to live as slaves." In 1822, Denmark Vesey of South California formed a plan to free his fellow slaves. That wonderful movement shook the whole empire of slavery." this is Garnets Speech. I trust him because he has been a slave and he know what he talking about. On the other hand, Whipper believes the bible does not approve of war. Whipper said just and necessary war or physical self defense goes against the letter and spirit of the bible." But I don't agree what he says

Polish: "Were these methods used by abolitionists at the time?"

Praise: "You've summarized the two perspectives well here!"

Praise: "Nice job supporting your reasons with quotes, explanation and evaluation!"

Polish: "How could you argue against ("rebut") this point?"

Goal: "Continue using H2W to plan and organize your essay. It really helps! Remember to rebut opposing side arguments."

FIGURE 7.4. Aaron's Essay for Investigation 5

In the mid 1800's William Whipper & Henry Garnet gave speeches On ways to abolish slavery, in which Whipper supported non-violence, and Garnet supported violence. The historical question that came up was weather it was better to use non-violence or violence to abolish slavery. People disagreed because some wanted violence and some did not. My personal answer to the historical question was non-violence is the best way to abolish slavery. ¶ I belive non-violence is the best way to go because violence will just lead to more & more violence. A quote that supports this is the quote that says "Human punishments are not effective in getting rid of human evils. Human bodies have been cut with whips and prisions have been built. But the increase of crime has kept pace with the genius of punishment." this supports my avrgument because it shows the more you try to force somebdy to stop doing something the more it makes them want to do it. This idea was convincing to me because it was illustrated with a powerful message.

I also belive non-violence is the best way to go because violence is against christianity. One quote that supports this idea says "I do not approve of the often made claim that the teachings of the bibble justify war." this supports my avrgument because it shows how violence goes against the bibble. This is reliable to me because it is accurate according to what I know about christianity.

It may also be avrgued that violence is the best way to go. A quote that supports this says "Brothers rise up. Fight for your lives & for your liberties. this supports violence because it is telling people that they have to fight for whatever they want. This is reliable to me because it conveys a very strong message.

When all of the facts on both sides are considered, I think non-violence is the best way to abolish slavery. I think violence Is the worst way to go because it will just cause lots of war & Death. non-violence is the best way because it keeps the peace but still lets you get your point across.

Praise: "Good choice of quote to support your argument!"

Polish: "Why would this have been an effective way to end slavery at that time?"

Polish: "Why might this be an ineffective way to free slaves at that time?"

Goal: "Remember to think about the historical context when answering the historical question. That means using information about what was going on at the time to support your conclusion."

civil rights movement of the 1950s and 1960s); this is something she tends to struggle with. Tamia does recognize that nonviolence is not the same as nonaction (e.g., she cites protests, petitions, and boycotts accurately). As we noted with Aaron's earlier work, Tamia's teacher might work with her on effective responses to opposing arguments.

Aaron (Figure 7.4) continues to benefit from using the *H2W* to structure and elaborate on his arguments. As we saw earlier, this investigation challenges students to step away from a modern perspective to understand the methods and arguments of the abolitionists. Aaron's first supporting paragraph manages to capture the rationale of nonviolence from a historical perspective. However, the second supporting paragraph slips into arguing why nonviolence is moral, rather than a more effective way to end slavery. Similarly, in his rebuttal, he focuses on why violence is justified rather than why it is more effective than moral persuasion. A teacher might use this opportunity to help Aaron keep sight of the historical question when planning his essay.

LESSON PLANS AND MATERIALS

Teachers and students will need the following: Lesson plans (Figures 7.5–7.7) Investigation 5 packet (clipboard with overview, timeline with map, reading and writing process overview, Garnet speech, and Whipper speech found after the lesson plans in Figure 7.8), Additional materials for this investigation (abolitionism background cards in Figure 7.9, Structured Academic Controversy directions in Figure 7.10), Disciplinary literacy tools (*IREAD*, Planning Your Essay graphic organizer, *H2W*, Essay Response Template, and Reflection Guide in Appendix A), and overhead projection capacity (to share annotations and plans).

FIGURE 7.5. Lesson Plan, Day 1: Background Knowledge, Reading Comprehension, and Historical Reading

Materials: **Investigation 5 student packets, *IREAD*, Planning Your Essay graphic organizer, H2W, Essay Response Template, Projector, Abolitionism background cards**

Suggested time: **1 hour per day**

INTRODUCTION

1. Review the goal for each step of an investigation to help students see that everything they do contributes to the final goal of writing an evidence-based argument.

    a. Start at the bottom of the graphic on page 3 of the student packet. Have students respond and write a goal for each step (e.g., what is our goal when we WRITE an historical essay? How does a good PLAN help us write? What is our goal when we develop a good plan? How do good annotations and judgments based on *IREAD* help us plan? What is our goal when we read? How does a good understanding of the HISTORICAL QUESTION help us read? What is our goal when reading the question?). Then explain that from the very beginning of an investigation, everything we do prepares us to write a good essay.

2. Warmup: If you want someone to stop doing something that's wrong, how could you persuade him or her?

3. Introduce the historical question for this investigation and connect it to the warmup (e.g., Slavery had continued in the United States for 200 years. In the 1800s it divided the country more and more, eventually leading to the Civil War. White and Black Americans—mostly from the North—tried to end slavery. They disagreed over the best way to end slavery).

BACKGROUND INFORMATION

4. Overview: Read page 1 of the packet and preview vocabulary (e.g., *abolitionism, abolitionist, oppressor, persecution*).

5. Review and discuss the timeline and map on page 2 of the student packet.

    a. Find where each state, territory, or region noted on the timeline is on the map.

    b. Consider the balance of slave and free states in 1820: How many states were slave states? How many were free? Based on the timeline, do you think slavery was on the rise, on the decline, or staying the same?

    c. Put the date of each speech in the packet on the timeline.

6. Abolitionism card activity: In groups, have students look over the cards and organize them into two rows—one row with cards that use nonviolent tactics to end slavery and one row with cards that use more aggressive action to end slavery.

    a. Discuss: What were different nonviolent tactics people used? What were the effects of the slave rebellions? How could the actions in each card be used to end slavery?

HISTORICAL READING WITH DOCUMENT 1

7. Set expectations for using *IREAD* to increase student independence (e.g., give students 20 minutes to read and analyze the Garnet speech, use a timer and give reminders about the time, prompt students after 10 minutes to move on to *EAD*, signal remaining time, etc.).

8. Prompt students to read and annotate the Garnet speech using *IREAD*.

9. Debrief: Share annotations and check for understanding of the speech.

10. Closure: What about Garnet's speech was useful in thinking about the question?

FIGURE 7.6. Lesson Plan, Day 2: Historical Reading and Planning

INTRODUCTION

1. Remind students to read the documents today with the goal of identifying and evaluating evidence for each side. This will help them plan and write their essays in response to the historical question.

2. Have students recall the historical question and on which side of the controversy Garnet and Whipper were.

3. Tell students that today they will annotate the Whipper document, judge both sides, and plan their essays.

HISTORICAL READING WITH DOCUMENT 2

4. Set expectations for using *IREAD* so students can become more independent (e.g., give students 20 minutes to read and analyze the Whipper speech, use a timer and give reminders about the time, prompt students after 10 minutes to move on to *EAD*, signal remaining time, etc.).

5. Prompt students to read and annotate the Whipper speech using *IREAD*.

6. Debrief:

   a. Share annotations and check for understanding of the speech.

   b. What about Garnet's speech was useful in thinking about the question?

HISTORICAL THINKING AND READING: MAKING JUDGMENTS

7. Use *EAD* of *IREAD* to make judgments. Discuss in pairs or as a class reasons to trust and doubt each document. Remind students to consider the reliability of the authors, influence of context, and/or facts and examples each author uses to make their judgments, as well as how these sources relate to the historical question.

8. Debrief as a class and have students write down 2–3 judgments on each document.

PLANNING

9. Think-pair-share: What was the most effective way to free slaves before the Civil War, non-violence or more aggressive action?

10. Review our goal: to convince someone with a different perspective that your argument is strongest; give convincing evidence and say why it is convincing.

11. Ask students to use the Planning Your Essay sheet (Appendix A) and their documents to select and organize content for each paragraph of their essay.

    a. Remind students of the resources they have, including the background, timeline, map, primary sources, plan, *H2W*, and transition words and phrases on *H2W*.

    b. Remind students that they will share and reflect on their essays tomorrow after they compose them.

FIGURE 7.7. Lesson Plan, Day 3: Historical Writing

INTRODUCTION

1. Warmup: What evidence and judgments of evidence support your argument?

2. Remind students of their primary goals when composing: to persuade someone who has a different opinion that your argument is strongest by using convincing evidence and explaining that evidence. They will use the plan, judgments, and annotations from the previous 2 days to write their essay.

COMPOSING

3. Give students 5 minutes to finish their planning from the previous day, if necessary.

4. Ask students to compose their essay. Give them 45–50 minutes to do so.

   a. Highlight the supports students have, including the background, timeline, map, primary sources, plan, H2W, and transition words and phrases on *H2W*.

   b. Use a timer and set to 45–50 minutes *(save 10 minutes at the end for reflection)*. Tell students to aim for about 8–10 minutes per paragraph and prompt them to move on every 8–10 minutes.

   c. Circulate around the room as students work. Show them how to find content from their documents, to use their plan to write sentences, and to use the *H2W* guide and transition phrases. Look for students who are struggling and offer support by:

      i. Asking which side they will take.

      ii. Asking them to explain which evidence they will use and how it supports their argument.

      iii. Showing them transition phrases that may be useful for each paragraph.

      iv. Suggesting that they move on to the next paragraph if they're spending too much time on any one paragraph.

   d. Students may need encouragement. Reinforce their efforts with participation points or praise. *If students are struggling, encourage them to write one, not two, supporting paragraphs.*

REFLECTION

Be sure to save the last 10 minutes for reflection, even if students haven't completed their essays

5. Students should pair up with someone who wrote a different argument and share their essays.

   a. Students should consider how someone could interpret the same issues differently.

   b. Students should react to their partner's essay according to how it meets writing goals. Ask them to complete their partner's "Reflection Guide" based on their essay.

6. Direct students to switch back to their own papers and think about their partner's assessment.

   a. Ask students whether they agree with their partner's assessment. If not, allow them to make changes to the "Reflection Guide."

   b. Using this information, ask each student to identify at least one goal for improvement for his or her next essay (in the "I am working on" box).

FIGURE 7.8. Materials: Investigation 5 Packet

Name: _____ Class: _____ Date: _____

INVESTIGATION #5:

WHAT WAS THE MOST EFFECTIVE WAY TO FREE SLAVES IN THE U.S. BEFORE THE CIVIL WAR: NONVIOLENCE* OR MORE AGGRESSIVE ACTION?

In the mid-1800s, the movement to end slavery, or abolitionism, began to move forward and develop in the United States. Abolitionists included White and Black Americans, mostly from the North.

African-American abolitionists had different ideas about how to free slaves in the United States. Some argued that immediate aggressive action should be taken to end slavery, while others thought more peaceful tactics would be most successful.

What do you think made the most sense in this time period? Take out your pens and get ready to investigate!

WORD BANK
***Nonviolence:** In this time period, nonviolence was often called "moral 'suasion" or moral persuasion."

FIGURE 7.8. Materials: Investigation 5 Packet, Continued

Name:_____ Class:_____ Date:_____

Events related to slavery in the U.S.

1793. Eli Whitney patents the cotton gin, making cotton production more profitable. The market value of slaves increases as a result.

By 1804, the nine states north of Delaware had freed slaves or adopted gradual freedom plans.

1807. Congress makes it illegal to import slaves starting in 1808.

1820. The Missouri Compromise admits Maine to the U.S. as a free state and Missouri as a slave state. Slavery is banned in the northern half of the Louisiana Purchase above the 36°30' line.

By 1837, President Andrew Jackson's Indian removal policies opened up 25 million acres to white settlers and their slaves in the Southeastern U.S.

SLAVE AND FREE AREAS AFTER THE MISSOURI COMPROMISE.

Source: The map is from J.W. Redway, *The Redway School History: Outlining the Making of the American Nation* (New York: Silver, Burdett, and Comapny, 1910), p. 250.

FIGURE 7.8. Materials: Investigation 5 Packet, Continued

Name:_____ Class:_____ Date:_____

The Reading and Writing Process

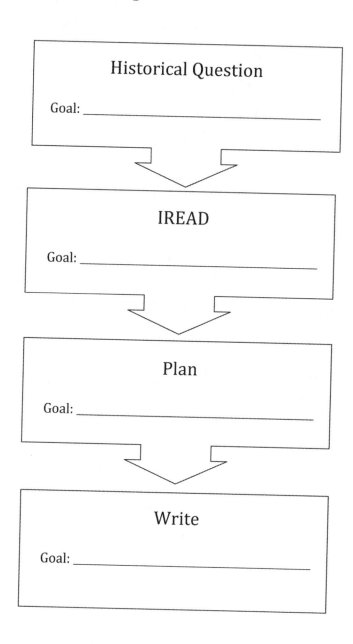

Thinking through each part of the process will help you write a better historical argument!

FIGURE 7.8. Materials: Investigation 5 Packet, Continued

Name:_____ Class:____ Date:_____

 Garnet Speech

Head Note: African-American abolitionists had different ideas about how to free slaves in the United States. Henry Highland Garnet was born into slavery in 1815, and later escaped with his family in 1824 through the Underground Railroad. Here, Garnet calls on slaves to take aggressive action in order to end slavery.

Brothers, your oppressors try to make you as much like animals as possible. Once they have stopped you from thinking and asking questions, and once they have made your life bitter, then American slavery has done its perfect work.

It is sinful for you to willingly give in to such terrible conditions. It is your duty to respect and obey the Ten Commandments. If you do not obey them, you will surely upset God. He requires you to love him completely, to love your neighbor, to study the Bible, to bring up your children to respect God's laws, and to only worship Him. But slavery goes against God and His laws. Being a slave does not destroy your moral responsibility to God. Neither God, nor angels, nor just men command you to suffer for a single moment. God would smile upon every effort that slaves might make to free themselves.

Look around you. Notice your loving wives who struggle with pain too terrible for words! Hear the cries of your poor children! Remember the whippings your fathers suffered. Think how many tears you have cried upon the soil that you have farmed. Remember that as native-born American citizens you deserve all the rights that are granted to the freest men. Then go to your enslavers and tell them that you are determined to be free. If you want to be free this is your only hope. Unfortunately, there is not much hope of freedom without shedding blood. But, it is better to die as free men, than to live as slaves.

In 1822, Denmark Vesey of South Carolina formed a plan to free his fellow slaves. That wonderful movement shook the whole empire of slavery. Slaveholders were overwhelmed with fear. As a result of Vesey's threatening plan, the slave states seriously considered freeing the slaves. But once the threat of a slave revolt went away, the slaveholders stopped talking about freeing slaves.

There was Joseph Cinque, the hero of the Amistad in 1839. He freed a whole shipload of his fellow men on the high seas. And he now sings of liberty on the sunny hills of Africa. Those who have died fighting for freedom are remembered. Those who are living are honored.

Brothers, rise up! Fight for your lives and liberties. If every slave throughout the land fights then the days of slavery are numbered. You cannot be more oppressed than you have been. You cannot suffer greater cruelties than you have already. It is better to die as free men than to live as slaves. Remember that there are four million of you!

Source: Excerpt adapted from Henry Highland Garnet's speech, "Call to Rebellion," to slaves in the United States. August 21, 1843.

FIGURE 7.8. Materials: Investigation 5 Packet, Continued

Name:_____ Class:____ Date:_____

 **Whipper Speech**

Head Note: Some African-American abolitionists wanted to end slavery using peaceful tactics such as moral persuasion. Moral persuasion meant that abolitionists modeled good behavior and convinced people to use reason rather than to fight with force. William Whipper's African-American mother was a servant for his European American father. Here, William Whipper explains why moral persuasion is the best way to end slavery.

I do not approve of the often-made claim that the teachings of the Bible justify war. In my opinion, the Bible is the greatest enemy of war. As soon as the Bible is fully understood and followed, wars and fighting will stop. I believe that every argument in favor of what people call a "just and necessary war" or physical self-defense goes against the letter and spirit of the Bible. Such arguments for war should be rejected. Arguments for war are not about justice. Arguments for war are an attack on Christianity.

It is a deadly mistake to believe that the only way to maintain peace is always to be ready for war. The spirit of war can never be destroyed by all the killings and persecutions the human mind can create. The spirit of defeating others feeds war. War has never been, nor can ever be, conquered by more war. Human punishments are not effective in getting rid of human evils. Human bodies have been cut with whips and prisons have been built. But the increase of crime has kept pace with the genius of punishment.

If mankind ever expects to enjoy peace, they must be ready to let go of their rude passions. They can only do this by using their reasoning powers. If people want to overlook attacks and insults of others, they must look for protection in something higher than human power. They must place their faith in God to protect them from danger. Without this they will soon fall prey to the evil tricks of their enemies. Our reasoning powers ought to be the controls of a boat that guide us through the shallow waters and quicksands of life.

I have tried to show that reason is a great safeguard, against passion. It helps us in periods of the greatest trouble and difficulty. If there is a single class of people in these United States, who must follow this duty it is the free and enslaved colored population of this country. We live among people who believe that slavery is legal. More people sympathize with slave owners than slaves. So, we must continue calmly onward, with self-denial, patience and perseverance.

Let it always be our goal to live in a spirit of unity with each other. We must support one common cause by spreading our influence for the good of mankind. We will hope that the time will come when universal peace will triumph throughout the world.

Source: Excerpt adapted from William Whipper's speech, "Non-Resistance to Offensive Aggression." September 1837

FIGURE 7.9. Additional Materials: Abolitionism Background Cards

DIFFERENT ABOLITIONIST EFFORTS

1801 George Washington's slaves are freed according to his will. In 1797, he wrote that he wished there was a policy to get rid of slavery gradually in the United States.	1831 Nat Turner leads a slave rebellion in Virginia and is executed. This led to the execution of hundreds of Blacks. The Virginia legislature considered ending slavery, but didn't.
By 1804 The nine states north of Delaware had freed slaves or adopted gradual emancipation plans.	1833 The first meeting of the New York Anti-Slavery Society is held. About 200 anti-slavery societies are organized in the North around this time to protest slavery.
1822 Denmark Vesey and his followers are executed in South Carolina because they tried to rebel against the slave system. The state organized a patrol system to prevent further threats.	1838 After escaping slavery, Frederick Douglass becomes a leading spokesman for ending slavery. He starts an abolitionist newspaper 9 years later called *The North Star.*

FIGURE 7.10. Structured Academic Controversy Extension

STRUCTURED ACADEMIC CONTROVERSY DIRECTIONS*

Historical Question: What was the most effective way to free slaves in the United States before the Civil War: nonviolence or more aggressive action?

Side A	Side B
Nonviolence was the most effective way to free slaves in the United States before the Civil War.	More aggressive action was the most effective way to free slaves in the United States before the Civil War.

1. Form groups of four. Within each group, assign two students to prepare Side A and two students to prepare Side B.
2. Partners prepare Side A or Side B
   a. Find evidence that supports their assigned side of the argument. Craft position.
3. Position presentation
   a. Side A presents the evidence from the texts that support their assigned position.
   b. Side B *restates* to Side A's satisfaction.
   c. Side B presents the evidence from the texts that support their assigned position.
   d. Side A *restates* to Side B's satisfaction.
4. Consensus-building
   a. Abandon roles/sides.
   b. Build consensus regarding the question (or at least clarify where differences lie), using supporting evidence.

*These directions are adapted from S. Wineburg, D. Martin, & C. Monte-Sano, *Reading Like a Historian* (New York: Teachers College Press, 2011), pp. 45–47. See Appendix B for a generic version of these directions that can be used with any investigation or question as well as a note-taking sheet to guide students' thinking.

CHAPTER 8

Was the United States Justified in Going to War with Mexico in 1846?

Overview of Chapter 8

Investigation	Foundational Concepts	Disciplinary Literacy Practices	CCSS Links	C3 Links	Principles of Teaching
Investigation 6: *Was the United States justified in going to war with Mexico in 1846?*	Reading, thinking, and writing are interconnected activities in studying history	Students integrate reading, analysis, planning, and composing independently	RI.5.6 (p. 14) RI.5.8 (p. 14) RI.5.9 (p. 14) RH.6–12.1 (p. 61) RH.6–12.2 (p. 61) RH.11–12.3 (p. 61) RH.6–12.6 (p. 61) RH.6–12.8 (p. 61) W.5.1a–d (p. 20) W.5.9b (p. 21) WHST.6––12.1a-e (p.64) WHST.6–12-4 (p. 66) WHST.6–12.5 (p. 66) WHST.6–12.9 (p. 66)	D2.His.1.6–8 D2.His.4.6–12 D2.His.6.6–8 D2.His.10.6–8 D2.His.13.6–8 D2.His.16.6–12 D3.2.6–8 D3.4.6–12 D4.1.6–12 D4.4.6–12	Adapt the curriculum to students' needs while continually emphasizing disciplinary thinking and writing

Cognitive apprenticeship Stage 5, promote independence |

INVESTIGATION 6 BUILDS on the content in Investigations 4 and 5 regarding the expansion of slavery and causes of the Civil War. Here we ask, *"Was the United States justified in going to war with Mexico in 1846?"* Students build an argument in response to conflicting sources, a pro-Democratic newspaper that supported the war and an anti-war senator. Over the 3-day investigation, reading, thinking, and writing are interconnected with studying history. Students begin their writing by analyzing past work and establishing goals. Reflection and goal-setting set the stage for reading and analysis, as well as planning and composing. As students integrate literacy practices with greater independence, they should start to move through reading, thinking, and writing in a more fluid, iterative manner, and with a greater sense of purpose.

The teachers who helped develop this curriculum commented that student confidence increased noticeably by this point. They found students more invested, willing to complete the assignment, and less resistant than earlier in the year. A student with a learning disability missed the 1st day of the investigation, but to the teacher's surprise, the next day this student decided to go through the documents on her own and catch up. At this point in the year, the hard work of modeling and coaching students through historical reading, thinking, and writing begins to reveal itself. Because not every student will show the same level of progress, we offer ideas to use with students who continue to struggle.

HISTORICAL BACKGROUND

In July 1846, a simple act of rebellion gave birth to a lasting voice of social protest. Henry David Thoreau refused to pay his taxes because he disagreed with U.S. involvement in the Mexican American War, which he believed would extend slavery. From jail, Thoreau wrote his now-famous essay *Civil Disobedience*. He explained, "If a thousand men were not to pay their tax-bills this year, that would not be a violent and bloody measure, as it would be to pay them, and enable the State to commit violence and shed innocent blood. . . . There are thousands who are in opinion opposed to slavery and to the war, who yet in effect do nothing to put an end to them."[1]

> *Teachers Reflect.* "Where some of them had written three or four sentences for Investigation 1, now they're writing five paragraphs. When we compared [Investigation] 6 to 1 and they saw how much they've grown— even if they don't want to admit it—you can tell there's a sense of pride."

Thoreau was not alone in his anti-war sentiments. The poet James Russell Lowell wrote, "Ez fer war, I call it murder,—/ There you hev it plain an' flat."[2] Prominent leaders like Henry Clay and John C. Calhoun also opposed the war, arguing that President Polk had provoked Mexico. A little-known freshman congressman named Abraham Lincoln critiqued the president in a series of speeches that made him unpopular in his home state of Illinois, where people supported the war.[3] Leading abolitionists such as William Lloyd Garrison and Frederick Douglass spoke out against the war as well.

Still, the vote to declare war passed both houses of Congress, and popular opinion supported it.[4] The U.S. decision to annex Texas in 1845 had heightened tensions; Mexico believed that Texas was its territory, while President Polk regarded it as independent. When the Mexican Army and American troops clashed near the Rio Grande, Polk declared that the Mexican government had "invaded our territory and shed the blood of our fellow citizens on our own soil."[5] A song printed on the front page of the *New York Herald* in May 1846 captured popular sentiment regarding the war:

The Mexicans are on our soil,
In war they wish us to embroil;
They've tried their best and worst to vex us,
By murdering our brave men in Texas,
     Chorus—We're on our way to Rio Grande,
     On our way to Rio Grande,
     On our way to Rio Grande,
     And with arms they'll find us handy.[6]

In an editorial in the *Brooklyn Daily Eagle*, Walt Whitman wrote, "Mexico must be thoroughly chastised . . . we are justified in the face of the world."[7]

With so much popular and political support, why was this war so divisive? The larger backdrop issues of expansionism, Manifest Destiny, slavery, and U.S.-Mexico relations offer clues to understanding this controversy.[8]

Expansionism and "Manifest Destiny"

The United States had long focused on expanding its territory, but in the 1840s the pace of expansionism accelerated. The 1803 Louisiana Purchase, 1819 purchase of Florida, 1845 annexation of Texas, 1846 settlement of the Oregon Territory, 1848 Treaty of Guadalupe Hidalgo, and 1853 Gadsden Treaty enabled the United States to push past the Mississippi River to the Pacific Ocean.[9] In 1845, the journalist John O'Sullivan coined the term *Manifest Destiny* to describe America's God-given right to expand across the continent in the context of the Texas annexation.[10] O'Sullivan wrote that those who opposed war acted "in a spirit of hostile interference against us, for the avowed object of thwarting our policy and hampering our power, limiting our greatness and checking the fulfillment of our manifest destiny to overspread the continent allotted by Providence for the free development of our yearly multiplying millions." He believed the United States should annex Texas, and that Manifest Destiny justified that position. Richard White reminds us that it's difficult to assess the extent of O'Sullivan's influence, since coining the term can't tell us how many people actually believed in it.[11] Nonetheless, the term became shorthand for expansionist settlement. Those in favor of war and expansion argued that the United States needed more land for its growing population, and for the stability and strength of its economy (free trade was a popular argument in favor of the war). Some nationalistic historians describe the war as a triumph for the United States.[12] Others cite the 1830 Indian Removal Act as part of the country's expansionist trajectory, pointing out how a sense of racial superiority characterized America's God-given mandate to cover the continent.[13]

Yet Manifest Destiny can be overused as a blanket explanation for all of Western history. When Manifest Destiny dominates historical interpretation, it can confine the study of the West to the period between that Cherokee Removal and Little Bighorn, and feature Anglo Americans as key actors. White's work broadens and complicates this conventional frame, arguing that the West has been shaped by evolving and complex relationships among many different groups of people over time.[14]

The Influence of Slavery

Territorial acquisition had significant implications for the institution of slavery. Initially, it looked like slavery would simply die out. The Northwest Ordinance of 1787 banned slavery in the Northwest Territory, and Congress had made importing slaves illegal starting in 1808. An equal number of slave and free states preserved the balance of power in Congress between North and South. The Missouri Compromise of 1820 maintained this balance when Maine was admitted to the Union as a free state and Missouri as a slave state. But the preservation of land north of the 36°30′ latitude line (with the exception of Missouri) as free favored those against expanding slavery. The annexation of Texas as a slave state, and with it, the prospect of adding land via the Mexican American War, threatened this balance and fueled sectional tensions.

Northern Whigs accused Polk of deciding to extend slavery into land gained from Mexico. They gathered behind an anti-slavery amendment to an appropriations bill that would have banned slavery in any new territory (i.e., the Wilmot Proviso), but it did not pass. Outnumbered in the House of Representatives, Southern states now dominated the Senate. The balance of power in Congress was maintained until the Kansas-Nebraska Act of 1854 repealed the Missouri Compromise, allowing new states to decide whether to be slave or free (popular sovereignty). Although some historians question whether the divisiveness caused by the Mexican American War echoed the North-South sectionalism that characterized the antebellum era, the war certainly lit a spark.[15] Historians tend to agree that anti-war critics believed the purpose of the war was to extend slavery.[16]

U.S.–Mexico Relations

The colonization, independence, and annexation of Texas, as well as Mexico's transition from Spanish colony to independent nation, and the interactions between Mexico and the United States, all contributed to the imminent war. David Weber's work is notable in explaining both Mexican and U.S. perspectives of this borderland, and its holistic view of the Southwest as a region.[17] After Mexico gained independence from Spain in 1821, Anglo Americans began to settle in the Mexican state of Coahuila y Tejas.[18] By encouraging immigration from the United States, Mexico hoped to strengthen the buffer zone that northern Coahuila y Tejas formed between its core and raiding Comanche.

Historians Pekka Hämäläinen and Brian DeLay challenge the traditional Western narrative, that of a monolithic Anglo American force victimizing Native Americans.[19] The Comanche had a strong political system and market economy, extracting resources and labor from the borderlands and dominating the Southwest. DeLay points out that the Mexican government essentially ignored its northern states' pleas for help while trying to manage other concerns. Hämäläinen argues that while Comanche exploitation of Mexican colonial territories increased their power and prosperity, it significantly weakened Mexico's hold over the northern frontier.

Although earlier immigrants to the region had agreed to become Mexican citizens and adopt Catholicism, Americans in the northern Mexican territory ignored such promises and kept their own language, schools, and slaves, turning a blind eye to the Mexican Constitution's prohibition of slavery. In short, they stayed separate from Mexicans in the region. Although American settlers outnumbered Hispanics in the northern part of Coahuila y Tejas, Hispanics constituted the majority population of the region. When a centrist Mexican government moved to restrict American immigration, outlaw slavery, and increase taxes, the American settlers began to discuss rebellion.

In 1834, General Santa Anna became dictator and put a new constitution in place. At first the colonists adopted their own constitution in hopes of reforming the Santa Anna government. But concerns over settlement, tariffs, and slave ownership led the colonists to rebel in a conflict known as the Texas Revolution. Although they were overwhelmed by Mexican troops at the Alamo, Texans ultimately defeated the Mexicans and became an independent country in 1835. The Treaty of Velasco established the Mexican-Texas border at the Rio Grande; however, the Mexican Congress never approved it, and the government did not recognize Texan independence.[20]

American Texans wanted to be annexed to the United States, but they represented a small part of the four distinct communities that considered the region their own: the Comanche in the north, who continued to raid neighboring towns; the Apache in the west, who also raided towns and traveling groups; Mexicans, many of whom considered Texas theirs; and the American Texans, who faced the paradox of inviting themselves into a democracy while at the same time they subordinated their former Mexican rulers. It took 9 years for the U.S. government to make up its mind. Some believed that more land would enrich the country; others worried that Texas would become a slave state and upset relations with Mexico. When the United States finally annexed Texas in 1845, they upheld the boundary at the Rio Grande, despite Mexican protestations that the border was farther north, at the Nueces River.

President Polk sent U.S. Minister Slidell to Mexico to negotiate, but with little sensitivity to the instability of the Mexican government. Troops under Zachary Taylor were sent to the Rio Grande border. Claiming the Americans had invaded, the Mexican Army attacked Taylor's troops. Polk exhorted Congress to declare war, stating that American blood had been shed on American soil. Joseph Wheelan explains: "When Polk asserted that Mexico had started the war by rejecting negotiations and sending troops across the Rio Grande to bushwhack American dragoons, most Americans believed him."[21] The press portrayed Mexico as an enemy, stereotyping Mexicans as early as the Texas Revolution.[22] Eventually, Generals Zachary Taylor and Winfield Scott led the United States to victory, and 2 years later the war ended with the Treaty of Guadalupe Hidalgo. But it wasn't until after the Civil War that conflict with the Comanche and Apache settled the boundaries of the region.

LITERACY PRACTICES STUDENTS WILL LEARN

Reading History

Students may begin to read and analyze primary sources in a more integrated way in this investigation, blending the aspects of *IREAD* into their reading rather than doing one at a time.[23] Expect students to jump between steps as they make sense of a source; that's a good sign. Experienced readers don't source a document in its entirety before they notice its context, nor do they need to know all the historical details embedded in a document before forming inferences and judgments. When we created *IREAD*, we itemized ways of reading and thinking to make them explicit and accessible to students. The first time students confront a historical text, they don't have to read like an expert. Instead, they can take small steps, trying out a different aspect of historical reading during the initial investigations. Time is set aside to encourage students to notice historical details in sources, and then use them to make inferences. As your students develop facility with historical reading, they will blend different practices as they begin to analyze complex historical texts like historians. As one teacher noted, "They are actually [evaluating] while they read the first time, which shows that they are actually having a conversation with the document."

A persistent challenge facing history teachers is how to provide students with content knowledge to support their reading. Background knowledge and reading are deeply entwined, a fact that becomes noticeable in this investigation as students are prompted to develop knowledge of a complicated topic on their own (see Figure 8.4, Lesson Plan, Day 1). Without background knowledge or historical context, students will have a hard time engaging in the critical reading and thinking that this curriculum targets. Teachers can help students by situating each investigation in a broader historical context and the specific time period.

The exercise for students is to make sense of historical content, analyze the map, and construct a timeline of related events, so that they have all the tools they need to read historically and construct rational arguments. Some teachers augment this lesson with film clips, textbook readings, or lectures. Others spend time on the timeline and map, pushing students beyond placing events in chronological order to thinking about how each event related to the Mexican American War, or tracking events related to slavery, using the map and key. Elise Fillpot's *Bringing History Home* curriculum suggests creating a timeline over the course of the entire year[24]—this will help students connect one investigation to the broader historical background. In other words, presenting background knowledge isn't restricted to the first 15 minutes of an investigation.

Careful historical reading will provide opportunities to teach background knowledge *as* students read. If students struggle with sources or their annotations miss a particular point, teachers can highlight the background that students need in order to work with the sources. For instance, the word *annexation* in the pro-war newspaper article confused some students. Teachers then reviewed the concept and gave examples. They also observed that as students read and thought about the question, it was important to explain the role of slavery in the Mexican American War controversy. Many did so by having students look at maps to grasp the larger historical context that led up to the Mexican American War.

The primary sources in this investigation contain details that call for additional knowledge, especially about the Whig and Democratic parties. Though some Whigs supported the war, Senator Corwin did not, nor did prominent Whigs from the North and South such as Henry Clay. Most Democrats and the public favored the war, yet longtime compromiser John C. Calhoun did not. Hostilities were already under way when these statements were produced. As Corwin and the staff writer delivered their positions, Congress was already debating whether to allocate money for the war effort. In February 1847, when Corwin wrote, the United States continued to recruit American soldiers to fight in the war.[25] Around the time the pro-war staff writer responded, General Winfield Scott's troops made their way to Mexico City (which they occupied by September 14 of that year).

Beliefs about Manifest Destiny and the expansion of slavery continued to shape views of the war. Such perspectives also influenced these authors' interpretation of events and the evidence they use to make their points. For example, both authors cite Minister John Slidell's mission to meet with Mexican officials to support their arguments. The pro-war staff writer criticizes Mexico for its treatment of the ambassador, whereas Corwin finds fault with Slidell's behavior. Where Corwin questions the goal of expansion, the staff writer asserts that the United States acted in defense of Texas. These excerpts represent some of the debate that occurred in the 1840s over the Mexican American War, and previews the impending Civil War. As they blend background knowledge with sourcing, contextualization, and critiquing authors' arguments, students will start to see texts as part of a larger conversation that took place in the United States at this time.

Writing History

Sometimes students see the investigation questions in a different light and miss the point of a controversy. They may try to synthesize new knowledge, but they may not be able to express their thoughts in writing. One common response we saw involved who was to blame for the Mexican American War ("The Mexicans started the Mexican American War."). Often, students have a better understanding than they can convey in a thesis statement. Because learning about the topic independently contributes to the challenge of composing a response and selecting evidence, encourage students to discuss U.S. actions at the time and whether they were appropriate, given the events and issues of the day. Some teachers found that the term *justified* was difficult for students and substituted language (i.e., "Who was responsible for the Mexican American War?" or "Should the conflict with Mexico be called the 'Mexican American War' or the 'U.S. Invasion of Mexico'?").

Another problem can arise when students, working independently, ignore the planning stage in favor of reading and composing. A brief time spent planning makes composing easier and the written product stronger. One solution may be to grade or assign extra points for student plans as well as essays.

At this point, many students understand how to structure an essay and what to include, even if they are still working on executing a written argument. They may need to be reminded that a good historical argument is not just about format or including the components of an essay (claim, evidence, explanations, evaluations, rebuttal), it's about the *quality* of such elements. Writing a historical essay requires interpretation, consideration of evidence that has bearing on a historical question, and how different sources shed light on that question. Remind students that their purpose is to convince others, using evidence and critique to back up their claim and sharing how such evidence led them to make their claim.

Ideally, students should work toward developing nuanced interpretations of the historical controversy. However, as students grasp the concept of argument, they may oversimplify their claims and think of one source as right and another wrong (see Figure 8.1). Try to move students away from black-and-white thinking about either text; each source has its strengths and weaknesses in considering the historical question. No text is all right or all wrong. Instead of placing authority in a single text such as a textbook, have students analyze the merits and limitations of *each* document when addressing the central question. A student could discuss one source in each of the first two body paragraphs, using the third body paragraph to reconcile the different perspectives in an interpretation that takes both sources into account. This is an alternative text structure that more naturally supports complex historical thinking, but doesn't always lead to an argument.

Reflection and goal-setting allow students to become more purposeful as they transition toward greater independence. In reflecting on their writing, students can identify if they are meeting expectations. One teacher asked students to write two positive comments and one helpful hint on a peer's essay, and found that their feedback reflected many of the ideas she had explained while using this curriculum. Another teacher felt the combination of having students set goals and focus on their improvement helped their writing. These teachers didn't simply hand the Reflection Guide to students; one modeled how to reflect by comparing the Reflection Guide to sample essays. He thought out loud and pointed out where the essays met expectations or fell short. He also talked through how one might improve the aspects of the essay that fell short. Developing student proficiency with reflection gives them the power to determine their direction as they begin an investigation, and can guide their work throughout.

FIGURE 8.1. Student Work Sample Emphasizing One Source as Right.

> After reading information on both side
> of the arguement I thought that Document A
> was correct. This docuement stats that

HOW TO TEACH THIS INVESTIGATION

What's New in This Investigation?

Students are given less time for reading and writing in this investigation. With their teachers' encouragement, they continue to work more independently. Day 1 prepares students for independent work—they reflect on past writing, set goals, develop a timeline of events, and review their overarching purpose. This day can help students work more purposefully. On the 2nd day, they read and analyze *both* primary sources and begin to plan. Students can finish planning on Day 3 if necessary, but should spend their time composing a final essay.

Teaching Principles

This investigation focuses on Stage 5 of the cognitive apprenticeship model ("Promote independence"). Students can work with or without scaffolds, transitioning away from using *IREAD*, *H2W*, and planning sheets. Teachers will need to adapt the curriculum to students' needs, aligning changes to the targeted disciplinary thinking and literacy practices. Students have shown growth in disciplinary literacy when teachers pay attention to their thinking and expect them to do more on their own. Of course, teachers may need to alter expectations for students within the same class, prompting some to be more indpendent while giving others more support.

> *Classroom Notes:* Help students learn to manage their time by displaying time using an electronic timer. Make occasional references to where students should be during each of the final two investigations.

Pushing students to work independently can require positive reinforcement, and questioning rather than telling. One teacher needed to set clear parameters and then let students think through the material before she engaged with them. She explained, "Sometimes I would tell them literally, 'I'm just going to walk away from you right now, but I know you can do this. And I'm going to come back and look at this in 5 minutes.'" Rather than responding directly to a question, this teacher asked students to figure it out themselves and then followed up, gradually increasing the amount of time students worked independently. This often meant that students had something to say when the teacher returned, allowing for conversation and shifting students out of a dependent mode. The teacher continued the conversation with students who had completed their essays early. While other students were still composing, the teacher could read through "finished" essays and use questions to prompt students' thinking and rewriting.

One teacher's biggest challenge was letting students consider the material and form their own opinions: "I always want to say something to try to help, but realized that sometimes they need that struggle, they need that wait time to think and really look at it." He realized he was doing too much of the talking, taking responsibility for thinking away from his students. His challenge was to shift from providing answers to asking questions, and allowing space so that students had time to process material on their own. These teachers found that as changing roles shifted authority in the classroom away from them and to the students, student independence increased.[26] On the other hand, leaving students to their own devices before they're ready won't lead to progress. Adapting to students' needs is crucial; this could mean reteaching or spending more time guiding students before setting them loose to work independently.

> *Classroom Notes.* Another way to promote independence is to tell students that you will allow them "three lifelines" (as on *Who Wants To Be a Millionaire*), or three opportunities to ask for help. Keep a visual record of each time you help a student and encourage the student to figure queries out on his or her own.

Things to Keep in Mind

Students were most successful when given clear structure and expectations. Within structured environments, students worked with minimal teacher support. Teachers created conditions for success by arranging the class so that students reflected, created their own timelines, and understood their purpose. Students were less successful in classrooms where the teacher did not clarify goals at the outset or offer reminders about time, spoke to the whole class for an extended period (making individual work difficult), or allowed students to talk throughout the lesson (making it difficult for students to concentrate and take their work seriously). Independence doesn't just mean setting students loose to do whatever they want. Teachers play an important role in providing structure and high expectations.

If students need continued support to reach those high expectations, we offer three examples from teachers who have used this curriculum. One strategy that's useful with English language learners involves spending time on U.S. history and culture. One teacher noticed that students who were new to the United States didn't have the same knowledge about U.S. history and had difficulty with the investigations. She grouped English language learners together to go over the background information: what was going on at the time, why it was important historically, and how it affects us today. Sharing historical context was crucial for these learners. In addition, pointing out "Helpful Phrases" on the back of *H2W* gave them vocabulary to express ideas.

Other teachers worked with struggling students in groups. They could establish attainable, concrete expectations for students challenged by the curriculum. Some students continued to write one supporting and one rebuttal paragraph through the sixth investigation; others just included evidence rather than critiquing it. One teacher described her approach when she said, "I was able to sit with those kids and say, 'Okay, let's just choose three things that we understand. We may not understand all of this, but what do we understand?' . . . In the end I asked, 'Okay, write an introduction, supporting, and rebuttal and maybe a conclusion' for two or three of the kids. Just setting a different goal for a smaller group, I think they were a lot less frustrated. They were trying to keep up with everybody else . . . and they weren't there." Teachers also used this time to review student work; point out competencies demonstrated in their annotations, plans, or essays; and identify next steps (e.g., "Why don't you add a little more here?"). Positive reinforcement where warranted, followed by tangible, achievable goals, helped struggling students to learn.

Last, teachers asked questions and used dialogue to help struggling students express their ideas and reason about the material by pulling them into discussion (either whole class, small groups, or one-on-one). One teacher reminded students to "look at the documents" and prompted students' thinking by asking, "Why *would* you trust this author, why *wouldn't* you?" Whether dropping in on a conversation or drawing out student ideas, teachers used dialogue to help students process the material and push their thinking, a move that supported all students.

HOW MIGHT STUDENTS RESPOND?
STUDENT WRITING AND TEACHER FEEDBACK

Because students had less support and time for reading and writing in Investigation 6, it was not uncommon for some to lose some ground in this last investigation. As in Investigations 4 and 5, students may struggle with the historical question where they must evaluate a policy and reconcile opposing perspectives on historical events. Once again, it is important that students focus on their background knowledge to evaluate the documents. The historical context for this unit may present challenges for students unfamiliar with the time period, so teachers may want to provide explicit support.

Compared with her accomplishments in Investigation 5, Tamia's essay shows less progress (Figure 8.2). However, she is now working with less support from her teacher and peers, and may be more focused on comprehension than on argument. In her annotations, she identifies and summarizes main points and notes key passages that reveal the authors' perspectives. In her essay, she argues her point primarily by recounting events in a way that highlights Mexico's role in justifying U.S. actions. But it is unclear whether she is answering the prompt literally or not (focusing on who shot first to answer the historical question about the beginnings of the Mexican American War), and her argument is again hard to follow, particularly at the end. In fact, her essay suggests that she may have struggled with comprehending the events, leaving less time to plan what she would write. In hindsight, Tamia may not have

FIGURE 8.2. Tamia's Essay for Investigation 6

The mexicans started the mexican American war in texas had disputed all area. The american troops were sent war to protect the land but mexico started to ~~xxxxx~~ shoot troops and the people thought the U.S. had gone to to war but mexico started unfairly. Mexico and the U.S. had agreed to resolve their disagreements. But if mexico didn't want to except the peacefullness it probably would still be war going on now. Mexico murded two officers and attacked troops for no reason. Sent forces to protect past mexico went to for and got killed. President polk tried to gain land from mexico by offering money, he told his commandors to prepare possibly for war with texas in 1845. Since mexico started fire but didn't know they were coming with an plan.

Praise: "I like how you use the background, head note and text to write this essay."

Polish: "Relate this back to the historical question—Was the US justified in going to war with Mexico? If so, why?"

Polish: "Don't forget to address Corwin's views in document 2. Why might some people say that the US was not justified in going to war?"

Goal: "Make sure you address the historical question directly in your essays. Continue to follow the H2W format to make sure you have a complete essay."

FIGURE 8.3. Aaron's Essay for Investigation 6

In 1846 the U.S. and mexico began fighting the mexican-
American war. The controversy was over if the U.S. was
justified or not with going to war with mexico. People
disagreed because some thought the U.S. was justified and
others did not. I think the U.S. was not justified in
going to war with mexico.

The strongest reason I think the U.S. was
not justified is because they crossed into the disputed
territory. A quote that supports my aurgument says
"The president said he would take texas at mexico's exspent."
This supports my aurgument that the U.S. not justified
because the U.S. taking texas at mexico's exspense was
like the first straw of the war. I found this information
beliveable because I was written by a member of a U.S.
political party, & he would not go againist his own goverment
unless what he was saying was true.

> Polish: "Why was it wrong for the US to enter the disputed territory with troops? Your quote should address this question."

been ready to work independently for this unit and may have benefited from reviewing the documents with a peer to better grasp the content. Or she may still need more time to master reading, planning, and writing. Ideally, next year she will return ready to pick up where she left off in this investigation and continue refining her skills.

Aaron (Figure 8.3) was more successful at using background knowledge to answer the historical question in this investigation. He moved a little further away from a literal interpretation of the prompt and examines ways in which the United States provoked an international incident. But even here, he could pay more attention to the legitimacy of Texan independence or its claim to the disputed territory. Although Aaron decided to "use better judgments" when he set a goal for the investigation, he judged the credibility of each source without using context and argumentation to evaluate the documents. He also needs to rebut opposing arguments to leave the reader with a clearer sense of why he has drawn his conclusion.

FIGURE 8.3. Aaron's Essay for Investigation 6, Continued.

Another reason I belive the U.S. was not justified is mexico tried to tell the U.S. taking texas would cause war. A quote that supports this says "Mexico humbly begged the president not to take texas. Mexico said that taking texas might disturb the peace between our contries". This quote supports my ~~orig~~ avigument that the U.S. was not justified because mexico tried to warn the U.S. but they purposely ignored mexico Knowing very well a war could be started. I find this imformation also to be reliable because this speech was given to the senate, and if they thought it was false they would have imediatly tried to defend their ~~countr~~ contries name.

> Praise: "I like how you focus on the motives of the US here."

On the other hand, people might have thought the U.S. was justified because they were fired upon first. A quote that explains this says "Mexico murdered 2 officers and attacked some troops in texas for no reason" This would show why the U.S. was justified because if the U.S. was fired on first they have the right to defend themselves. I find this imformation somewhat beliveable because it was written for the public to see, so if it was a lie there would have been a uproar.

> Polish: "Rebut this argument. How might you defend Mexico's actions in this incident?"

When all of the facts on both sides are considered, I still think the U.S. was not justified in going to war with mexico.

> Goal: "Remember to explain your evidence and consider how evidence from both documents support your conclusion."

LESSON PLANS AND MATERIALS

Teachers and students will need the following: Lesson plans (see Figures 8.4–8.6), Investigation 6 packet (overview page with map, newspaper article, and Corwin speech found after the lesson plans in Figure 8.7), Additional materials for this investigation (Sample Essay Cards in Figure 8.8), Disciplinary Literacy tools (*IREAD*, *H2W*, Essay Response Template, and Reflection Guide in Appendix A), overhead projection capacity, and students' essays from earlier investigations.

FIGURE 8.4. Lesson Plan, Day 1: Preparation for Independent Work

Materials: **Investigation 6 student packets, *IREAD*, *H2W*, Essay prompt sheet, Sample Essay Cards, Projector, student essays from earlier investigations**

Suggested time: **1 hour per day**

INTRODUCTION

1. Give an overview of the next 3 days and how this investigation is similar to and different from previous investigations.

    a. This is not a typical 3-day investigation. The 1st day is focused on helping students think about the main goal in writing a history essay and preparing them to work independently. It is a day of transition from working with support to working more independently. The 2nd and 3rd days include the typical parts of investigations: reading and annotating documents, planning, composing, and giving students practice to independently use all of the strategies they have learned so far.

    b. If teachers choose, students can write a final essay using primary documents ("posttest") after this investigation to show how much they've learned.

REVIEW WRITING GOALS

2. Review the purpose of writing a historical argument: to convince someone that the evidence supports your response to the historical question.

3. Use the Sample Essay Cards to review how a whole essay fits together to make a convincing argument (see Figure 8.8, Additional Materials, below). Explain that these cards are paragraphs from one student's essay.

    a. In groups of five, students read the cards and put them in order according to the *H2W* structure. Students can decide which paragraph will be the introduction, which paragraph will be a supporting paragraph, and so on.

    b. Ask students how they know which is the right order for these paragraphs, that is, introduction/supporting/rebuttal/conclusion.

    c. Students should justify why they put paragraphs in a particular order and/or explain what each one is.

    d. Key ideas from this activity include:

        i. Introductory paragraph should clearly state the writer's position.

        ii. Supporting paragraphs include evidence to support the position.

        iii. Rebuttal paragraph doesn't argue against the position in the introduction but supports it by showing a weakness in the opposing side.

        iv. Concluding paragraph shows both sides and then gives a reason why the writer's position is the stronger one.

FIGURE 8.4. Lesson Plan, Day 1: Preparation for Independent Work, Continued

REFLECT ON STUDENTS' PROGRESS AND SET GOALS

4. Review progress students have made from the start of the year until now. Ask them to look at their past essays and find an improvement they are most proud of accomplishing. Students may look at their yellow cards, if helpful.

5. Ask students to share in groups at their tables, or to share with the class.

6. Ask students to make a final goal for the day and write it on the packet for Investigation 6. (Sample goals are to explain evidence, to judge evidence, to ensure that the essay makes sense, writing five paragraphs, not asking for help unless I'm completely stuck, etc.)

BACKGROUND INFORMATION

7. Together, read the background information on page 1 of the student packet for Investigation 6, look at the map on page 1, and read the headnote for each document.
    a. Review the Historical Question with students.
    b. Identify where the Rio Grande is on the map.
    c. Identify the "disputed area" of land that both Mexico and the United States considered theirs.

8. Ask students to create a timeline on the top of page 2 of the student packet.
    a. Ask students to include three key events that are relevant to this investigation. They can refer to the background on page 1 and the headnotes for help.
        i. Share and put these dates on a timeline for students to see if they need this support.
    b. Ask students to add the dates of each document to their timeline.
        i. Share and put these dates on a timeline for students to see if they need this support.
    c. Ask students what they would need in order to make a timeline on their own next time.

REVIEW THE PLANNING PROCESS

9. Note that students will create a planning page. Discuss how they can plan their essays. Ask students to discuss how they have planned for earlier investigations (e.g., what worked?).

10. Record students' discussion so that everyone can share planning ideas.

11. If students need support, record these ideas on the visualizer or projector:
    a. Write the numbers 1, 2, 3, 4, 5 on a blank planning page for each paragraph.
    b. Beside each number, write a personal reminder *next to each number* (what's most important, what might you forget) about each paragraph, using *H2W*.
    c. Write on the documents as you plan. You can remind yourself what to select by putting "reason, quote, explain, and judge" or "R, Q, E, and J" next to numbers 2–4.

ENCOURAGE INDEPENDENCE

12. Encourage students to work independently, by explaining they can ask for help up to three times (these can be called "lifelines") each of the next 2 days. This can encourage students to solve challenges on their own.

13. If students need more support to continue to make progress, adapt and give them support where necessary.

FIGURE 8.5. Lesson Plan, Day 2: Historical Reading and Planning

INTRODUCTION

1. Decide whether to give students a document-based essay as a posttest. If you do, explain that these are the last 2 days for students to practice what they have learned, and that taking a posttest will help you compare how they did on the test to the first essay they wrote. On the test, students will need to manage their time independently. Since students will have 2 days to read, plan, and write, today and tomorrow can serve as a practice test for students to try working on on their own.

2. Review the historical question together and discuss what it means.

3. Ask students to review their timelines from yesterday to remember the context of this historical question.

    a. Ask students to find one detail in the background information or timeline that they can use in the introduction of their essay when they write later.

HISTORICAL READING AND THINKING

4. Help students to think about how to manage their time as they read and analyze each document.

    a. Let students know that they will have about 20 minutes to do *IREAD* for each document. (Either 4 minutes per letter or 10 minutes for *IR* and 10 minutes for *EAD*. Or they can do all of the letters at the same time as they read each document.)

    b. Remind them every 5 minutes about how much time is left to read each document.

5. Prompt students to read and annotate the staff writer's article using *IREAD*.

    a. Circulate to check for understanding. Offer support *only if a student asks* you for help.

6. Prompt students to read and annotate the Corwin's speech using *IREAD*. Follow same procedure as with the first document.

7. Compare sources and make judgments:

    a. Use *EAD* of *IREAD* to make judgments. Discuss or think about reasons to trust and doubt each document. Remind students that they may consider the reliability of the authors, the influence of context, and/or the facts and examples each author uses to make their judgments, as well as how these sources relate to the historical question.

    b. Debrief as a class and have students write down two to three judgments on each document.

CLOSURE AND REFLECTION

8. Debrief the process of reading and judging independently to help students think about how to approach reading and judging in the future. Ask them:

    a. How did annotating and judging go for you today?

    b. What went well? What was challenging?

    c. What do you want to keep in mind next time you annotate and judge documents?

FIGURE 8.6. Lesson Plan, Day 3: Planning and Historical Writing

INTRODUCTION

1. If students will complete the posttest, this will be their last practice essay. Next time they will show everything they have learned by reading, planning, and writing on their own.

2. Encourage students to keep the disciplinary literacy tools nearby so they can consult them to remember what to do.

3. Push students to work independently by explaining that they can ask for help up to three times (using "lifelines"). This can encourage students to solve challenges on their own.

PLANNING

4. Ask students to create a planning page and use their documents to select and organize content from the packet for each paragraph.

   a. Circulate around the room but do not offer assistance unless asked.

   b. Encourage students to try to work on their own, but step in after 3–5 minutes if a student is struggling.

COMPOSING

5. Direct students to begin composing their essays.

   a. Use a timer and set to 45 minutes. Tell students to spend 8–10 minutes per paragraph. Remind students every 8–10 minutes to move on to the next paragraph.

   b. Circulate around the room as students work. Make a tally mark on students' papers if you show them how to find content from their documents, how to use their plan to write sentences, and how to use the *H2W* guide and transition phrases.

   c. Suggest that students move on to the next paragraph if they're spending too much time on any one paragraph.

   d. Students may need encouragement. Reinforce students' efforts or accomplishments with participation points or praise. If students are struggling, encourage them to write one, not two, supporting paragraphs.

CLOSURE

6. What was hard? What was easier than students expected? Tell students that they are now ready to show everything that they learned this year on the final document-based essay.

FIGURE 8.7. Materials: Investigation 6 Packet

Name_____

Class_____

Date_____

INVESTIGATION #6:

Was the U.S. justified in going to war with Mexico in 1846?

Directions: Read the documents, consider both perspectives, and develop an argument in response to the question: *Was the U.S. justified in going to war with Mexico in 1846?* Use evidence from the documents to support your argument. Remember what you have learned about reading and writing with documents.

[*Justified= right, did they have a good reason for the action taken]

Background: Before 1835, Texas was a part of Mexico. In the Texas Revolution, the Texans defeated the Mexicans. Mexico did not accept the 1836 treaty that gave Texas rights to all of the land north of the Rio Grande (even though the Mexican General signed it). Texas was an independent country for 10 years before the U.S. annexed [added] Texas to its territory. People in the U.S. questioned whether adding Texas helped the U.S. by adding more land and resources, or hurt it by expanding slavery and dividing the Northern and Southern states. Texans wanted to join the U.S., but Mexico did not want to lose Texas. After Texas was added to the U.S., Mexico and the U.S. disagreed about the location of the border between them. Both thought the disputed area (see map below) was a part of their country. President Polk sent troops to this disputed area in March 1846. Mexicans saw this as an invasion and attacked U.S. troops. This was the start of the Mexican American War. People disagreed about whether the U.S. should have gone to war with Mexico and if the U.S. unfairly started this war.

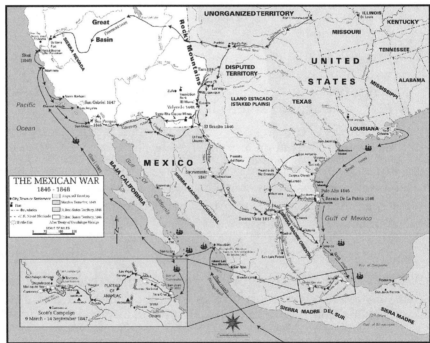

Source: Mexican-American War Overview, Wikimedia Commons. Retrieved March 24, 2014, from http://commons.wikimedia.org/wiki/File: Mexican war overview.gif

FIGURE 8.7. Materials: Investigation 6 Packet, Continued

Name:_____ Class:_____
Date:_____

 **A Staff Writer's Pro-War Newspaper Article**

Head note: When the U.S. added Texas to its territory in 1845, Mexico kicked out the U.S. ambassador and stopped working with politicians from the U.S. Later when the U.S. sent a representative (Minister Slidell) to Mexico, he was not welcomed. In 1847, most Democrats supported the war with Mexico.

Newspaper articles and Congressmen believe the annexation of Texas is one of the causes of the Mexican American War. We do not deny that it has to do with the war. But Mexico alone is responsible for making the annexation of Texas a problem. The annexation of Texas was not an act of war on our part. Texas was an independent country like other nations of the earth. The most powerful European governments recognized its freedom. Texas had the power to choose to become a member of the U.S. There is no good reason why the annexation of Texas would offend Mexico.

After a lot of angry communication, Mexico and the U.S. agreed to discuss and resolve our disagreements. We sent our minister, Mr. Slidell, in good faith and Mexico promised that they would receive him. We sincerely offered friendship. These efforts only led to new insults. Mexico was unwelcoming and misled our minister. Slidell's life was hardly safe in the hands of such untrustworthy people. The treatment of Mr. Slidell and the harmful effect of this event on our national honor are causes of this war.

A Mexican force threatened to attack Texas. Texas was worn out from its struggle for independence and needed our assistance. When we acted, there was no great military effort as if we had some grand plan. We merely ordered troops to protect a distant post, as we have done for years with the rivers and prairies of the far west. The instructions were to avoid all aggressive conduct towards Mexico and the Mexicans unless in self-defense. The Mexicans took the lead with their usual craftiness and love of blood. Mexico murdered two officers and attacked some troops in Texas for no reason. Mexico was not willing to accept our peace offering. Mexico must be charged with a deliberate plan to make war.

Source: Excerpt adapted from the newspaper article "The Mexican War: Its Origin and Conduct." Written by a staff writer for the pro-Democratic newspaper, *The United States Magazine and Democratic Review.* April 1847.

FIGURE 8.7. Materials: Investigation 6 Packet, Continued

Name:_____ Class:____
Date:_____

 **Corwin's Speech**

Head Note: The President of the U.S. (President Polk) wanted to expand the territory of the U.S. at this time. Although he tried to gain land from Mexico by offering money, he also told his commanders to prepare for the possibility of war after adding Texas to the U.S. in 1845. Senator Corwin gave this speech to the U.S. Senate when they debated whether to give more money to the U.S. military effort in Mexico.

The U.S. President ignored the protests and needs of Mexico before the war. Mexico humbly begged the President not to take Texas. Mexico said that taking Texas might disturb the peace between our countries. But our President was still unstoppable. Mexico begged the President to leave Texas alone. If Texas were independent, let her enjoy her independence. If Texas were free, let her enjoy her liberty. The President said no. He said we would take Texas at Mexico's expense.

At last the President was told that Mexico was willing to have a low-level U.S. government official come to negotiate a quiet settlement about the Texan boundary. Instead, the U.S. President sent a more important government official—a minister—and demanded a public welcome worthy of a minister. The Mexican President at the time was in trouble in his country and losing power. He begged Minister Slidell not to force a reception at that time. Slidell was told that the Mexican people were so agitated that he must wait. What did Slidell do? He said, "You shall meet with me *now.* You shall recognize me as minister and not as a simple official. You shall treat me as though the most peaceful relations existed between the two countries." From Slidell's letters it is perfectly clear that if Mr. Slidell had acted as a humble official to work out the Texas boundary, treaties and not bullets would have solved the problem. But the U.S. President wanted a powerful war, not a peace process. He threw down the pen of the diplomat, and picked up the sword of the warrior.

We are fighting this war for territory, for "room." But why? Look at the U.S. It extends from the Alleghany Mountains to the Pacific Ocean. It can support more people than will be in the whole Union for one hundred years to come. And yet Americans persist in the ridiculous assertion, "I want room." The need for room is an outrageous excuse for war. In the future, people will see this is a lie we created to cover up our greed for land that is not ours.

Source: Excerpt adapted from Senator Corwin's speech to the U.S. Senate in Washington, D.C. February 11, 1847. Senator Corwin was a member of the Whig party.

FIGURE 8.8. Additional Materials: Sample Essay Cards

During the 1800s people didn't know how to free slaves, with force or by peaceful action. Some Americans think slaves should fight and god would be happy whenever slaves fight for their freedom. Others think slaves should follow nonviolence, so people disagree about the best way to end slavery. To me the most reasonable answer is to work for freedom without violence.

William Whipper says, "The spirit of defeating others feeds war." He is saying that with war will come more war, and there will always be pain and hate. The author had a slave mother, so he probably knows and had experience of slavery. This is convincing since if people don't let go of harsh feelings, there will be a cycle of revenge.

"We must support one common cause by spreading our influence for the good of mankind." I think this quote means that you have to wait because at the moment nothing can be done about slavery. Whipper realizes that slavery is legal and there are too many supporters for it to end right away. Unfortunately that makes sense in 1837, given the state of the Abolitionist movement.

Henry Garnet believes that slaves should fight to end slavery. He says, "fight for your lives and liberties." This means that slaves should fight and live or die trying. This totally goes against God, even though he uses the bible to justify his words. The author must not understand the bible, since violence isn't tolerated. It seems that Whipper understands the bible more since the Ten Commandments tell us not to use violence.

Nonviolence would be the best way for victory for slaves, at least if they believe in god. Although some abolitionists believe in violence, I believe that fighting will always lead to more deaths of the innocent. Your faith should be in God to protect you. Fighting back and killing is against God. God would never want humans to fight he always strives for peace.

CHAPTER 9

Assessing Historical Thinking and Writing Outcomes

> ***Teachers Reflect.*** "One thing I really liked is [the curriculum] didn't necessarily focus on the 'high' kids or the 'low' kids or the 'middle' kids. It could be molded into whatever you wanted . . . you can't do that with a normal worksheet. . . . I felt like you could meet every person, every child, where they were and I really liked that aspect of it. . . . The top kids weren't pigeonholed into doing something remedial that was boring for them. They could push it further with the right questions. The kids that really needed that extra help, they could just get that paragraph. Maybe that was all they could really write and do well at. . . . They had to take responsibility for it because it was not just a worksheet. It was about their writing so it put the focus of responsibility back on them."

WHAT'S THE POINT?

RETURNING TO THE big picture, it's time to review what all this effort is for: namely, to cultivate historical thinking and literacy practices. These investigations were designed to target the disciplinary use of evidence in students' argument writing.

To capture that outcome, we examined students' essays for argument writing, historical thinking, and facility with composing (as measured by the length of their papers), and found growth for each criterion. By integrating literacy and history, students not only learn required content, but also critique historical sources; question and analyze; construct their own interpretations; and develop ways of thinking, reading, and writing that will lay the foundation for continued success.

The outcomes of this curriculum reflect the Common Core's emphasis on creating arguments with clear and coherent writing; strengthening writing through planning; and gathering evidence from texts to support analysis (e.g., WHST.1a–e, WHST.9). In addition, it targets many reading outcomes listed in the Common Core—both for reading history and informational texts (e.g., RH.1 or RH.6, as well as RI.6 or RI.9). The curriculum embodies key aspects of the C3 Framework as well, given its roots in social studies concepts, inquiry practices, and literacy (e.g., Dimension 2-History, Dimension 3, Dimension 4).

Regardless of the particular technical language, this curriculum targets disciplinary writing by opening up history to interpretation and by fostering analytical and literacy practices that support historical inquiry.

ASSESSING STUDENTS' PROGRESS TOWARD OUTCOMES

While these are all worthy goals, teachers may wonder how to know what students have learned or when they have reached the goals set for them. Typically, social studies assessments feature multiple-choice questions that can obscure student reasoning and limit conclusions about a student's understanding and skills. These assessments don't track the types of thinking and writing emphasized here. Implementation of the Common Core will add more assessments that include writing, but it is unclear how many simultaneously embrace history.

The essay, plan, and annotations students draft during each investigation will offer ongoing assessment opportunities, but it's vital to gauge student progress from the beginning of the curriculum until after they've finished. Having students complete a historical writing task at the start of the lessons affords a baseline to establish where students are, before introducing the ideas and skills in their courses. For some students, seeing where they are at the beginning of the year also helps them "buy in" or commit to working on writing historical arguments during the year. Having students complete a parallel task after they've done the curriculum will let teachers track their progress.

The pre- and posttests used in our research do just that (see Appendix C).[1] These assessments offer a way to analyze student learning in history and writing, and can even be used as final exams to measure students' progress toward key course goals. Whether they teach history in a literacy-rich way or use an inquiry-oriented approach, alternative assessments like these can provide evidence of student learning and make a case for this approach to teaching history. The chance to have a window into student work on parallel tasks from before and after the major learning opportunities helped us improve the curriculum and our professional development efforts every year. In the same way, by collecting data on student progress, teachers can better meet their students' needs and grow as educators.

Administering a pre- and posttest is just the first step. As Chapter 2 made clear, reading and reflection on student work help teachers gain insight (i.e., examining student progress over time with Figure A.12, the Analysis of Student Writing Worksheet in Appendix A). We also share methods of measuring student progress through examples and rubrics, keeping the CCSS and C3 at the forefront, since these documents can greatly influence social studies teachers' assessments.

FIGURE 9.1. One Student's Conclusion Paragraph for His Evidence-Based Argument

> I think slaves were not all free after the civil war because in some places they lived a good life but in others they lived as though they were still slaves. Not all are free. Some still fear and even hide. In my opinion they are neither free nor slaves.

Clarifying Text Types and Purposes

First, we looked at whether students used the sources to build an argument or to summarize ideas in the texts, an important distinction when students are starting to see that history is not a fixed set of information but open to interpretation. This reorientation opens the door to analyzing evidence and developing claims—key ingredients in disciplinary thinking and argument writing.

An effective argument has a central interpretation or claim that ties everything together (see Figure 9.1). The inclusion of evidence and explanation or analysis is purposefully linked to a central claim. Each paragraph preceding the conclusion in Figure 9.1 does just that, using evidence and analysis to support the claim reiterated above. In contrast, a summary translates the sources into a writer's own words or generalizes about a time period (see Figure 9.2). The overall tone is descriptive, akin to the CCSS emphasis on writing informative/explanatory texts. Students may also want to write a narrative which tells a story by reporting a sequence of events.

Elements of narrative and summary writing often appear in arguments. Narrative writing can be used in argument or summary writing.[2] In such cases, choosing where to start and end and what to include would constitute interpretation. Frequently, students just list events without establishing any cause-and-effect relationships. The main way to determine whether an essay is argumentative is to check if it is oriented around a central claim.

Identifying Changes in Students' Argument Writing

In learning to write arguments, students usually start by making a claim, before discovering that more than one interpretation is possible. They go on to provide and explain evidence that supports their claim. Ideally they will evaluate the quality or credibility of evidence in making their argument, which calls

FIGURE 9.2. One Student's Summary of Informational Texts

In the document (Doc 1) it says that the African Americans did not realize that they were free. What the African Americans need is encouragement, Advice and strenghth. An Association has soon been Orqaniced which was called the Savannah Educational Association.

In document 2 the African Americans need protection. Because they have been holding meetings they seemed to have been earning hatred and spite of the people who did not agree with their opinions. Colored men were also getting hurt and beaten for No reason but nobody does anything about it.

for disciplinary thinking. Finally, they work on organizing their ideas and evidence into a coherent statement that includes an introduction and conclusion.

In assessing the argumentative nature of student writing, we looked at two criteria: substantiation and rebuttal. We created an analytic trait rubric that allowed us to score each criterion separately. Rubrics were based on an initial analysis of student work while keeping in mind research into argumentation and historical thinking. Below are excerpts of student work that identify key areas of accomplishment and convey what student growth looks like.

For some students, simply making a claim can be a major accomplishment (see Table 9.1 for the "substantiation" rubric); getting them to share evidence that led to their claim may feel like a herculean task. Students can fail to provide evidence that's relevant to their claim or specific enough to be compelling. They also need to explain the relationship between the evidence and the claim, or how the evidence supports the claim. Finally, our progression specifies the importance of including credible evidence. The various ways in which one may evaluate evidence are often determined by the discipline in which the argument is being made. In history, a consideration of reliable evidence might mean an analysis of the author, the context of the document, and how the particular source has bearing on a historical question. Ultimately, substantiating a claim is crucial to both historical thinking *and* argumentation.

Early stages of rebuttal (see Table 9.2) involve recognizing more than one interpretation or perspective is possible in response to a historical question, and that the evidence doesn't only support one interpretation. Eventually students see that different responses are possible, but in the meantime they may

TABLE 9.1. A Substantiation Rubric with Descriptors and Excerpts from Students' Essays

Score	Rubric Descriptor	Student Essay Excerpts that Illustrate Different Levels of Substantiation
0	(a) No position or claim. OR (b) No support.	"I agree with Side A because it is right. Side B says that."
2	(a) The position is clear. There is clear and relevant support in the essay, but evidence is not drawn from the documents. OR (b) The position is clear. There is clear and relevant support drawn from the documents without explanation.	"Yes, because in Document 1 it say that the African kids went to school. And Charlotte said that she never saw children so eager to learn the alphabet, [the] majority of students learned quickly, and the older one worked in the fields [from] early mornings to 11:00 or 12:00."
4	The position is clear. Evidence is clearly drawn from the documents to support a claim, the link to the claim is clearly established, AND the strength of the evidence or reasoning is evaluated to add support to the claim. *Note: In evaluating, students must not only make a judgment but also share their reason for their judgment (i.e., their evaluation must be explained or they must show their reasoning).*	"After reading information from both sides, I feel African-Americans were not free after the Civil War. Document B says, 'But when we are at the midnight hour, our lives threatened and the Laws fail to protect or help us, the only thing we can do is defend ourselves.' This quote is saying African Americans are still being 'harassed' and nobody is doing anything to help them. This point makes sense because the whites didn't necessarily feel comfortable with 'negroes' around them."

present different perspectives without comparing or elaborating on them. Students tend to elaborate on opposing positions, and may state why they believe their claim is stronger in the face of challenging evidence or counterclaims. A student may also reconcile multiple perspectives without "choosing" which one to support. Ultimately, students not only cite and explain opposing arguments, but also address them to restore the strength of their own position.

Tracking Students' Historical Thinking

Historical thinking isn't a single outcome, but different ways of thinking and historical concepts that promote understanding history as an act of interpretation. Curriculum developers and researchers focus on different aspects of historical thinking, so the range of possible goals for disciplinary thinking is worth noting.[3] We believe that disciplinary use of evidence is a key to writing good arguments, which is one reason we integrate historical thinking into literacy practices. To that end, we focus on perspective recognition and contextualization. We developed these rubrics by analyzing student writing,

TABLE 9.2. A Rebuttal Rubric with Descriptors and Excerpts from Students' Essays

Score	Rubric Descriptor	Student Essay Excerpts that Illustrate Different Levels of Rebuttal
0	No mention, acknowledgment, or recognition of opposing sides.	*In one two-page essay, a student described the perspective of Mr. Lynch, an African American minister, regarding the question. The student never acknowledged an opposing perspective.*
2	(a) Opposing sides are presented and clearly distinguished or juxtaposed but are not drawn from the documents. (They may or may not be elaborated on). OR (b) Opposing sides are drawn from the documents and are distinguished or acknowledged but are not elaborated on.	"Yes they was free but . . . the colords would get beet shot knock out could for now reason and the police didn't do nothing about it."
4	Opposing sides are presented and drawn from the documents. In addition, opposing sides are elaborated on. There is an explicit rebuttal, critique of evidence, or reconciliation of opposing views. The student may not take one side in the end, but the student demonstrates the ability to critique at least one side.	"In some ways they were free. Like they could go to school and to church. But the truth was that they were not free. They could go to school but people were predigest against them. Like in the letter Hamilton wrote in 1866. This letter tells us how they were attacking a schoolhouse. . . . So in a way they were free but still they weren't free from the attacks and the hatered. . . . " "The colored people were free but were not treated like they were. These are 24 people that have these promblems maybe more. The document A says they have been free which they are but doesn't know how people treating them. I can conclude that the colored people were free but were not getting all the rights they should have gotten."

looking for markers of progress starting at the basic level and becoming more sophisticated.

We frame perspective recognition as an orientation to primary sources that recognizes the constructed nature of these sources (see Table 9.3 for excerpts of our rubric alongside student samples). Through word choice and explanations, writers indicate that primary sources are created by people in social situations and represent people's ideas. They are not to be read literally as "The Truth," but rather as one way of thinking about a topic, influenced by the author's context. Students' essays sometimes treat such ideas as fact, and students can use information without representing its origins (a less advanced level of perspective recognition). More advanced essays recognize that the ideas and information in a primary source come from someone living in a particular time and

TABLE 9.3. A Rubric for Perspective Recognition with Descriptors and Excerpts from Students' Essays

Score	Rubric Descriptor	Student Essay Excerpts that Illustrate Different Levels of Perspective Recognition
0	Presents evidence from documents as student's own perspective (e.g., reports as though factual, does not mention documents or where information came from).	"Most of the slaves went to school if they were slaves or freed. Some white people wanted to close schools for Africans, but the Africans refused too."
2	Mentions the author(s) (e.g., "According to Lynch . . ." "The author says . . .")	"The author states that 'many grown people want to know how to read.' This shows that . . ."
4	In using evidence/explanation to support an argument, the writer evaluates the authors' perspectives (e.g., discusses reliability, trustworthiness, credibility) OR evaluates the authors' position as a reporter.	*Student quotes a source, explains it, and then writes:* "This is also reliable because it is the voice of the African Americans and had 24 signatures." Or "Captain Hamilton is very reliable because he actually was their to witness some things and was a soldier in the U.S. army."

place. Given the historical question under consideration, authors may be reliable in some ways and fallible in others. Students must consider the credibility of authors and whether they were in a good position to explain the events that they share.

When writers contextualize, they situate their essay in a time and place and connect their subject matter to events or issues that have bearing on their topic. When writers fail to contextualize, their statements aren't grounded in time or in the topic of their essay. At the novice level, contextualizing means observing concrete details of the primary sources (e.g., Level 2, the date or place in which a source was written), or citing what was happening, without necessarily drawing meaning from or connecting those events (Level 1). Later students will integrate context in support of their claims, applying context to evidence to make inferences or draw conclusions. Eventually they will be able to explain the relationship between historical events and their topic, as well as place their argument in its historical setting (see Table 9.4).

Revisiting Tamia's and Aaron's Writing

Applying these considerations—analysis of text types and purposes, argumentation, and historical thinking—to Tamia's and Aaron's posttests reveals growth and areas for improvement. For both students, the posttests represent their work after they engaged in our curriculum and moved from guided to independent practice, without tools like *IREAD*, *H2W*, or the planning graphic organizer. Such completely independent work gives us insight into how students may internalize the curriculum by the end of the year.

In her pretest, Tamia argues that African Americans were free after the

TABLE 9.4. A Rubric for Contextualization with Descriptors and Excerpts from Students' Essays

Score	Rubric Descriptor	Student Essay Excerpts that Illustrate Different Levels of Contextualization
0	(a) No context mentioned or inaccurate contextual information overwhelms accurate contextual information. OR (b) Student uses anachronisms (e.g., makes a chronological mistake or uses information from another time period without noting the different era) or generalizations not specific to the time period.	"The African Americans were free because of Reconstruction. Reconstruction started the Civil War . . ."
2	Includes factual details about the context of the documents themselves (e.g., mentions the time, place, or audience of the documents). This information might come from the documents, headnotes, background information, or source lines.	"One reason is a quote from an excerpt adapted from a letter written by Captain C. M. Hamilton in 1866 to the Office of the Adjutant General in Washington, D.C. . . . "
4	(a) The writer notes relationships between historical events or situates the documents or argument in their historical setting. OR (b) Demonstrates an understanding of the time period (e.g., the norms and beliefs of the Reconstruction era). Writer goes beyond the specific information in the documents.	"Supposeably James Lynch is seeing that the African Americans are showing that they are free, and little by little are losing 'fear' they once had. This is non reliable because, it was written in the year 1865. That was when they were just starting off. Of course it was going to be 'easy.' But in the year 1867 (2 years after) is when others envied African Americans and got meaner. This was written 2 years 'before,' it's old news. If James Lynch were to go see them now, who knows what he would say."

Civil War. To support her claim, she cites two examples: a story found in one primary source and Rosa Parks' act of civil disobedience (an event from a different era that does not apply to the time period of the prompt). Throughout her essay, Tamia appears to be more focused on the concept of African American protest as a path to equal rights, straying from the point of the question (to consider the concept of freedom in the context of the Reconstruction era).

Tamia's posttest is more compelling from a historical standpoint, though similar in length and structure. It reminds us that structure alone does not make a good historical essay: The quality of reasoning and understanding of context are also important. This time Tamia focused on the concept of freedom for African Americans after the Civil War. She grounds her reasoning and evidence in primary sources and historical context. In sharing evidence from James Lynch, she recognizes his authorship and tries to evaluate his credibility (e.g., "he must have been a slave"). Tamia also acknowledges multiple perspectives and some degree of complexity when she notes that the 24 African Americans who wrote the letter were free (we think she means "technically free"), but the way they were treated shows they weren't fully free.

Tamia's greatest weakness from an argumentation standpoint may actually demonstrate strength in her historical reasoning: She changes her thesis. Tamia appears to truly reason through the question *as* she reads and composes. She begins by arguing that African Americans were not free and uses a primary source to support her thesis. But when she considers a second primary source, Tamia finds the evidence and author convincing, and changes her thesis on that basis. Reconsideration of a historical question and interpretation based on new evidence are crucial steps in developing historical interpretations. Granted, if Tamia had thought through the evidence *before* starting to write, she might have composed a more coherent and compelling argument. Tamia minimized the role of planning half of the time that she used this curriculum (i.e., she had no written plan)—precisely a part of the writing process that can address this issue. Students often report information when they do not have a plan to guide them in writing an argument. So our biggest piece of advice for Tamia at this point is to develop a plan before writing (and to revise the plan as she writes, if necessary), but we applaud her reasoning in the posttest.

Aaron makes an argument in both his pre- and posttest; he does not summarize information. In his pretest, Aaron clearly states a claim and focuses on it throughout the paragraph. His evidence is comprised of brief examples (former slaves allowed to go to church and school) and he does not elaborate on or evaluate his sources. The last sentence oversimplifies the issue at hand—that although slavemasters no longer existed, the sources indicate poor treatment of African Americans by Whites angry about post–Civil War changes.

Aaron's posttest argument is more convincing for several reasons. He argues a claim consistently, including two supporting reasons, evidence for each reason, and an explanation for how each piece supports his claim. In addition, his evidence is specific and persuasive, as he integrates quotations from the sources. Aaron does not, however, recognize the sources of the quotations, and he writes about the reliability or credibility of those sources in a simple and not always historical way ("This information was convincing to me because of my prior knowledge").

Aaron recognizes multiple perspectives in his rebuttal paragraph, although he does not explicitly reconcile an opposing perspective that he raises or explain clearly why his interpretation is stronger. In historical terms, Aaron's thinking is more complex than it was at pretest. He recognizes that privileges existed, but also sees that African Americans' enjoyment of those privileges was limited by the times. Aaron's main challenge is to situate and evaluate his evidence, recognizing their sources and evaluating their credibility, while explaining why his interpretation is stronger than the opposing one noted in his rebuttal. In short, our advice to Aaron is to express more of the thinking behind his choices.

MOVING FORWARD

Improving argument writing and historical thinking is hard work, but the changes we have observed after only six investigations are noteworthy. In trying out this approach, you may find that you are on your feet—circulating around the room, modeling core practices, attending to students' thinking, and reading essays. At first, this may seem like a lot to do, but we advise sticking with it. The reward is worth it. Students will be more prepared for their next steps in school as well as their civic and job responsibilities later in life. In closing, we discuss some of the challenges this kind of teaching presents, as well as suggestions for managing them.

Cognitive Apprenticeship Revisited

Teaching literacy and complex ways of thinking requires teachers to be very explicit. The disciplinary literacy tools, adapted primary sources, Planning Your Essay sheets, and timelines are all pieces of the curriculum that scaffold learning.

But scaffolding through tools such as these is only meant to be temporary. Our curriculum helps students to gradually become more competent and integrate new ideas and practices. Eventually we encourage teachers to fade students' use of the supports that have been built into this curriculum, as students learn to think, read, and write on their own. *IREAD* and *H2W* are helpful in large part because they provide a systematic means to execute some of the cognitive strategies that historians have been observed to engage in. Yet expert practices will always be more complex than tools. That's why it's important to push student thinking once they've mastered the basic ideas and practices embedded in these supports. Teachers often notice that students who understand how to plan write less of a plan as they gain competence in composing; in many cases, students continue to plan mentally (without creating written plans that are visible representations of their thinking). Whether students stick with the tools or move beyond them, the cognitive apprenticeship model requires gradually shifting control to students so they can employ targeted practices with greater purpose and independence.

Making the transition from extensive teacher modeling to independent student work or thinking beyond what the tools offer is not easy. Judging when a student is ready to take on more responsibility, to employ the strategies with less support, is challenging. The answer will differ depending on the student. When some students move toward independence too quickly, they can become lost or frustrated. Other students who demonstrate they're ready to think through sources or plan an essay can become bored or disengaged, given too much control.

Here's one solution: Try out this curriculum with a colleague so you can discuss your progress with a peer. Review the lesson plans together and figure out how to use the ideas in your classroom. Another approach involves using the Analysis of Student Writing Worksheet (Figure A.12, Appendix A) to guide analysis of student work, troubleshoot problem areas, and identify ways to help students make progress.

Formative and Summative Assessment

We encourage teachers to analyze student work throughout the year, not just the beginning and the end. Such monitoring helps teachers decide when to push students toward greater independence or give more support. When it comes to formative assessment throughout the year, teachers can learn a lot by circulating and having conversations with students. Looking at annotations or plans, for example, can lend insight into their comprehension of sources and interpretive thinking. One way to balance the demands on teachers' time is to administer the pre- and posttests to the whole class, but read through only a subset. This way teachers can extract and share examples of strengths as well as areas for improvement. An abbreviated analysis is often enough to glean lessons that can be applied to future work with students. Sharing feedback and examples with the class, and having a conversation about those ideas, can be more effective than leaving students to their own devices.

Extending this Work

Six investigations are a very short time in which to master complex practices. Yet the students whose teachers implemented this curriculum improved their historical thinking and argument writing significantly, compared with those students who were not exposed to these lessons.[4] Extending this kind of learning opportunity across multiple years of experience has the potential to be far more influential than a single year. To create a comprehensive experience for students, working with social studies teachers across and within grade levels to establish goals for historical thinking and argument writing would be ideal. Fortunately, both the C3 Framework and Common Core set out goals for students at different levels, so teachers can rely on or adapt existing guidelines. Goals from year to year could follow a reasonable progression, where teachers work together on goals at each grade level.

Questions might include: What are the major tasks that give students opportunities to learn and demonstrate those goals? What scaffolding or tools would help students work toward them? Teachers may share student work to determine the kind of support students need moving forward; in fact, this has been among the most powerful professional development activities we have seen. Looking at student work helps teachers understand the goals and develop a sense of the challenges students face.

In addition to working with social studies teachers, we recommend coordinating this approach with English/Language Arts teachers, special educators, and ESL teachers. The goals can be adapted to include disciplinary thinking in different content areas along with argument writing. Students can learn that subject areas rely on different ways of thinking, but by being explicit

TABLE 9.5. Foundational Concepts and Teaching Principles Behind This Curriculum

Foundational Concepts	Teaching Principles
• Use historical argument, or interpretation, as a foundational frame.	• Pose central historical questions that have multiple possible answers and present historical sources to investigate.
• We learn history by analyzing and questioning historical sources and artifacts.	• Develop background knowledge of historical topics to support students' thinking and literacy practices. • Use developmentally appropriate representations of content or tasks.
• Reading, thinking, and writing are interconnected activities in studying history.	• Take a cognitive apprenticeship approach to instruction. • Adapt the curriculum to students' needs while continually emphasizing disciplinary thinking and writing.

about such differences and using common terminology teachers can help them navigate the differences. Ultimately, the curriculum shouldn't be just a 1-year project, but a commitment by a department, interdisciplinary team, or multi-grade-level team to multiple years of focused work with students.

Not every educator can convince schools to work toward a common set of goals, but they can reach out through professional organizations, social networking, or district networks to create a professional learning community. By working together, teachers can articulate goals for students, define major tasks and tools to reach those goals, and analyze student work to monitor student progression.

If some teachers want more investigations, or to customize an investigation to a specific history course, they can develop materials on their own or apply the disciplinary literacy tools to an existing inquiry-oriented, text-based history curriculum.[5] Those developing materials on their own should keep the foundational concepts and teaching principles in mind as the basis of literacy-rich history instruction (see Table 9.5).

When you discover primary sources on your own, you may need to adapt them. Try to identify the segment of text that is most helpful in terms of your central question. Then consider vocabulary or sentences that might be challenging for students and include a word bank, substitute words, or phrases in brackets, and include a headnote and attribution to offer key information that supports historical reading.[6]

In order to gain insight into how students work with a text, we generally start by having a student read and think aloud about a document. In defining a central question, we worked iteratively among the standards, available primary sources, and background research on a historical topic to find questions that call for argument or interpretation (rather than leading students to summarize or asking closed questions with only one right answer). When integrating literacy tools, a cognitive apprenticeship model will make reading, writing, and thinking practices explicit, regardless of content and grade level. Assessments of student thinking and writing can determine when and how to transition toward independence. Preparing materials is time-consuming—all the more reason to work with colleagues on this endeavor.

Regardless of whether you use these materials, develop your own, or work with a team, we end with some encouraging words from a teacher who learned that listening to his students, attending to their thinking and literacy practices, and responding to their work helped him and his students grow:

> It's not a rigid step-by-step thing. Be flexible. Meet students where they are. They just need to be exposed to different things and to look at the student growth. You're not going to get a home run every time; you're not going to get your students to do everything. You might have students who are better at one part. They might have an excellent discussion but can't translate into writing. As it grows . . . find out what each student needs the most help with, what the pitfall for each kid is and then . . . [give] them the part that they need. At first you need to put it all out there. . . . Just try to give them everything and let the students pick what works for them and what doesn't and figure out how you can bring them along.

By offering these materials, we hope we have provided teachers the chance to focus on student thinking and writing rather than worrying about concocting a lesson in time for the next class. We are eager to get feedback, questions, and suggestions, so we encourage teachers to stay in touch as they try out these materials in their classrooms.

Epilogue

THIS BOOK IS the result of a study we completed over a 3-year period in one school district in the Mid-Atlantic United States, with funds from the federal government. We worked in more than a dozen schools, and provided professional development to more than 30 teachers who used our curriculum intervention for a full year. Fifteen teachers allowed us to give pre- and posttests to children who did not work with our curriculum; their students' essays served as comparison data. In all, we collected historical essays from more than 6,000 8th-grade students, and analyzed the work from a stratified random sample of just under 1,400 students. We took care to balance the number of struggling, average, and advanced readers and to select equivalent numbers of students from teachers who used our curriculum and those who did not, considering known factors such as students' ethnicity, gender, and status as an English language learner or having a disability.

Reports outlining these details are beyond the scope of this book. Suffice it to say that we have and continue to make conference presentations and publish research articles that describe important teacher and student learning outcomes, using both quantitative and qualitative methodology. Interested readers may learn more about the basis of our conclusions from these sources, which describe our data analyses and inferences more fully.[1] These reports explain the significant and meaningful learning outcomes in students who completed the majority of the curriculum provided in this book. Such progress depended in large part on dedicated teachers. The extent to which both teachers and students engaged meaningfully with these lessons made a real difference; therefore, we strongly encourage teachers to use all, rather than portions of, the investigations.

Disciplinary Literacy Tools and Additional Writing Supports

FIGURE A.1 *IREAD* Foldable—Front

I READ

Identify the author's argument in response to the historical question.
- Which side is the author on?
- How would the author respond to the historical question?

Read each paragraph and ask about the author's main idea.
- What is the author describing in this ¶?
- What is the main idea of this ¶?
- Does this main idea relate to or answer the historical question? How?

Examine the author's reliability.
- Who wrote this document and what judgments can we make about him/her?
- Why did s/he write this? *Clue= Type of document, audience, & occasion for writing*

Assess the influence of context.
- How might place have influenced the writing of this document? *Clue= Compare document location to location of events*
- What else was going on at this time in history? *Clue= Identify historical events & when docs were written.*

Determine the quality of the author's facts and examples.
- What facts or examples does the author give to support his/her argument?
- How do facts or examples support the author's argument?
- Where do the facts or examples come from?

FIGURE A.2. *IREAD* Foldable—Back

Identify the author's argument in response to the historical question.

- Put a big box at the bottom and write the author's main argument.

Author believes the colonists fired first.

Read each ¶ and ask about the author's main idea.

- Underline sentences that tell you the author's main idea.
  OR
- Write the main idea in 3–4 words next to each ¶.

Soldiers marched all night

Examine the ★ author's reliability.

- ★Star★ information about the author, his/her purpose, type of document, audience, and occasion for writing.

  AND

Judge: Write 1 reason to doubt the author and 1 reason to trust the author.

Assess the influence of context.

- Put →arrows← next to information about the context—dates of docs, location, & historical events.
- Make timeline.
  AND

Judge: Given what else was going on at this time/place, write why the author's argument does/ doesn't make sense.

Determine the quality of the author's facts & examples.

- Put boxes around facts and examples the author uses to support his/her argument.

  AND

Judge: Write why the author's facts and examples are/are not convincing.

I READ

Identify the author's argument in response to the historical question.

-Which side is the author on?
-How would the author respond to the historical question?

Read each paragraph and ask about the <u>author's main idea.</u>

-What is the author <u>describing</u> in this paragraph?
-What is the <u>main idea</u> of this paragraph?
-Does this <u>main idea</u> relate to the historical question? How?

Soldiers marched all night

Examine the author's ★ reliability ★.

-Who wrote this document and what judgments can we make about him/her?
-Why did s/he write this document? ***Clues***: ★ Type of document ★ audience ★ and ★ occasion for writing ★

 Judge: Write 1 reason to doubt and 1 reason to trust the author.

Assess the influence of context. ←

-How might →place← have influenced the writing of this document? ***Clue***: Compare document location to location of events.
-What else was going on at →this time← in history? ***Clue***: Identify →historical events← and compare to when documents were written.

Judge: Given what else was going on at this time/place, write why the author's argument does/doesn't make sense.

Determine the quality of the author's facts and examples.

-What facts or examples does the author give to support his/her argument?
-How do facts or examples support the author's argument?
-Where do the facts or examples come from?
-Which facts or examples are most persuasive?

-*Judge: Write why authors' facts/examples are/are not convincing.*

How to Write Your Essay

Introduction. (1) Recap the event or issue (include who, what, when, and where). (2) Write one sentence that explains the historical question. (3) Tell why people disagreed about the dilemma or events. (4) Write an answer to the historical question, taking care to include the name and/or author perspective.

↓

Supporting paragraph. (1) Introduce your strongest reason that supports your argument. (2) Select a quote or other evidence that will convince a skeptic of your argument AND state who/where this evidence comes from. (3) Explain how your quote or evidence supports your argument. (4) Explain your judgment of (a) the author's reliability, (b) the influence of context, and/or (c) the quality of the author's facts and examples.

↓

Supporting paragraph. (1) Choose another reason to support your argument. Repeat the above (2)→(4). Select a quote or other evidence– convince someone of your argument!

↓

Rebuttal paragraph. (1) Choose the strongest reason, quote, or other evidence that goes against your argument, but explains the other perspective. (2) Select a quote that someone who has the opposite perspective might agree with. (3) *Rebut*, or *reject* the opposing evidence *by explaining your judgment* of (a) the author's reliability, (b) the influence of context, and/or (c) the quality of the author's facts and examples.

↓

Conclusion. (1) Write your answer to the historical question by comparing the two documents and explaining why someone should choose your perspective over the other perspective. Connect your ideas to what was happening in the historical context.

HELPFUL PHRASES FOR WRITING HISTORICAL ARGUMENTS

Introducing your argument	After reading [write down authors of each document], After reading information from both sides,
Introducing a reason that supports your argument or perspective	[Name of person or group]'s speech, diary, letter, or document gives many reasons why [something about the controversy] happened. Another reason why [the perspective of your argument makes sense] is that . . . [explain an idea that supports your thinking].
Introducing a quote	In [Name of location/Date], [Name of person] wrote that, ". . . ." In [Name of location/Date], [Name of group of people] wrote that, ". . . ."
Explaining a quote	His/Her quote supports my argument because . . . His/Her quote shows that . . .
Judging your evidence	Author's reliability I trust/doubt this author because . . . The author is a better source of information because . . . This author knows more about . . . This author is more likely to understand . . . This author is reliable/dependable because . . .
	Influence of context Compared to other people's views at the time/in this place, this author . . . Given what else was going on at this time/place, the author's argument makes sense because . . . Other events in history that support this argument include . . . because . . . Another event in history that relates to this was when . . .
	Quality of the author's facts and examples This author's facts/examples are convincing because . . . This point makes sense because . . . The author supports this point by showing that . . . The author backs this up with facts/examples by saying/such as . . .
Adding to what you have already written	Another reason why this is true is that . . . Moreover . . . In addition . . .
Including ideas from another perspective	On the other hand . . . It may also be argued that . . . While . . . [Name of the person with the opposing perspective] had a different point of view. S/he believed that . . .
Rejecting/refuting another perspective	[Name of person or Describe evidence] was more reliable [explain] But there is a problem with [his/her] thinking because . . .
Wrapping things up	When all of the facts on both sides are considered, While it may never be answered conclusively, the available evidence strongly suggests that . . .

Planning Your Essay

Introduction.

(1) Recap the event

(2) Explain the historical question

(3) Why people disagreed

(4) Your answer to the historical question

↓

Supporting paragraph.

(1) Strongest reason

(2) Quote (Label **Q1** on document or note here)

(3) Explain

(4) Judge (Label **J1** on document or note here)

↓

Supporting paragraph.

(1) Strongest reason

(2) Quote (Label **Q1** on document or note here)

(3) Explain

(4) Judge (Label **J1** on document or note here)

↓

Rebuttal paragraph.

(1) Strongest reason that <u>goes against</u> you

(2) Quote (Label **Q3** on document or note here)

(3) Explain

(4) Judge and explain why you reject an opposing perspective (Label **J3** on document or note here).

↓

Conclusion. (1) Explain why someone should choose your perspective over another.

MY EVIDENCE-BASED ARGUMENT

CENTRAL HISTORICAL QUESTION: _____

_____

Based on your historical detective work, write your interpretation of the central historical question above. Cite evidence to support your answer.

SAMPLE ESSAY #1: THE BRITISH FIRED THE FIRST SHOT AT LEXINGTON GREEN

Many people don't know who fired the first shot at Lexington Green. Some say it was the Patriots. Some say it was the Redcoats. It wasn't clear. Based on my resources and research, I believe that the Redcoats started the Revolutionary war.

The Patriots gave more evidence why it wasn't them who shot the first shot. They told the judges, with explicit details, how the British attacked them first. The minutemen explained that about 5 o'clock in the morning, they were leaving. While their backs were turned on the British troops, the British attacked them. This is very convincing because they lived in very religious times, so if someone swore on a bible to the judge, they were telling the truth.

The Patriots claim that they were fired on while their backs were turned to the Redcoats. They were the ones who were killed and wounded. If they fired first the Redcoats would have been killed or wounded. The Patriots actually had 33 more witnesses than the Redcoats so this is actually more believable.

Lieutenant Barker wrote in his diary right after the attack. He may have written lies about what had taken place. Barker had stated that he saw a large group of people at Lexington Green and that they had started shooting at his troops but I don't believe him. The Minutemen said they didn't show up at Lexington until they heard their drumbeat. Even when they did, not everyone was there at the same time, as opposed to what was stated in document 1.

These are the reasons that led me to think that the British shot the first shot. The minutemen gave more evidence why it wasn't them who shot first. And Barker does not back up his statement that the Patriots were firing on his troops first. So it must have been the British who shot first because they had to bring the colony back under their control.

SAMPLE ESSAY #2: THE MINUTEMEN FIRED THE FIRST SHOT AT LEXINGTON GREEN

Who fired the first shot at Lexington Green? Hmm maybe we will never know. Personally I think that the Colonists fired first. I say this for numerous reasons.

Barker said his men did not want to attack the Patriots. He wrote that, "On our coming near, they fired one or two shots." In other words, the minutemen were waiting for the British to arrive and started the fight. They also could have shot first because they were mad that the British kept making them pay taxes.

The Minutemen said earlier that they were expecting a war. They said, "Some of our group were making their way toward Lexington Green. Our men began to leave." But you don't walk home when the enemy is approaching. Barker said that his men rushed in on them, but his men only fired after the Minutemen fired one or two shots.

On the other hand, the Minutemen said, "To our knowledge not a gun was fired by any person in our group." But this was said by only 34 out of 300 Minutemen who swore that the British fired first. So in the group, in all the confusion, someone else may have fired. The 34 were trying to protect themselves from British and knew who did but the others didn't know and refused to give a false statement.

For these reasons I say the minutemen fired the first shot. Their information is not accurate and the British have no reason to lie to themselves because the document is written from John Barker to the British. The British said they were prepared and when the Patriots fired they rushed into firing without any orders. The minutemen fired the first shot and caused the American Revolution.

SAMPLE ESSAY #2: SHAYS AND HIS FOLLOWERS WERE REBELS

Shays' Rebellion took place in Massachusetts in the late 1780s. Local men interfered with court trials that put some farmers and debtors in jail. In response, the state used soldiers to stop the mobs from closing courts. People disagreed about the government's right to send people to jail for not paying their taxes and whether Daniel Shays' actions were patriotic or not. After reading documents from two points of view, I believe Daniel Shays and his men were rebels.

Abigail Adams wrote a letter to Thomas Jefferson explaining why Daniel Shays and his men were no better than common criminals. She wrote "the Courts have been shut down in several counties." This is a problem because you can't just shut down the courts when you disagree with a ruling. At this time, the U.S. had just established itself as its own country with its own laws. If people ignored these laws, the new country couldn't succeed.

Moreover, Adams worried that Shays and his men were causing real harm to our young nation. She argued that, "this mob of rebels wants to weaken the foundation of our country, and destroy the whole fabric of our nation." Her concern makes sense because she wrote her letter just after the Revolutionary War when the United States government was weak. Since she knew so many people involved in the founding of the country she probably understood what the new nation needed to be successful.

Some may say that Daniel Shays and his men were fighting for freedom by protesting unfair taxes. As Mr. Gray complained, "Money from taxes and fees should be set aside to pay off the foreign debt." But Abigail Adams noticed that people were not paying taxes because they spent their money on foolish things, so they could not use it to support the government. If the people didn't have enough money to pay their taxes, they shouldn't be allowed to complain how the government spent its money.

While Shays had the support of many people, I believe he was a rebel. He misled people. In addition, he and his men shut down courts, stopping our government from being able to fully do its job. Although some leaders accused the government of mishandling taxes, in truth, most people were not paying them. When all of the facts on both sides are considered, Daniel Shays and his followers were working against the interests of our country.

SAMPLE ESSAY #1: SHAYS AND HIS MEN WERE FREEDOM FIGHTERS

Shays' Rebellion took place in Massachusetts, in the late 1780s. Local men interfered with court trials that put some farmers and debtors in jail. In response, the state used soldiers to stop the mobs from closing courts. People disagreed about the government's right to send people to jail for not paying their taxes and whether Daniel Shays' actions were patriotic or not. After reading information from two sides, I believe Daniel Shays and his men were freedom fighters.

Daniel Gray's speech gave many reasons why people started to rebel against the government. One reason was, "people who have stepped up to demand rights for themselves and others are likely to be put in jail." So, the American government was acting just like England before the Revolutionary War. This is convincing because putting a person in jail simply for protesting is "unlawful punishment."

Another reason why these men seem like freedom fighters is that Daniel Shays and his men were protesting unfair taxes. The government was using tax money to help "the rich get richer." In other words, the nation did not pay off foreign debt or solve the country's problems. Daniel Gray's speech about the reasons for Shays' actions is reliable. Gray probably had a good idea of what was going on because he gave his speech in the same region and time period as these events happened.

On the other hand, Abigail Adams thinks Shays and his men are rebels. She believes that they want "to weaken the foundation of our country and destroy the fabric of our new nation." Her quote shows that she thinks America would be hurt by unrest, or quarrels, of any kind. But there is a problem with her thinking because Shays was not trying to weaken the country at all. He saw the problems of the new nation and wanted to strengthen the government by using taxes to pay off the national debt.

Daniel Shays and the men who followed him were true freedom fighters. They protested unfair punishment for poor farmers who landed in jail for unlawful reasons. They did not like the way the government wanted to use its tax money. While Abigail Adams thought Shays was only stirring up trouble, he was really trying to end unjust laws. In sum, Shays and his followers wanted to make our new country a nation to believe in.

FIGURE A.10. Reflection Guide, Front

Your Purpose: Convince your reader that your argument is the strongest and most convincing.
Your Audience: Readers who are not familiar with the documents you used and the historical controversy you are addressing.
Directions: For each investigation, select 2 things you think you have done well and describe them in the boxes below. Then select 1 area that you would like to work on and describe how you are going to improve.

Goal (check each goal you completed below and explain your progress to the right) :	1 I am good at	I am working on	2 I am good at	I am working on	3 I am good at	I am working on
Introduction I used *H2W* to create four sentences (with all parts in my introduction).						
My introduction sets up the controversy well.						
Support ¶ 1 I gave a reason, a quote, explanation, and judgment to support my argument.						
My ideas are convincing and support my argument.						
Support ¶ 2 I gave a 2nd reason, a quote, explanation, and judgment to support my argument.						
My ideas are convincing and support my argument.						
Rebuttal ¶ I gave a reason against my view in support of the other side. I rejected a quote by explaining my judgment of a problem with the other side.						
My rebuttal rejects the opposing side well.						
Conclusion I compared both sides, explained why my view is best, and linked my ideas to the context.						
My conclusion ends with evidence that considers both sides but sticks to my point of view.						

FIGURE A.11. Reflection Guide, Back

Your Purpose: Convince your reader that your argument is the strongest and most convincing.

Your Audience: Readers who are not familiar with the documents you used and the historical controversy you are addressing.

Directions: For each investigation, select 2 things you think you have done well and describe them in the boxes below. Then select 1 area that you would like to work on and describe how you are going to improve.

Goal (check each goal you completed below and explain your progress to the right):	4		5		6	
	I am good at	I am working on	I am good at	I am working on	I am good at	I am working on
Introduction — I used H2W to create four sentences (with all parts in my introduction.						
My introduction sets up the controversy well.						
Support ¶1 — I gave a reason, a quote, explanation, and judgment to support my argument.						
My ideas are convincing and support my argument.						
Support ¶2 — I gave a 2nd reason, a quote, explanation, and judgment to support my argument.						
My ideas are convincing and support my argument.						
Rebuttal ¶ — I gave a reason against my view in support of the other side. I rejected a quote by explaining my judgment of a problem with the other side.						
My rebuttal rejects the opposing side well.						
Conclusion — I compared both sides explained why my view is best, and linked my ideas to the context.						
My conclusion ends with evidence that considers both sides but sticks to my point of view.						

FIGURE A.12. Analysis of Student Writing Worksheet (For Teachers)

Student Name: _____   Mod: _____   Reading Level: _____

Essay Component	Inv.#1 LEX.GR.	Inv.#2 SHAYS	Inv.#3 POLIT.PA.	Inv. #4 INDIAN	Inv. #5 ABOLIT.	Inv. #6A TX IND.	Inv. #6B MX WAR
Introduction							
Shares relevant background							
Explains why people disagree							
Answers the historical question							
Supporting Paragraph(s) (put more than one check if multiple)							
Supports the argument with evidence							
Explains how evidence supports arg.							
Judges the ideas, evidence, or source							
Rebuttal Paragraph							
Shares evidence for the opposing perspective							
Explains how evidence supports arg.							
Rebuts opposing evidence by explaining a problem with source quality or evidence.							
Conclusion							
Answers the historical question							
Compares the two documents							
Tells why student's interpretation or perspective is more convincing							

190

Optional Teaching Materials

FIGURE B.1. Sample Approach to Establishing a Learning Environment

Good detectives . . .

 …are focused on learning.

 …cooperate with their partners and teacher.

 …keep others from getting off track.

 …think about evaluating and using evidence.

FIGURE B.2. Structured Academic Controversy Directions

Historical Question: _____

_____

_____

_____

Side A   Side B

_____   _____

_____   _____

_____   _____

I. Form groups of four. Within each group, assign two students to prepare Side A and two students to prepare Side B.

II. Partners prepare Side A or Side B

    a. Find evidence that supports their assigned side of the argument. Craft position.

III. Position presentation

    a. Side A presents the evidence from the texts that support their assigned position.

    b. Side B restates to Side A's satisfaction.

    c. Side B presents the evidence from the texts that support their assigned position.

    d. Side A restates to Side B's satisfaction.

IV. Consensus-building

    a. Abandon roles/sides.

    b. Build consensus regarding the question (or at least clarify where differences lie), using supporting evidence.

These directions and the note-taking sheet are adapted from S. Wineburg, D. Martin, & C. Monte-Sano. *Reading Like a Historian* (New York: Teachers College Press, 2011), 45–47.

FIGURE B.3. Structured Academic Controversy Notes

1. Gather the evidence for one position, present it, and take notes on evidence presented for the alternate position.

	Evidence supporting the position that	Evidence supporting the position that
	_____ (Side A).	_____ (Side B).
Source 1 Author/ date:		
Source 2 Author/ date:		

2. After each pair has presented their evidence, discuss which evidence is most convincing.
   - Convincing evidence: (write out quotation and where it came from)
   - What is convincing about this evidence?
   - Unconvincing evidence: (write out quotation and where it came from)
   - What makes this evidence unconvincing?

3. What was the best way to free slaves in the United States before the Civil War: nonviolence or more aggressive action? Explain which position is best supported by the evidence.

FIGURE B.4. Sample Vocabulary Supports

SHAY'S REBELLION VOCABULARY PREVIEW

DOCUMENT A

taxing heavily	To make people pay a lot of money to the government.
petitioning	Asking for help or for something from the government.
debt	Money you have to pay or you owe.
imprisonment	Going to jail
credit	The extra money you have left over after spending.

FIGURE B.5. Sample Activity to Introduce Interpretation, Evidence, and Perspective*

FOOD FIGHT MYSTERY

Let's pretend that 3 days ago, there was a huge food fight in the cafeteria. The principal wants to know *who started the fight.* Whoever started the fight will receive 10 days of out-of-school suspension. The administrative team has narrowed down their search to two possible culprits. The team has just looked at statements from different sources to uncover the instigator. Unfortunately, the stories are different.

Discuss with a partner and take notes:

Why might there be different stories about the same event?

Why might people see or remember the event differently?

Below is a list of people who wrote statements (or, authors). Look at the list of authors.
  1. The teacher on lunch duty at the time of the fight.
  2. The two students who have been accused of starting the fight.
  3. A student who was not involved in the fight, but sat at the table where the fight began.
  4. The school administrator on lunch duty at the time.
  5. A student who was involved in the fight, and who is best friends with one of the accused culprits.

Discuss with a partner and take notes:

How might each statement differ and why?

Which statement might be most trustworthy? Why?

*We are indebted to Denise Meadows Miles for putting this "mystery" together.

Assessing Student Progress

FIGURE C.1. Pretest and Posttest Materials

COVER

Name: _____ Date: _____

Teacher: _____ Mod: _____

Were African Americans free after the Civil War?

Directions: Read the documents and develop an argument that considers both sides of the issue in response to the question: Were African Americans free after the Civil War?

Use evidence from the documents to support your argument.

Remember what you know about reading and writing with documents.

Background: Reconstruction was the period of time after the Civil War between the North and the South. During Reconstruction, former slaves discovered new rights. Many of them went to school and church for the first time during Reconstruction. Some people did not want former slaves to have the same rights as White people. These people tried to stop former slaves from attending school and church. In these documents, the authors explain what it was like for some former slaves who wanted to go to school and church.

You may use this page as you prepare your essay.

FIGURE C.1. Pretest and Posttest Materials, Continued

TEST A MATERIALS

Forten's Article

Charlotte Forten was an African American from the North who went to the Sea Islands in South Carolina at the end of the Civil War to teach newly freed slaves. Slaves in the Sea Islands were freed and could go to school and work for money earlier than in the rest of the South.

"Life on the Sea Islands" from *The Atlantic Monthly*

The first day at school was rather difficult. Most of my children were very small and restless. Some were too young to learn the alphabet. These little ones were brought to school because the older children had to take care of them and could not come without them. After some days, I found little difficulty in managing and quieting the tiniest and most restless spirits.

I never before saw children so eager to learn, although I had several years' experience in Northern schools. Coming to school is a constant delight to them. They come here as other children go to play. The older ones work in the fields for money from early morning until 11:00 or 12:00, during the summer. Then they come into school, after their hard work in the hot sun, as bright and as excited to learn as ever.

The majority of students learn very quickly. Many of the grown people want to learn how to read. It is wonderful how a people who have been so long crushed to the earth can have so great a desire for knowledge, and such an ability for reaching it. One cannot believe that the arrogant English race, after centuries of such an experience as these people have had, would do any better. And I get angry at those in the North and the South who criticize the colored race as inferior while they themselves use every means in their power to crush and shame them, denying them every right and privilege, closing every path to improvement.

Daily the long-oppressed people of these islands are demonstrating their capacity for improvement in learning and labor. What they have accomplished in one short year exceeds our greatest expectations.
by Charlotte Forten
May & June 1864

Source: Excerpt adapted from Charlotte Forten's article in The Atlantic Monthly, "Life on the Sea Islands," May and June, 1864.

FIGURE C.1. Pretest and Posttest Materials, Continued

TEST A MATERIALS

Hamilton's letter

Captain Hamilton, a Northerner in the U.S. Army, was posted in Florida after the Civil War. Here, Hamilton writes to the U.S. Army officer in charge of organizing and supporting soldiers about events at a school in the region where he is posted.

Florida, 1866

Dear Sir:

The night school has been frequently disturbed. One evening a mob called the teacher out of the schoolhouse. When the teacher showed himself, he was faced with four revolvers, and a man with a threatening expression of shooting him, if he did not promise to quit, and close the school.

The freedmen, who were now able to protect themselves, came to his aid promptly and the mob broke up.

About the 18th or 19th of the month, I was absent when an alarming riot took place at the school. The same mob threatened to destroy the school that night. The freedmen, learning this, gathered at the school in self-defense.

I understand that not less than forty colored men armed to protect themselves, but since their plans became known to the mob, the rowdy men only moved about in small groups, and were wise enough to avoid a collision.

[Hamilton's signature]

Source: Excerpt adapted from a letter written by Captain C. M. Hamilton in 1866 to the Office of the Adjutant General in Washington, D.C.

FIGURE C.1. Pretest and Posttest Materials, Continued

TEST B MATERIALS

Lynch's Letter

Lynch was an African American minister from Baltimore who worked as a missionary and teacher in Savannah, Georgia, during Reconstruction.

Savannah, January 4, 1865

My Dear Sir:

I have been here for some days. The lack of supplies and the shortage of jobs—all these had the effect of causing our people to stand on the threshold of freedom like the rescued passenger of a ship on a barren sea-shore, wet and shivering with the cold blast of the storm. They needed encouragement, advice, and strength to go forward and act like free men.

I am happy to say their confidence has been growing every day and they seem to lose that fear which slavery had made a second nature. There are so many very intelligent colored persons in Savannah. We have been holding large meetings of the colored citizens. The interest has been great, and the promise of good being done is bright.

The Government has given us three large buildings:

1."Bryant's Negro Mart" (reads the sign over the door). It is a large three-story brick building. We are going to use it for a school.

2. The Stiles house on Farm Street, formerly used as a rebel hospital. We will also use it for school purposes.

3. A large three-story brick building on the lot next-door for a hospital for freedmen.

We have organized an Association called the Savannah Educational Association. Members are made up of the pastors and members of the colored churches. There are five very large colored churches in this city; four of them will seat one thousand persons each. Three have fine organs. That the colored people built such churches is astonishing. Hundreds of colored people are joining the Association.

We have talked to some of the most intelligent of the colored young men and women to find out their qualifications for teaching and selected nine. This makes use of the ability and intelligence held by the colored people, and gives them confidence and encouragement.

Refugees are continually coming in and filling up the city. Oh, how much books are needed! We could use right away a thousand spelling-books, if we had them.

James Lynch

Source: Excerpt adapted from a letter written by James Lynch to the New York Freedman's Relief Association, January 4, 1865, Savannah, Georgia.

FIGURE C.1. Pretest and Posttest Materials, Continued

TEST B MATERIALS

Letter from 24 African Americans

In 1867, Congress divided the South into five military districts to ensure rights for African Americans. In this letter, African Americans from one town write the commander of their military district to describe their complaints and ask for protection.

Calhoun, Georgia, August 25, 1867

General:

We the Colored people of the town of Calhoun desire to call your attention to the Situation that now exists.

On the 16th day of the month, we held a political meeting of the Union Republican Party. The Colored people of the County attended it all together. Since that time we seem to have earned the hatred and spite of people who did not agree with the opinions that we shared in that meeting.

We see the hatred of these people in several ways. Their first act was to deprive us of the privilege to worship any longer in their Church. We have found a church of our own. But, they threaten us if we hold meetings in it.

There have been houses broken open, windows smashed and doors broken down in the dead of the night, men rushing in, cursing and swearing and firing their Pistols inside the house. Colored men have been knocked down and beaten for no reason and yet the police do not notice it at all. We would open a school here, but are almost afraid to do so since we have no protection for life or limb.

We wish to do right, obey the Laws and live in peace and quiet. But when we are attacked at the midnight hour, our lives threatened and the Laws fail to protect or help us, the only thing we can do is defend ourselves. Yet we wish to avoid all such conflicts.

We respectfully ask that a few soldiers be sent here. We believe it is the only way we can live in peace until the Election this fall.

[Twenty-four signatures]

Source: Excerpt adapted from a letter written by 24 African Americans from Calhoun, Georgia, to the commander of the Third Military District, August 25, 1867.

FIGURE C.2. Tamia's Pretest

> **WERE AFRICAN AMERICANS FREE AFTER THE CIVIL WAR?**
>
> **Directions**: Review the documents you read yesterday and develop an argument that considers both sides of the issue in response to the question: Were African Americans free after the Civil War? Use evidence from the documents to support your argument.
>
> Write your essay on the lined paper.

What I think is that African Americans where Free. after civil war because the slaves got rediscover-ed or should I say discovered new rights After the Civil war. Like in one document I guess there was a man who was free and he opened up a school for slaves ann some mobs or robberies of an different race had heard about the school and was trying to shut it down. So he stood up and now that he stood up now colored boys or men can go. Also in an document alot of colored children can go to school and church with being treated the same way and they can be treated equal.

Our people stood up and fought in the civil war so they can be treated right. The man was tired of the mobs so he stood up. like For example, Rosa parks they wanted her to move in the back of the bus she was tired and refused too so she was tired of being treated unfair. Now when we get on the bus we can sit wherever. so after civil war since they was tired they fought in civil war and now have equal rights.

FIGURE C.3. Tamia's Posttest

WERE AFRICAN AMERICANS FREE AFTER THE CIVIL WAR?

Directions: Review the documents you read yesterday and develop an argument that considers both sides of the issue in response to the question: Were African Americans free after the Civil War? Use evidence from the documents to support your argument.

Write your essay on the lined paper.

NO, african Americans were not free after the Civil War. I say that because in the letter from 24 african Americans they may have been free but they still was getting robbed, windows smashed and doors broken down in the night time. Pistols being fired. colored men been getting beaten for no reason and the police acting like nothing was going on say they had to defend themselves. So I disagree african Americans were not free after civil war. In lynch's letter I agree because he was an african american who was free. I say that because he said that he was there for some days and said the things that happen. He says that at first the african americans was scared but each and everyday they have gained there confidence has grown. The slaves had lost there fear. So he must have been an slave and must have gone through alot so I say yes they were free after world war I agree.

FIGURE C.4. Aaron's Pretest

WERE AFRICAN AMERICANS FREE AFTER THE CIVIL WAR?

Directions: Review the documents you read yesterday and develop an argument that considers both sides of the issue in response to the question: Were African Americans free after the Civil War? Use evidence from the documents to support your argument.

Write your essay on the lined paper.

After the civil African americans were free. Many people think that African-Americans, were not free because there was still very bad segregation. But they were free because now they had a lot more privigies. They were allowed to go to church, to learn and go to school, and to to do lots of other things. And they could do all of this without haveing the anxiety of a slave master or slave-owner trying to find them so they can be whipped and killed.

FIGURE C.5. Aaron's Posttest

WERE AFRICAN AMERICANS FREE AFTER THE CIVIL WAR?

Directions: Review the documents you read yesterday and develop an argument that considers both sides of the issue in response to the question: Were African Americans free after the Civil War? Use evidence from the documents to support your argument.

Write your essay on the lined paper.

In 1865 & 1867 two letters were written about the freedom of coloreds in georgia. The historical question is were blacks free after the civil war? People disagreed because some thought blacks were free and others did not. I personally think coloreds were not free after the civil war.

The strongest reason I think blacks were not free after the civil war is they were not allowed simple rights like being able to go to church. A quote that supports this says "Their first act was to deprive us of the priviladge to worship any longer in their church. We have found a church of our own but they threaten us if we hold meetings in it. This supports my idea that blacks were not free after the civil war because they did not even have simple constitutional rights like freedom of religion. this information was conving to me because the authors used convincing facts and examples.

FIGURE C.5. Aaron's Posttest, Continued

The second strongest reason I think blacks were not free after the civil war is, they did not have government protection like non-colored people. A quote that supports this says "colored men have been knoked down and beaten for no reason and yet the police do not notice it at all". This supports by idea because it shows police would not protect blacks from being beaten or even killed. This information was convincing to me because of my prior knowlage.

On the other hand people might say blacks were free after the civil war because they were allowed to go to school and use hospitals. A quote that supports this says "The government have has given us three buildings, 2 we intend to use for schools". This supports my idea because before the civil war blacks were not even allowed to go to school. This information may have been convincing to the other side because, It was written by a minister.

After all of the facts on both sides are considered I still think blacks were not free after the civil war.

Notes

Chapter 1

1. Specifically, the Common Core State Standards set out for English Language Arts and Literacy in History/Social Studies, Science, and Technical Subjects highlight those skills most relevant to our work as social studies educators. See Council of Chief State School Officers (2010).

2. A group of state education agencies, social studies, and disciplinary organizations collaborated to create the C3 Framework to provide states with voluntary guidance for upgrading existing social studies standards; it was published by the National Council for the Social Studies (NCSS) in August 2013. You can access the C3 Framework at http://www.socialstudies.org/c3.

3. The following researchers share evidence of this approach: Bain, "Rounding Up Unusual Suspects," 2080-2114; Kiuhara, Graham, and Hawken,"Teaching Writing," 136.

4. Compare to Paxton, "Influence of Author Visibility," 197–248.

5. This includes major aspects of Dimensions 1–4 of the C3 Framework: asking questions, applying disciplinary concepts, evaluating sources and using evidence, and communicating conclusions.

6. For other examples of this approach see Bain, "They Thought the World Was Flat?," 179–213; Reisman, "'Document-Based Lesson,'" 233–264; VanSledright, *In Search of America's Past*.

7. A grant from the Institute of Education Sciences, U.S. Department of Education (Grant No. R305A090153) to the University of Maryland funded this project. We have 3 years of data with 2,500 8th-graders per year that support claims about the effectiveness of this curriculum.

8. These are key historical concepts outlined in Dimension 2: Applying Disciplinary Tools and Concepts (NCSS, C3 Framework, pp. 45–59).

9. For more on adapting historical documents, see Wineburg and Martin, "Tampering with History," 212–216. Given that one-third of the students we encountered read 2 or more years below grade level, we used Lexile scores to adapt primary sources to a 6th-grade level while still highlighting controversial or complex ideas for more advanced readers.

10. We share our research findings more fully in recent papers. For example, see De La Paz, Felton, Croninger, and Monte-Sano, "Developing Historical Reading."

11. This historical question and the primary sources we use were constructed as part of the Amherst History Project in the 1960s (see Brown, 1996, for more on this project); it was adapted by Sam Wineburg in his seminal work on identifying expert and novice ways of historical reading and thinking (e.g., Wineburg, 2001). Wineburg, Martin, and Monte-Sano (2011) feature this historical question, the two sources, and supporting materials in *Reading Like a Historian: Teaching Literacy in Middle and High School Classrooms*.

12. To consider this idea further, read Wineburg and Schneider, "Bloom's Taxonomy," 56–61.

13. In *Writing Standards for Literacy in History/Social Studies, Science, and Technical Subjects 6–12*, the very first goal states that students in grades 6–8 will "write arguments focused on discipline-specific content" CCSSO (*Common Core*, p. 64).

14. For a great introduction to this concept, see Holt, *Thinking Historically*.

15. Wineburg, *Historical Thinking*.

16. CCSSO, *Common Core*, 61.

17. CCSSO, *Common Core*, 39. The Common Core's focus on "informational texts" is most similar to historical texts, but in the context of history the term is misleading. Disciplinary literacy in history requires more than simply drawing information out of a text, something the new standards recognize as well. While historical texts must be included alongside informational texts in standard textbooks, they should have attributes that distinguish them. To use an obvious example, authors of historical texts are generally not around to explain what they wrote. Instead, historical texts are the residue of long-ago interactions or situations that must be resurrected if we are to understand them. Compared to an easily replicated lab experiment, historical texts have been crafted in a different time and place that cannot be re-created. We must imagine what life was like "back then" if we are to make sense of what a long-dead author meant to say. As a result, historical reading is as much about the subtext embedded in the artifact as it is the literal meaning of written words. In other words, if readers of history pay attention only to the information in a text, they miss a great deal of its historical meaning and significance.

Page 31 of the Common Core defines informational text for grades K–5 as secondary sources used in place of textbooks from which students extract information. Although this definition broadens to include arguments and opinion pieces for grades 6–12, the shift is a subtle one and may not adequately highlight the usefulness of historical texts for skilled readers. For example, in 1963 Dr. Martin Luther King Jr. responded to White clergymen who wanted racial segregation to be resolved in the courts, not through public protest. In his "Letter from a Birmingham Jail," Dr. King presents a rationale for nonviolent protest, using evidence to support how he thinks the civil rights movement should be conducted. Calling such historic documents "informational text" classifies them as inert information rather than provocative messages that lead students to engage with the ideas presented, understanding that by doing so, they are taking part in a historic national conversation.

18. See NCSS, *C3 Framework*, 14, for an overview of the C3 Framework, or pp. 45–49 for Dimension 2-History (in particular, the disciplinary concepts and tools this curriculum highlights include context, perspectives, historical sources and evidence, and argumentation), pp. 52–53 for Dimension 3, and pp. 57–59 for Dimension 4.

19. For more on this idea, see Moje, "Foregrounding the Disciplines," 96–107.

20. For example, see Hynd, Holschuh, and Hubbard, "Thinking Like a Historian," 141–176.

21. Paxton, "Influence of Author Visibility," 197–248.

22. See Wineburg and Martin, "Tampering with History," 212–216.

23. Collins, Brown, and Holum, "Cognitive Apprenticeship," 6–11, 28–46. For an adaptation of this model see Harris and Graham, "Self-Regulated Strategy Development," 277–309.

Chapter 2

1. Cf. Collins, Brown, and Holum, "Cognitive Apprenticeship," 6–11, 28–46.

2. Brown and Campione, "Psychological Theory," 289–325; Palincsar and Brown, "Reciprocal Teaching," 117–175.

3. Collins, Brown, and Holum, "Cognitive Apprenticeship," 6–11, 28–46.

4. Harris and Graham, "Self-Regulated Strategy Development," 277–309.

5. Studies of students with high-incidence disabilities primarily involve students with LD, but demonstrate the value of SRSD with those identified with ADHD, autism spectrum, and behavior disorders.

6. Harris and Graham's six types of self-regulation may be useful for students with disabilities. Self-regulation ranges from *problem definition*, to the *focusing of attention*, *coping*, *self-evaluation*, *self-control*, and *strategy implementation*, e.g., "the first step in writing an essays is to understand and evaluate historical evidence."

7. Engle and Conant, "Guiding Principles," 399–483.

8. For examples, see De La Paz, "Effects of Historical Reasoning Instruction," 137–156; De La Paz and Felton, "Reading and Writing," 174–192.

9. We adapted previous work from Fuchs and Fuchs to develop our "Good Detectives" poster. See Fuchs et al., "Peer-Assisted Learning Strategies," 174–206.

10. Fuchs and Fuchs' *Peer-Assisted Learning Strategy* (http://kc.vanderbilt.edu/pals/) may be helpful for students who are not able to decode text independently. See Fuchs, Fuchs, Mathes, and Simmons, "Peer-Assisted Learning Strategies: Making Classrooms More Responsive to Diversity," 174–206 or see http://www.promisingpractices.net/program.asp?programid=143 for some background.

11. Graham, Harris, and Hebert, *Informing Writing*.

12. Popham, "What's Wrong," 72–75.

13. Newkirk, "Mania for Rubrics," 41.

14. Ball and Cohen, "Developing Practice," 3–31.

Chapter 3

1. The Amherst Project on American History originally developed curriculum materials centered on this question and these primary sources, among others, in the 1960s. For more on this foundational work see Brown, "Learning How to Learn," 267–273. Sam Wineburg adapted and used this question and two of the same primary sources that we use in his seminal research on historical sensemaking and reading. See Wineburg, "Historical problem solving: A study of the cognitive processes used in the evaluation of documentary and pictorial evidence," *Journal of Educational Psychology, 83*(1), 73–87, 1991. Published by the American Psychological Association. Reprinted and adapted with permission.

2. For this quote and a description of the competition between the towns, see pp. 17–18 of Wineburg, Martin, and Monte-Sano, *Reading Like a Historian*.

3. For more on her interpretation, see Lepore, "Paul Revere's Ride." Although people remember Revere, some mistake his role—see Sarah Palin's comments about warning the British in Warner, "Lexington and Concord."

4. See the following for more on the events that immediately followed the Battle of Lexington and Concord: Allen, "Lexington and Concord;" Warner, "Lexington and Concord;" Worcester Polytechnic Institute, "Lexington and Concord."

5. For additional resources on the American Revolution see the Library of Congress's in-depth narrative overview of the Revolutionary time period (1763–1783), including links to dozens of relevant primary sources to extend students' thinking, at http://www.loc.gov/teachers/classroommaterials/presentationsandactivities/presentations/timeline/amrev/. PBS has a website and documentary entitled, *Liberty! The*

American Revolution, which provides a wealth of resources: http://www.pbs.org/ktca/liberty/. Steven Mintz and Sara McNeil's Digital History includes a range of resources on this time period: http://www.digitalhistory.uh.edu/era.cfm?eraID=3&smtID=1. For additional primary sources to use in the Battle of Lexington inquiry, see Wineburg, Martin, and Monte-Sano, *Reading Like a Historian*. See also Steven Mintz and Sara McNeil's "exploration" at Digital History: http://www.digitalhistory.uh.edu/active_learning/explorations/revolution/revolution_battles.cfm.

6. For more information about the Proclamation of 1763 and resources for teaching it, see http://teachinghistory.org/history-content/ask-a-historian/25374. Scholars have increasingly emphasized the American Indian perspective on the Seven Years' War. For more on this perspective, see Anderson, *Crucible of War*; Dowd, *A Spirited Resistance*.

7. See Worcester Polytechnic Institute's description of events immediately preceding the deployment of British troops as well as a catalogue of key players involved at http://www.wpi.edu/academics/military/lexcon.html.

8. This quotation comes from a Williamsburg, VA, Committee of Correspondence, found at http://nationalhumanitiescenter.org/pds/makingrev/crisis/text8/vacommrlexingtonconcord.pdf. To investigate colonists' reactions further, see the complete site housed at the National Humanities Center, http://nationalhumanitiescenter.org/pds/makingrev/crisis/text8/text8read.htm.

9. Birnbaum, *Red Dawn at Lexington*, vii.

10. Ibid., vii–viii.

11. See Galvin, *The Minute Men*, 5.

12. See Fischer, *Paul Revere's Ride*, xv.

13. Ibid.

14. A transcript of the original Barker diary can be found at the Library of Congress (see pp. 398-400), http://memory.loc.gov/cgi-bin/query/r?ammem/ncps:@field(DOCID+@lit(ABK2934-0039-99)) or at Cornell's digital library, http://digital.library.cornell.edu/cgi/t/text/pageviewer-idx?c=atla;cc=atla;rgn=full%20text;idno=atla0039-4;didno=atla0039-4;view=image;seq=00404;node=atla0039-4%3A1. A transcript of the original Minutemen Testimony can be found at Northern Illinois Library, http://lincoln.lib.niu.edu/cgi-bin/amarch/getdoc.pl?/var/lib/philologic/databases/amarch/.2475.

15. For more on these ideas see Jitendra and Gajria, "Main Idea and Summarization," 198–218.

16. This differs slightly from Wineburg's (2001) characterization of sourcing, which includes looking at the author, author's motivation, and type of document as well as the date the author created the document. Here we leave consideration of the date for contextualization (step A of *IREAD*) to let students attend to both sets of information and use the information to draw inferences about the meaning and reliability of the document.

17. For the full study see Kiuhara, Graham, and Hawken, "Teaching Writing," 136–160.

18. For more on these ideas see Wineburg, *Historical Thinking*.

Chapter 4

1. See Cogliano, *Revolutionary America*.

2. For more on this see Leonard Richards, *Shays's Rebellion*.

3. Nash discusses this idea in Nash, *The Unknown American Revolution*.

4. To access an image of the original, go to http://shaysrebellion.stcc.edu/shaysapp/artifactPage.do?shortName=gazette_crostick6jun87&page=.

5. You can find this primary source at http://lcweb2.loc.gov/ammem/gwhtml/gwhome.html, The George Washington Papers at the Library of Congress, 1741–1799.

6. Franklin in a letter to Governor Bowdoin, March 6, 1787. You can find this primary source at http://memorialhall.mass.edu/collection/itempage.jsp?itemid=17456&img=0&level=advanced&transcription=1.

7. You can find this primary source at http://memorialhall.mass.edu/collection/itempage.jsp?itemid=16484&img=0&level=advanced&transcription=1.

8. See Humphrey, *Revolutionary Era*.

9. You can find this primary source at the Library of Congress, Thomas Jefferson to Colonel Edward Carrington, January 16, 1787, Thomas Jefferson Papers, Series 1, General Correspondence.

10. You can find this primary source at the Library of Congress, Thomas Jefferson to James Madison, January 30, 1787, Thomas Jefferson Papers, Series 1, General Correspondence. Or go to http://shaysrebellion.stcc.edu/shaysapp/people/home.do for excerpts from it.

11. Colton's history, "'. . . Unwilling to Stain the Land . . .': Conflict and Ambivalence in Shays' Rebellion" (2007), can be found by searching "Shays Rebellion" at http://www.nps.gov/spar/index.htm. Also, Leonard Richards (2002) explains the Regulators' perspective in detail and their intent to modify the existing government.

12. Cogliano takes this view in Cogliano, *Revolutionary America*.

13. See Szatmary, *Shays' Rebellion*, 128.

14. For more on this idea, see Colton, "Shays' Rebellion."

15. Colton reports this conversation in Colton, "Shays' Rebellion," 13.

16. For a transcript of the original text of Gray's speech, go to http://shaysrebellion.stcc.edu/shaysapp/artifact_trans.do?shortName=gazette_dg27dec86&page. For the original text and a transcript of Abigail Adams's letter, go to: http://myloc.gov/Exhibitions/creatingtheus/Constitution/RoadtotheConstitution/ExhibitObjects/OpinionofRevoltinMassachusetts.aspx.

Chapter 5

1. For example, the Virginia and Kentucky Resolutions proposed that states nullify laws, but soon after that the Supreme Court asserted its right to declare laws unconstitutional.

2. Our Documents includes an original image of one of the Acts and full transcripts of the Alien, Alien Enemies, and Sedition Acts. Go to http://www.ourdocuments.gov/doc.php?flash=true&doc=16. The Avalon Project at Yale includes full transcripts of the Alien and the Sedition Acts as well as the Virginia and Kentucky Resolutions. Go to http://avalon.law.yale.edu/subject_menus/alsedact.asp. The full text of all four acts can be found at the Library of Congress, http://www.loc.gov/rr/program/bib/ourdocs/Alien.html. If you work with stronger readers or if you have more time, these documents offer a chance to compare the actual Acts to the U.S. Constitution directly as well as a chance to read the original texts.

3. The National Archives presents a series of documents focused on the case of Thomas Cooper, a lawyer and newspaper editor convicted under the Sedition Act for publishing a broadside that criticized President John Adams. This is a nice opportunity to understand the Sedition Act and its impact as well as to consider the concept of freedom of the press. Go to http://www.archives.gov/education/lessons/sedition-case.

4. For example, see Gragg, "Order vs. Liberty," 24–28, 56–59.

5. See Miller, *Crisis in Freedom*.

6. See Taylor, "Alien and Sedition Acts," 63–76.

7. The Library of Congress houses additional historical sources that could complement this investigation and provide extensions for students who can handle additional commentary, including the opposition of one Virginia Congressman, http://www.myloc.gov/Exhibitions/creatingtheus/BillofRights/FormationofPoliticalParties/Ex-

hibitObjects/CongressmanDeclares.aspx; a petition from Virginia, http://www.myloc.gov/Exhibitions/creatingtheus/BillofRights/FormationofPoliticalParties/ExhibitObjects/OppositiontoAlienandSeditionActs2.aspx; a petition from New York, http://www.myloc.gov/Exhibitions/creatingtheus/BillofRights/FormationofPoliticalParties/ExhibitObjects/OppositiontoAlienandSeditionActs2.aspx; and a statement from Virginia legislators who supported the Acts and opposed the Virginia Resolution, http://www.myloc.gov/Exhibitions/creatingtheus/BillofRights/FormationofPoliticalParties/ExhibitObjects/VindicationofConstitutionalityofAlienandSeditionLaws.aspx.

8. For more on Blackstone and his influence see Taylor, "Alien and Sedition Acts," 63–76.

9. See Taylor, "Alien and Sedition Acts," 70–71.

10. See Miller, *Crisis in Freedom*, 168.

11. See Elkins and McKitrick, *Age of Federalism*, 700.

12. For example, Taylor, "Alien and Sedition Acts," 63–76.

13. This quote is in 4th paragraph from the bottom of Lynch's online article found at http://www.history.org/foundation/journal/winter07/alien.cfm.

14. Rael, *Reading, Writing, and Researching*.

15. For the original Kentucky Resolution, see http://memory.loc.gov/cgi-bin/ampage?collId=icufaw&fileName=bmc0105/icufawbmc0105.db&recNum=0&itemLink=r?ammem/fawbib:@field(DOCID+@lit(bmc0105. For a transcript of the original Massachusetts Response, see http://memory.loc.gov/cgi-bin/ampage?collId=lled&fileName=004/lled004.db&recNum=544.

16. For more on efforts to teach contextualization, see Nokes, Dole, and Hacker, "Teaching High School Students," 492–504; Reisman, "Reading Like a Historian," 86–112.

17. The field of argumentation that concerns itself with the analysis of elements of argument against disciplinary standards would be informal logic. See, for example, Toulmin, *The Uses of Argument*.

18. See Chambliss and Murphy, "Fourth and Fifth Graders," 91–115.

19. See Young and Leinhardt, "Writing from Primary Documents," 25–68.

20. See Wineburg and Martin, "Tampering with History," 214.

Chapter 6

1. For a description of John Ross, see Remini, *Andrew Jackson*.

2. For example, see Wallace, *The Long, Bitter Trail*.

3. For all Presidential State of the Union Addresses and Annual Messages, go to The American Presidency Project at http://www.presidency.ucsb.edu/sou.php. For this specific Address see http://www.presidency.ucsb.edu/ws/index.php?pid=29443.

4. For Jefferson's 1807 and 1808 Annual Message, see the following urls: http://www.presidency.ucsb.edu/ws/index.php?pid=29449 and http://www.presidency.ucsb.edu/ws/index.php?pid=29450.

5. Satz, *American Indian Policy*, 2.

6. Theda Perdue is an expert on the Cherokee. For an example of her work see Perdue, "The Conflict Within," 55–74.

7. For a more complete explanation of Cherokee women, see Perdue and Green, *The Cherokee Removal*.

8. See http://digital.library.okstate.edu/Kappler/Vol2/treaties/Che0288.htm for the 1828 treaty.

9. For resources on this topic see the PBS website, "Indian Removal, 1814–1858," at http://www.pbs.org/wgbh/aia/part4/4p2959.html.

10. Remini, *Andrew Jackson*, 160.

11. Jackson specifically said the following in his 1829 Annual Message to Congress: "Surrounded by the whites with their arts of civilization, which by destroying the resources of the savage doom him to weakness and decay, the fate of the Mohegan, the Narragansett, and the Delaware is fast over-taking the Choctaw, the Cherokee, and the Creek. That this fate surely awaits them if they remain within the limits of the States does not admit of a doubt. Humanity and national honor demand that every effort should be made to avert so great a calamity. . . . I suggest for your consideration the propriety of setting apart an ample district west of the Mississippi, and without the limits of any State or Territory now formed, to be guaranteed to the Indian tribes as long as they shall occupy it, each tribe having a distinct control over the portion designated for its use. There they may be secured in the enjoyment of governments of their own choice, subject to no other control from the United States than such as may be necessary to preserve peace on the frontier and between the several tribes. There the benevolent may endeavor to teach them the arts of civilization, and, by promoting union and harmony among them, to raise up an interesting commonwealth, destined to perpetuate the race and to attest the humanity and justice of this Government . . . This emigration should be voluntary, for it would be as cruel as unjust to compel the aborigines to abandon the graves of their fathers and seek a home in a distant land. But they should be distinctly informed that if they remain within the limits of the States they must be subject to their laws." For the complete speech go to http://www.presidency.ucsb.edu/ws/index.php?pid=29471.

12. Wallace, *The Long, Bitter Trail*, 56.

13. For student-friendly examples, see Ghere, "Indian Removal," 32–37.

14. Wishart, "Evidence of Surplus Production," 120–138.

15. Perdue, "The Conflict Within," 62.

16. Ibid., 66–67.

17. Remini, *Andrew Jackson*, 267.

18. Perdue, "The Conflict Within," 70.

19. See Remini, *Andrew Jackson*, 254–257, for an overview of these cases.

20. You can find a transcript of the original Cherokee Letter at http://dig.lib.niu.edu/teachers/lesson5-groupd.html—see the "Memorial of the Cherokee Indians," *Niles' Weekly Register* 38, no. 3, pp 53–54. We found the Boudinot Pamphlet in a book he authored and published in response to public attacks on the Treaty Party. The book is entitled *Letters and Other Papers Relating to Cherokee Affairs: Being a Reply to Sundry Publication Authorized by John Ross.* An electronic transcript is housed at the University of Georgia's Digital Library; see "Resolutions" dated October 2, 1832, pp. 11–13, http://neptune3.galib.uga.edu/ssp/cgi-bin/tei-natamer-idx.pl?sessionid=7f000001&type=doc&tei2id=pam012.

21. Wineburg, *Historical Thinking*.

22. For more on the role of audience and purpose in teaching students writing, see Duke et al., "Teaching Genre," 34–39.

23. See "Things to Keep in Mind" in Chapter 8 for ideas about how to circulate and support students.

24. For the originals, see note #20. For additional materials, see the History Teaching Institute lesson materials on Indian Removal at the Ohio State University: http://hti.osu.edu/history-lesson-plans/united-states-history/indian-removal; see also Ghere, "Indian Removal," 32–37, for additional teaching resources and primary sources on this topic. Additional materials include the original Indian Removal Act at http://www.mtholyoke.edu/acad/intrel/removal.htm, primary sources that show the debate about the Indian Removal Act at http://lincoln.lib.niu.edu/teachers/lesson5-cherokee.html, Charles Kappler's seven-volume collection of laws and treaties regarding American

Indians over time, first compiled in 1904 and now available online at http://digital.library.okstate.edu/Kappler, or Early Recognized Treaties with American Indians, a digital project from the University of Nebraska–Lincoln focused on treaties before the U.S. government took the lead in making treaties at http://earlytreaties.unl.edu.

Chapter 7

1. This question asks about effectiveness—what strategy would be more likely or effective in freeing slaves? We initially used the phrase "best way" instead of "most effective way," but we found that our initial language was ambiguous and led to personal judgments. As with our other questions, there's no right answer.

2. Steven Mintz and Sara McNeil's Digital History includes tremendous resources focused on slavery and anti-slavery in U.S. history, including their textbook with background, collections of primary sources, images, film and music, and lessons. See http://www.digitalhistory.uh.edu/era.cfm?eraID=6&smtID=1, accessed July 2, 2013. PBS's *Africans in America* is another incredible resource on African American history, with a resource-rich website that accompanies the documentary. See http://www.pbs.org/wgbh/aia/home.html, accessed July 2, 2013.

3. Newman, *Transformation of American Abolitionism*.

4. Newman characterizes these abolitionists as the second wave of reformers.

5. Stewart offers a good explanation of moral 'suasion and how it changed from 1830 to 1860 in Stewart, *Abolitionist Politics*.

6. Teachers can extend this investigation with speeches and writings by Garrison and Douglass. Douglass' autobiography (*Narrative of the Life of Frederick Douglass, An American Slave*) is a fantastic read, although longer. Both leaders wrote countless speeches and articles published in Garrison's paper, *The Liberator* (see the third entry in the Library of Congress's African American Mosaic, http://www.loc.gov/exhibits/african/afam007.html), or Douglass' paper, *The North Star* (see American Treasures at the Library of Congress, http://www.loc.gov/exhibits/treasures/trr085.html). For example, on the first page of Garrison's first issue in 1831, he wrote, "I will not equivocate—I will not excuse—and I will not retreat a single inch—AND I WILL BE HEARD."

7. Newman, *Transformation of American Abolitionism*, 6.

8. For more on Kantrowitz's interpretation, see Kantrowitz, *More Than Freedom*.

9. Horton and Horton, *In Hope of Liberty*.

10. Stewart, *Abolitionist Politics*, 5.

11. See "Henry Highland Garnet" biography on the PBS site, *Africans in America*, accessed July 2, 2013, at http://www.pbs.org/wgbh/aia/part4/4p1537.html.

12. See Harrold, *Rise of Aggressive Abolitionism*, 1. Garrison's reaction to Garnet's speech in 1843 shows a shift in his thinking from 1829 when Garrison reacted quite negatively to David Walker's Appeal—a similar call for slaves to rebel against their masters. For the full speech see http://www.pbs.org/wgbh/aia/part4/4h2931t.html.

13. Harrold, *Rise of Aggressive Abolitionism*, 2.

14. Lovejoy was an abolitionist who was defending his new printing press against an anti-abolitionist mob. Lovejoy had had three printing presses destroyed by anti-abolitionist mobs before his murder.

15. Stewart, *Abolitionist Politics*, 21–22.

16. Although resistance in the 1840s was more militant than its origins, the immediatist camp did not resort to violence until the Fugitive Slave Act of 1850, when immediatists turned their attention to federal slave catchers. And yet not all immediatists were comfortable with or supported this turn. The violent undercurrent of abolitionism came to the fore in John Brown's raid on Harpers Ferry in 1859, an event that shocked many immediatists and fell outside their conception of how to resist slavery. (See more

in Stewart for these changes. He frames Garnet's Address as distinct from John Brown's tactics, as opposed to Harrold, who frames John Brown's raid as the culmination of addresses like Garnet's.)

17. Stewart, *Abolitionist Politics*, 4.

18. Harrold's concluding chapter describes changes in the abolitionist movement in the 1840s and 1850s. He argues that even John Brown focused on assisted escape in the early 1850s and explains his transition to more violent methods. For an overview of Bleeding Kansas, see http://www.pbs.org/wgbh/aia/part4/4p2952.html.

19. Students can also read the original speeches for greater text complexity. For Whipper's original speech, go to the University of Detroit Mercy, http://research.udmercy.edu/find/special_collections/digital/baa/item.php?record_id=1312&collectionCode=baa. For a transcript of Whipper's full speech, go to Black Past, http://www.blackpast.org/?q=1837-william-whipper-non-resistance-offensive-aggression. For a transcript of Garnet's original speech go to the PBS site *Africans in America* located at http://www.pbs.org/wgbh/aia/part4/4h2937t.html.

20. For example, see Hynd, Holschuh, and Hubbard, "Thinking Like a Historian," 141–176.

21. Another solution is to incorporate more primary sources from websites cited in this chapter for students who are ready for the challenge and/or to discuss what additional evidence would help them respond to the question.

22. There are also generic SAC directions and a note-taking sheet in Appendix B that can be used with any investigation (Figures B.2 and B.3). See the following readings for more background on Structured Academic Controversies: Johnson and Johnson, "Critical Thinking," 58–64; Parker, "Learning to Lead Discussions," 125–149; Wineburg, Martin, and Monte-Sano, *Reading Like a Historian*.

23. See "Things to Keep in Mind" in Chapter 8 for ideas about how to circulate and support students.

Chapter 8

1. The full version of *Civil Disobedience* was published in 1849 and can be viewed here: http://www.ucs.louisiana.edu/~ras2777/judpol/thoreau.html. A 2003 children's book by D. B. Johnson paraphrases the story, describing a bear named Henry (Thoreau) who was arrested for not paying his taxes because he didn't want to support slavery. See Johnson, *Henry Climbs a Mountain*..

2. Published first in the *Atlantic Monthly* in 1846. Lowell later published this poem as part of a set in *The Biglow Papers* (1848).

3. Lincoln was not re-elected to Congress after giving these speeches and returned to his law practice before running for President in 1860. For the original versions of these speeches, see the Library of Congress's Web Guide to the Mexican American War at http://www.loc.gov/rr/program/bib/mexicanwar. For a shortened, transcribed version of Lincoln's December 1847 speech, see the Digital History site by Mintz and O'Neil at http://www.digitalhistory.uh.edu/disp_textbook.cfm?smtid=3&psid=3672. For a transcribed version of Lincoln's January 1848 speech, go to the American Memory project at the Library of Congress, http://memory.loc.gov/cgi-bin/query/r?ammem/mal:@field(DOCID+@lit(d0007400)).

4. Chavez refers to the vote as an "overwhelming majority" in Chávez, *War with Mexico*, 15. On public support for the war see Wheelan, *Invading Mexico*, 262. Polk's speech asking Congress to declare war on Mexico can be found at http://www.pbs.org/weta/thewest/resources/archives/two/mexdec.htm.

5. The full transcript of Polk's message to Congress can be viewed at http://memory.loc.gov/cgi-bin/ampage?collId=llcg&fileName=016/llcg016.db&recNum=829.

6. Chavez includes this song in Chávez, *War with Mexico*, 1–2. In addition to numerous pieces of sheet music on the Mexican American War, the Library of Congress compiled a Web guide for this topic that also includes broadsides, speeches, newspaper articles, political documents, maps, and images. See http://www.loc.gov/rr/program/bib/mexicanwar.

7. The full text of this source can be found in Chávez, *War with Mexico*, 82.

8. Episode 2 ("Empire Upon Trails") of the PBS documentary *The West* focuses on the period 1806–1848. The PBS website includes resources to accompany this episode, including visual and textual primary sources. See http://www.pbs.org/weta/thewest/resources/archives/two. Virginia Tech's website, "The Mexican-American War and the Media, 1845–1848," includes newspaper articles, images, and documents from the time period as well as timelines. See http://www.history.vt.edu/MxAmWar/INDEX.HTM#. The PBS site U.S.–Mexican War has extensive resources on this topic, including a detailed interactive timeline of the time period. Go to: http://www.pbs.org/kera/usmexicanwar/index_flash.html. Also, Steven Mintz's and Sara McNeil's Digital History has a background reading and primary sources devoted to this topic. See http://www.digitalhistory.uh.edu/teachers/lesson_plans/pdfs/unit5_9.pdf.

9. The *Choices* Program of Brown University houses a plethora of teaching materials for social studies teachers. One lesson includes a map of the expansion of the United States through treaties, war, negotiation, and purchase: http://www.choices.edu/resources/activities/we/images/westward-expansion.jpg.

10. O'Sullivan's article—"Annexation." *The United States Democratic Review*, 17(85) (July–August 1845): 5—can be found at Cornell's "Making of America" website: http://digital.library.cornell.edu/cgi/t/text/text-idx?c=usde;idno=usde0017-1. For additional primary sources on Manifest Destiny, see Steven Mintz's and Sara McNeil's *Digital History* page on the topic: http://www.digitalhistory.uh.edu/disp_textbook.cfm?smtID=11&psid=3843.

11. See White, *"It's Your Misfortune."*

12. For example, see Bauer, *The Mexican War*.

13. See Chávez, *War with Mexico*, and Foos, *A Short, Offhand Killing Affair*.

14. White, *"It's Your Misfortune."*

15. See Foos *A Short, Offhand Killing Affair*, 8–9.

16. See Wheelan, *Invading Mexico*, 261.

17. See Weber, *Mexican Frontier*.

18. The Center for American History at The University of Texas includes an overview of Texas history from Anglo American colonization of the Mexican region to annexation. The site includes background overview, images, and lesson plans: http://www.cah.utexas.edu/texashistory/annex/index.php. Yale Law School's Avalon Project houses primary sources on Texas independence through annexation at http://avalon.law.yale.edu/subject_menus/texmenu.asp.

19. See P. Hämäläinen, *Comanche Empire*, and DeLay, *War of a Thousand Deserts*.

20. Chávez offers a concise history of Texas colonization through annexation in Chávez, *War with Mexico*, 6–12.

21. See Wheelan, *Invading Mexico*, 263.

22. See Chávez, *War with Mexico*, 10.

23. Students can read the original sources for this investigation if they want more of a challenge at the Library of Congress's American Memory portal. For the *United States Democratic Review* article, "The Mexican War—Its Origin and Conduct," go to http://memory.loc.gov/cgi-bin/query/r?ammem/ncpsbib:@field(DOCID+@lit(AGD1642-0020-120_bib)). For Corwin's speech, go to the Library of Congress at https://archive.org/details/speechofmrcorwin00corw.

24. For ideas about how to create a class timeline throughout the year, see http://www.bringinghistoryhome.org/assets/bringinghistoryhome/timelines.pdf. For more information about *Bringing History Home*, a K–5 history curriculum that integrates reading and history, see http://www.bringinghistoryhome.org.

25. See February 1847 on the PBS interactive timeline for an example of a recruiting poster, http://www.pbs.org/kera/usmexicanwar/timeline_flash.html.

26. For more on this notion of authority in the history classroom—and the importance of shifting it from teachers and textbooks—see Bain, "Rounding Up Unusual Suspects," 2080–2114.

Chapter 9

1. We mixed up who received Test A and Test B for the pretest and then made sure that students received the opposite test form at the posttest (i.e., if one student completed Test A for the pretest, she completed Test B for the posttest, and vice versa). This is called counterbalancing. From a research standpoint, this ensures that the results are not determined by the test itself; teachers can decide if they wish to be this stringent or simply give everyone the same pretest and then switch to the other test form for the posttest.

2. CCSSO, *Common Core*, p. 65.

3. The *Reading Like a Historian* curriculum targets particular ways of reading and analyzing historical sources, including sourcing, contextualization, corroboration, and close reading. You can find examples of this curriculum at the Stanford History Education Group website, http://sheg.stanford.edu, and in Wineburg, Martin, and Monte-Sano, *Reading Like a Historian*. The *Historical Thinking Project* in Canada focuses on six historical thinking concepts: historical significance, evidence, continuity and change, cause and consequence, historical perspectives, and the ethical dimension. You can find their curriculum and assessment materials at the project web site, http://historicalthinking.ca, and in Seixas and Morton, *Historical Thinking Concepts*.

4. For more of the research results, see recent reports of this work such as De La Paz et al., "Developing Historical Reading."

5. Suggestions for additional curriculum materials like this include the following: Digital History, http://www.digitalhistory.uh.edu; Historical Thinking Matters, http://historicalthinkingmatters.org; the Historical Thinking project, http://historicalthinking.ca; the Internet Modern History Sourcebook, http://www.fordham.edu/Halsall/mod/modsbook.asp; the Library of Congress, http://www.loc.gov/teachers/tps; the National Archives, http://www.archives.gov/education; the National History Education Clearinghouse, http://teachinghistory.org; the Roy Rosenzweig Center for History and New Media, http://chnm.gmu.edu; the Stanford History Education Group, http://sheg.stanford.edu; World History for Us All, http://worldhistoryforusall.sdsu.edu.

6. For guidelines about adapting historical sources so that they're accessible to students, see Wineburg and Martin, "Tampering with History."

Epilogue

1. For reports of the research results, see De La Paz et al., "Developing Historical Reading," or De La Paz et al., "Historical Reading and Writing Apprenticeships."

Bibliography

Allen, Samantha. 2011. "Lexington and Concord Both Claim Last Word on First Shot." *Wicked Local Lexington*, July 29. Accessed June 25, 2013, http://www.wickedlocal.com/x2014916985/Lexington-and-Concord-both-claim-last-word-on-first-shot

Anderson, Fred. 2001. *Crucible of War: The Seven Years' War and the Fate of Empire in British North America, 1754–1766*. New York: Vintage.

Bain, Robert B. 2006. "Rounding Up Unusual Suspects: Facing the Authority Hidden in the History Classroom." *Teachers College Record* 108: 2080–2114.

Bain, Robert B. 2005. "'They Thought the World Was Flat?' Applying the Principles of *How People Learn* in Teaching High School History." In *How Students Learn: History in the Classroom*, edited by M. Suzanne Donovan and John D. Bransford, 179–213. Washington: National Academies Press.

Ball, Deborah, and David Cohen. 1999. "Developing Practice, Developing Practitioners: Toward a Practice-Based Theory of Professional Education." In *Teaching as the Learning Profession: Handbook of Policy and Practice*, edited by Linda Darling-Hammond and Gary Sykes, 3–31. San Francisco: Jossey-Bass.

Bauer, Jack. 1992.*The Mexican War, 1846–1848*. Lincoln, NE: Bison Books.

Birnbaum, Louis. 1986. *Red Dawn at Lexington*. Boston: Houghton Mifflin.

Boudinot, E. (1832). *Letters and Other Papers Relating to Cherokee Affairs: Being a Reply to Sundry Publication Authorized by John Ross* (pp. 11–13). Accessed at the University of Georgia Digital Library, http://neptune3.galib.uga.edu/ssp/cgi-bin/tei-natamer-idx.pl?sessionid=7f000001&type=doc&tei2id=pam012.

Brown, Ann L., and Joseph C. Campione. 1996. "Psychological Theory and the Design of Innovative Learning Environments: On Procedures, Principles, and Systems." In *Innovations in Learning: New Environments for Education*, edited by Leona Schauble and Robert Glaser, 289–325. Mahwah, NJ: Lawrence Erlbaum Associates, Inc.

Brown, Richard H. 1996. "Learning How to Learn: The Amherst Project and History Education in the Schools." *The Social Studies*, 87: 267–273.

Chambliss, Marilyn J., and P. Karen Murphy. 2002. "Fourth and Fifth Graders Representing the Argument Structure in Written Texts." *Discourse Processes* 34: 91–115.

Chávez, Ernesto. 2008. *The U.S. War with Mexico: A Brief History with Documents*. Boston: Bedford.

Cogliano, Francis D. 2009. *Revolutionary America, 1763–1815: A Political History*, 2nd ed. New York: Routledge.

Collins, Allan, John Seely Brown, and Ann Holum. 1991. "Cognitive Apprenticeship: Making Thinking Visible." *American Educator* 15: 6–11, 28–46.

Colton, Richard. *Shays's Rebellion: The Last Battle of the American Revolution*. U.S. National Park Service, Springfield Armory National Historic Site, Massachusetts, 2007. Accessed January 25, 2007, http://www.nps.gov/spar/historyculture/shays-rebellion.htm. (Shortened version: http://mskundinger.weebly.com/uploads/1/3/7/2/13720217/reading 5-2 shaysrebellion.pdf)

Council of Chief State School Officers (CCSSO). (2010). *Common Core State Standards for English Language Arts and Literacy in History/Social Studies, Science, and Technical Subjects.* Washington, DC: National Governors Association Center for Best Practices, Council of Chief State School Officers. Accessed August 27, 2012, http://www.corestandards.org/the-standards.

De La Paz, Susan. 2005. "Effects of Historical Reasoning Instruction and Writing Strategy Mastery in Culturally and Academically Diverse Middle School Classrooms." *Journal of Educational Psychology* 97: 137–156.

De La Paz, Susan, and Mark Felton. "Reading and Writing from Multiple Source Documents in History: Effects of Strategy Instruction with Low to Average High School Writers." *Journal of Contemporary Educational Psychology* 35 (2010): 174–192.

De La Paz, Susan, Mark Felton, Chauncey Monte-Sano, Robert Croninger, Cara Jackson, Jeehye Shim Deogracias, and Benjamin Polk Hoffman. "Developing Historical Reading and Writing with Adolescent Readers: Effects on Student Learning. Theory and Research in Social Education" (in press).

De La Paz, Susan, Chauncey Monte-Sano, Mark Felton, Robert Croninger, Cara Jackson, and Kelly Worland. "Historical Reading and Writing Apprenticeships for Adolescent Readers: Integrating Disciplinary Learning with Cognitive Strategies." Paper presented at the annual meeting of American Educational Research Association, San Francisco, CA, April 2013.

DeLay, Brian. 2009. *War of a Thousand Deserts: Indian Raids and the U.S.–Mexican War.* New Haven, CT: Yale University Press.

Dowd, Gregory Evans. 1993. *A Spirited Resistance: The North American Indian Struggle for Unity, 1745–1815.* Baltimore, MD: Johns Hopkins University Press.

Duke, N., Samantha Caughlan, Mary Juzwik, and Nicole Martin. 2012. "Teaching Genre with Purpose." *Educational Leadership* 69: 34–39.

Elkins, Stanley M., and Eric McKitrick. 1993. *The Age of Federalism: The American Republic, 1788–1800.* New York: Oxford University Press.

Engle, Randi A., and Faith R. Conant. 2002. "Guiding Principles for Fostering Productive Disciplinary Engagement: Explaining an Emergent Argument in a Community of Learners Classroom." *Cognition and Instruction* 20: 399–483.

Englert, Carol Sue, Taffy E. Raphael, Linda M. Anderson, Helene M. Anthony, and Dannelle D. Stevens. 1991. "Making Strategies and Self-Talk Visible: Writing Instruction in Regular and Special Education Classrooms." *American Educational Research Journal* 28: 337–372.

Fischer, David Hackett. 1994. *Paul Revere's Ride.* New York: Oxford University Press.

Foos, Paul. 2002. *A Short, Offhand Killing Affair: Soldiers and Social Conflict during the Mexican American War.* Chapel Hill: University of North Carolina Press.

Foreman, Grant. 1974. *Indian Removal: The Emigration of the Five Civilized Tribes of Indians.* Norman: University of Oklahoma Press.

Fuchs, Douglas, Lynn S. Fuchs, Patricia G. Mathes, and Deborah C, Simmons. 1997. "Peer-Assisted Learning Strategies: Making Classrooms More Responsive to Diversity." *American Educational Research Journal* 34: 174–206.

Galvin, John R. 1989. *The Minute Men. The First Fight: Myths and Realities of the American Revolution.* McLean, VA: Pergamon-Brassey.

Ghere, David L.1995. "Indian Removal: Manifest Destiny or Hypocrisy?" *Magazine of History* 9: 32–37.

Gragg, Larry. 1998. "Order vs. Liberty." *American History* 33: 24–28, 56–59.

Graham, Steve, Karen Harris, and Michael A. Hebert. 2011. *Informing Writing: The Benefits of Formative Assessment.* A Carnegie Corporation Time to Act Report. Washington, DC: Alliance for Excellent Education.

Graham, Steve, and Michael A. Hebert. 2010. *Writing to Read: Evidence for How Writing Can Improve Reading.* A Carnegie Corporation Time to Act Report. Washington, DC: Alliance for Excellent Education.

Hämäläinen, Pekka. 2008. *The Comanche Empire.* New Haven, CT: Yale University Press.

Harris, Karen R., and Steve Graham. 1992. "Self-Regulated Strategy Development: A Part of the Writing Process." In *Promoting Academic Competence and Literacy in School,* edited by Michael Pressley, Karen R. Harris, & John T. Guthrie, 277–309. San Diego: Academic Press.

Harrold, Stanley. 2004. *The Rise of Aggressive Abolitionism: Addresses to the Slaves.* Lexington: University of Kentucky Press.

Holt, Thomas C. 1990. *Thinking Historically: Narrative, Imagination, and Understanding.* New York: The College Entrance Examination Board.

Horton, James Oliver, and Lois E. Horton. 1998. *In Hope of Liberty: Culture, Community, and Protest Among Northern Free Blacks, 1700–1860.* New York: Oxford University Press.

Humphrey, Carol Sue. 2003. *The Revolutionary Era: Primary Documents on Events from 1776 to 1800.* Westport, CT: Greenwood Press.

Hynd, Cynthia, Jodi Patrick Holschuh, and Betty P. Hubbard. 2004. "Thinking Like a Historian: College Students' Reading of Multiple Historical Documents." *Journal of Literacy Research* 36: 141–176.

Jitendra, Asha K., and Meenakshi Gajria. 2011. "Main Idea and Summarization Instruction to Improve Reading Comprehension." In *Handbook of Reading Interventions,* edited by Rollanda E. O'Connor and Paricia F. Vadasy, 198–218. New York: Guilford.

Johnson, D. B. 2003. *Henry Climbs a Mountain.* Boston: Houghton Mifflin.

Johnson, David W., and Roger T. Johnson. 1998. "Critical Thinking Through Structured Controversy." *Educational Leadership* 45: 58–64.

Jordan, Ryan. 2004. "Quakers, 'Comeouters,' and the Meaning of Abolitionism in the Antebellum Free States." *Journal of the Early Republic* 24: 587–608.

Kantrowitz, Stephen. 2012. *More Than Freedom: Fighting for Black Citizenship in a White Republic, 1829–1889.* New York: Penguin Books.

King, Jr., Martin Luther. 1963/2000. Letter from Birmingham Jail. *Why We Can't Wait.* New York: Signet Classics.

Kiuhara, Sharlene A., Steve Graham, and Leanne S. Hawken. 2009. "Teaching Writing to High School Students: A National Survey." *Journal of Educational Psychology* 101: 136–160.

Lee, Carol D. 1995. "A Culturally Based Cognitive Apprenticeship: Teaching African American High School Students' Skills in Literary Interpretation." *Reading Research Quarterly* 30 : 608–631.

Lepore, Jill. 2010. "Paul Revere's Ride Against Slavery." *The New York Times,* December 18. Accessed June 25, 2013, http://www.nytimes.com/2010/12/19/opinion/19Lepore.html.

Lynch, Jack. 2007. "The Alien and Sedition Acts." *Colonial Williamsburg Journal,* Winter. http://www.history.org/foundation/journal/winter07/alien.cfm.

Miller, John Chester. 1951. *Crisis in Freedom: The Alien and Sedition Acts.* Boston: Little Brown.

Moje, Elizabeth B. 2008. "Foregrounding the Disciplines in Secondary Literacy Teaching and Learning: A Call for Change." *Journal of Adolescent & Adult Literacy* 52: 96–107.

Nash, Gary B. 2005. *The Unknown American Revolution: The Unruly Birth of Democracy and the Struggle to Create America.* New York: Viking Press.

National Council for the Social Studies. 2013. *The College, Career, and Civic Life (C3) Framework for Social Studies State Standards.* Silver Spring, MD: The National Council for the Social Studies.

Newkirk, Thomas. 2000. "A Mania for Rubrics." *Education Week* 20 (2): 41.

Newman, Richard S. *The Transformation of American Abolitionism: Fighting Slavery in the Early Republic.* Chapel Hill: University of North Carolina Press, 2002.

Nokes, Jeffery D., Janice A. Dole, and Douglas J. Hacker. 2007. "Teaching High School Students to Use Heuristics While Reading Historical Texts." *Journal of Educational Psychology* 99: 492–504.

Palincsar, Annemarie Sullivan, and Ann L. Brown. 1984. "Reciprocal Teaching of Comprehension Fostering and Comprehension-Monitoring Activities." *Cognition & Instruction* 1: 117–175.

Parker, Walter C. 2003. "Learning to Lead Discussions." *Teaching Democracy: Unity and Diversity in Public Life,* 125–149. New York: Teachers College Press.

Paxton, Richard J. 2002. "The Influence of Author Visibility on High School Students Solving a Historical Problem." *Cognition and Instruction* 20: 197–248.

Perdue, Theda. 1991. "The Conflict Within: Cherokees and Removal." In *Cherokee Removal: Before and After,* edited by William L. Anderson, 55–74. Athens: University of Georgia Press.

Perdue, Theda, and Michael D. Green. 2005. *The Cherokee Removal: A Brief History with Documents.* New York: Bedford St. Martin's.

Popham, W. James. 1997. "What's Wrong—and What's Right—with Rubrics." *Educational Leadership* 55: 72–75.

Pressley, Michael. 1979. "Increasing Children's Self-Control Through Cognitive Interventions." *Review of Educational Research* 49: 319–370.

Rael, Patrick. 2004. *Reading, Writing, and Researching for History: A Guide for College Students.* Brunswick, ME: Bowdoin College. Accessed July 20, 2012, http://www.bowdoin.edu/writing-guides.

Reisman, Avishag. 2012. "The 'Document-Based Lesson': Bringing Disciplinary Inquiry into High School History Classrooms with Adolescent Struggling Readers." *Journal of Curriculum Studies* 44: 233–264.

Reisman, Avishag. 2012. "Reading Like a Historian: A Document-Based History Curriculum Intervention in Urban High Schools." *Cognition and Instruction* 31: 86–112.

Remini, Robert V. 2001. *Andrew Jackson and His Indian Wars.* New York: Viking..

Richards, Leonard L. 2002. *Shays's Rebellion: The American Revolution's Final Battle.* Philadelphia: University of Pennsylvania Press.

Satz, Ronald N. 1975. *American Indian Policy in the Jacksonian Era.* Norman: University of Oklahoma Press.

Seixas, Peter, and Tom Morton. 2013. *The Big Six Historical Thinking Concepts.* Toronto: Nelson Education.

Smith, James Morton. 1956. *Freedom's Fetters: The Alien and Sedition Laws and American Civil Liberties.* Ithaca, NY: Cornell University Press.

Stewart, James Brewer. 2008. *Abolitionist Politics and the Coming of the Civil War.* Amherst: University of Massachusetts Press.

Szatmary, David P. 1980. *Shays' Rebellion: The Making of an Agrarian Insurrection.* Amherst: University of Massachusetts Press.

Taylor, Alan. 2004. "The Alien and Sedition Acts." In *The Reader's Companion to the United States Congress: The Building of Democracy,* edited by Julian E. Zelizer, 63–76. Boston: Houghton Mifflin.

Toulmin, Stephen. 2003. *The Uses of Argument,* 2nd ed. Cambridge, UK: Cambridge University Press.

VanSledright, Bruce. 2002. *In Search of America's Past: Learning to Read History in Elementary School.* New York: Teachers College Press.

Wallace, Anthony F. C. 1993. *The Long, Bitter Trail: Andrew Jackson and the Indians.* New York: Hill and Wang.

Warner, Gary A. 2011. "Lexington and Concord, Revisited and Revised." *Orange County Register*, July 1. Accessed June 25, 2013, http://articles.ocregister.com/2011-07-01/news/29734177_1_warning-shots-and-bells-paul-revere-british-troops.

Weber, David J. 1982. *The Mexican Frontier, 1821–1846.* Albuquerque: University of New Mexico Press.

Wheelan, Joseph. 2007. *Invading Mexico: America's Continental Dream and the Mexican War, 1846–1848.* New York: Carroll & Graf Publishers.

White, Richard. 1991. *"It's Your Misfortune and None of My Own": A New History of the American West.* Norman: University of Oklahoma Press.

Wineburg, Sam. 1991. "Historical Problem Solving: A Study of the Cognitive Processes Used in the Evaluation of Documentary and Pictorial Evidence." *Journal of Educational Psychology* 83: 73–87.

Wineburg, Sam. 2001. *Historical Thinking and Other Unnatural Acts: Charting the Future of Teaching the Past.* Philadelphia: Temple University Press.

Wineburg, Sam, and Daisy Martin. 2009. "Tampering with History: Adapting Primary Sources for Struggling Readers." *Social Education* 73: 212–216.

Wineburg, Sam, Daisy Martin, and Chauncey Monte-Sano. 2011. *Reading Like a Historian: Teaching Literacy in Middle and High School Classrooms.* New York: Teachers College Press.

Wineburg, Sam, and Jack Schneider. 2009/10. "Was Bloom's Taxonomy Pointed in the Wrong Direction?" *Phi Delta Kappan* 91: 56–61.

Wishart, David M. 1995. "Evidence of Surplus Production in the Cherokee Nation Prior to Removal." *Journal of Economic History* 55: 120–138.

Wong, Bernice Y. L. 1997. "Research on Genre-Specific Strategies in Enhancing Writing in Adolescents with Learning Disabilities." *Learning Disability Quarterly* 20: 140–159.

Worcester Polytechnic Institute. "The Battle of Lexington and Concord: A Brief History." Accessed June 25, 2013, http://www.wpi.edu/academics/military/lexcon.html.

Young, Kathleen McCarthy, and Gaea Leinhardt. 1998. "Writing from Primary Documents: A Way of Knowing in History." *Written Communication* 15: 25–68.

Index

About The Authors

Chauncey Monte-Sano is an associate professor of Educational Studies at the University of Michigan. A former high school history teacher and National Board Certified teacher, she currently prepares novice teachers for the history classroom and works with veteran history teachers through professional development programs. Her current research examines how history students learn to reason with evidence in their writing, and how their teachers learn to teach such historical thinking. She has won research grants from the Spencer Foundation and the Institute of Education Sciences and research awards from the National Council for the Social Studies and the American Educational Research Association. Her most recent scholarship can be found in the *Elementary School Journal,* the *Journal of the Learning Sciences, Social Education,* and *Phi Delta Kappan.* She has twice won the American Historical Association's James Harvey Robinson Prize for the teaching aid that has made the most outstanding contribution to teaching and learning history—once as part of the team who created the *Historical Thinking Matters* website (http://historicalthinkingmatters.org) and once for her book with Sam Wineburg and Daisy Martin, *Reading Like a Historian: Teaching Literacy in Middle and High School History Classrooms* (Teachers College Press, 2011). She can be contacted at cmontesa@umich.edu.

Susan De La Paz is an associate professor of Special Education at the University of Maryland. She has spent more than 15 years creating and validating writing curricula, first in English classes, and more recently within the discipline of history, helping teachers meet the needs of students with LD, struggling learners, and proficient and advanced learners in middle and high school classrooms. Her work employs cognitive apprenticeships to support adolescents' disciplinary thinking and as a vehicle for supporting inservice and preservice teachers. She won a Teaching American History Grant and led a Struggling Readers and Writers Grant from the Institute of Education Sciences, and has received funding from the American Educational Research Association. Her recent scholarship appears in *Written Communication, Journal of Literacy Research, Theory and Research in Social Education, Learning Disabilities, Research & Practice, Journal of Research on Technology in Education, Contemporary Educational Psychology,* and the *Journal of Learning Disabilities,* as well as the *Journal of Educational Psychology, Intervention in School and Clinic,* and *Exceptional Children,* among others. She has also written numerous book chapters on writing and disciplinary literacy. She can be contacted at sdelapaz@umd.edu

Mark Felton is a professor of Secondary Education at San José State University, San José, California. He currently prepares beginning teachers pursuing middle and high school teaching credentials and has developed a network of university-school partnerships to provide professional development to the veteran teachers who serve as teacher mentors. His research focuses on argumentation and the development of disciplinary thinking skills, particularly through the use of classroom discourse and deliberation. Most recently, he has focused on the acquisition and retention of scientific knowledge through peer-based argumentative reasoning in classroom settings. He has received a Struggling Readers and Writers Grant from the Institute of Education Sciences and a National Professional Development Grant from the Office of English Language Development. His most recent scholarship can be found in *Science Education, International Journal of Science Education, Contemporary Educational Psychology,* and *Informal Logic.* He can be contacted at mark.felton@sjsu.edu.